HARLEY-DAVIDSON
Evolution V-Twin
OWNER'S BIBLE™

by Moses Ludel

ROBERT BENTLEY
AUTOMOTIVE PUBLISHERS

HARLEY-DAVIDSON
Evolution V-Twin
OWNER'S BIBLE™

TABLE OF CONTENTS

The publisher encourages comments from the reader of this book. These communications have been and will be considered in the preparation of this and other manuals. Please write to Robert Bentley Inc., Publishers at the address listed on the top of this page.

This book was published by Robert Bentley, Inc., Publishers. Harley-Davidson Motor Company has not reviewed and does not warrant the accuracy or completeness of the technical specifications and information described in this book.

Library of Congress Cataloging-in-Publication Data

Ludel, Moses.
    Harley-Davidson Evolution V-twin owner's bible / by Moses Ludel.
      p.   cm.
    Includes index.
    ISBN 0-8376-0146-0 (alk. paper)
    1. Harley-Davidson motorcycle–Maintenance and repair. 2. Harley-Davidson motorcycle–Purchasing. I. Title
TL448.H3L83 1997
629.28'775–dc21
                           97-41253
                               CIP

Bentley Stock No. GOWH

00 99 98 97   10 9 8 7 6 5 4 3 2 1

The paper used in this publication is acid free and meets the requirements of the National Standard for Information Sciences-Permanence of Paper for Printed Library Materials. ∞

Harley-Davidson Evolution V-Twin Owner's Bible™: Moses Ludel's Hands-on Guide to Getting the Most From Your Motorcycle, by Moses Ludel

©1997 Moses Ludel, and Robert Bentley, Inc.

Manufactured in the United States of America

Front cover: 1991 Heritage Special owned by Deb Spano of Laramie, Wyoming, photo by Jeff Hackett. **Back cover** (clockwise from top): Duane and Toni Heiny ride the Virginia City truck route; FLSTS Heritage Springer sits outside Harley-Davidson of Reno; Evolution engines are special, whether stock or modified; Toni Heiny's Heritage Special Classic parked at Geiger Grade to watch the sunset; all photos by Moses Ludel.

ROBERT BENTLEY, INC. | AUTOMOTIVE PUBLISHERS

Information that makes
the difference.®

1734 Massachusetts Avenue
Cambridge, MA 02138 U.S.A.
800-423-4595 / 617-547-4170
e-mail: sales@rb.com
Web page: http://www.rb.com

INTRODUCTION

In 1963, on my fourteenth birthday, I tested for a license to operate a motor scooter on Nevada's public roadways. Limited to six and one-half horsepower and a 35 mph speed limit, a provisional scooter license was a modest place to start. My first cycle was pure American iron, a ruggedly constructed Cushman. Unlike the crop of Italian and Japanese scooters, the Cushman Husky engine boasted a solid iron block, tapered roller bearings on the crankshaft and a nearly indestructible design.

A well-worn '55 model, bought for eight dollars, that scooter had seen more than enough service. The conspicuous knock within the engine quickly proved fatal. My first ride into the rural countryside, filled with the rush of late spring air, the scent of barnyards and fresh alfalfa, and the sounds of crickets, abruptly came to a halt when a loose connecting rod separated from the crankshaft, snapped the camshaft in half and locked up the engine.

Here, my work in cycle mechanics and higher performance began. I pumped gas at a local filling station all summer and earned enough money to buy a larger displacement Super Eagle long-block and the other parts needed to revamp my Cushman. With a factory shop manual in hand, I painstakingly learned the details of a Tillotson side-draft carburetor, the Wico magneto, a centrifugal clutch, and the chain drive system.

So, too, I discovered firsthand what a hard-tail cycle with a "springer" front end is all about. Gradually, my chassis restoration came to match the "outlaw" eight horsepower engine. New wheel bearings, steering head bearings, brake lining and wiring made the high mileage scooter safer and more manageable.

As my cycling interests grew, I listened to old-timers, veteran riders who talked about their exploits on Harley-Davidson and Indian cycles. Tales of ancient V-twin flatheads and formidable Harley-Davidson knucklehead engines filled my head. When I rode a '58 Duo-Glide for the first time, cycling took on new meaning. For its era, no other motorcycle could match the smooth, high torque road feel of a Panhead engine or the balanced sensation of telescoping front forks and a hefty rear swing-arm with twin shocks. I can still recall my pulse quickening with each gear change and the steady rise of the swept speedometer needle.

By the early Seventies, I owned and operated an independent motorcycle repair shop. With a focus on chassis and engine performance, the shop's clientele included Harley-Davidson owners with Knucklehead, Panhead and Shovelhead V-twins. I took special interest in fine tuning and maximizing the reliability of these cycles. I either owned or had the opportunity to repair and test a broad range of road bikes. I experienced the handling, performance attributes and quirks of the H-1 and H-2 Kawasaki two-stroke triples, Honda twins and inline fours, the large displacement British twins and triples, Italian Ducatis and Moto-Guzzis, and the German BMW boxers.

Despite magazine promotion and pop interest in British and Japanese motorcycles, Harley-Davidson still held the most loyal and stable following. While the British bikes could outmaneuver a stock Harley, and high-tech Japanese engineering surpassed the rigid conventionality of America's only road motorcycle, there remained a tenacious, indomitable commitment among Harley-Davidson owners.

A traditional design and predictable nature have set Harley-Davidson apart in the American cyclists' psyche. Fundamental engineering, a hometown dealership base, and a long, colorful history have made Harley-Davidson motorcycles a significant part of the American experience and culture. No period in Harley-Davidson's Twentieth Century life-span, however, has been more exciting or infectious than the Evolution Era. From the early 1980s to the present, Harley-Davidson has raised owner volume and the prestige of America's premier motorcycle to unprecedented heights, breaking every sales and marketing expectation.

Evolution Era owners now range from traditional Harley-Davidson riders to crossover former sport bike owners. As for loyalty, ownership commitment and Harley-Davidson rider camaraderie, nothing can compare to a Harley Owners' Group (HOG) Rally or the annual events at Sturgis and Daytona Beach. The beat just grows stronger as the distinctive pitch and throaty roar of Harley-Davidson FX, FL, Sportster and Buell models roll on.

This book celebrates the entire Harley-Davidson ownership experience. From selecting the right new or used Evolution Era motorcycle, to the safe operation, routine maintenance and proper service of your Harley-Davidson "Evo," I strive to encourage and help you develop insight into your motorcycle and its mechanical needs.

My first riding took place on some of the loneliest highways in America. In such an environment, a rider learns respect for preventive maintenance, the philosophy that I promote throughout this book. Routine preventive care can make your riding experience safer and more satisfying, while reducing the risk of more costly major repair work. "Breakdown prevention" strategies contribute to greater engine, geartrain and electrical system reliability, a safer chassis and a longer life for your motorcycle. Within this book, you will learn why *all* my motorcycles have provided long and comparatively trouble free service.

In the performance sections, you will discover the important relationship between proven Harley-Davidson factory engineering and useful performance modifications. Safe motorcycling demands responsive handling and braking, an ultra-reliable engine and geartrain assembly, plus tires and wheels that provide the highest margin of safety and dependability.

Despite the extensive use of accessories, especially on touring cycles, ease of maintenance remains a hallmark of Harley-Davidson machines. Your motorcycle can provide a rewarding opportunity to sharpen mechanical skills. Equipped with this book and a genuine Harley-Davidson service manual for your model, you can perform many repairs on your own—or even tackle the full mechanical restoration of a higher mileage motorcycle.

For the do-it-yourself owner, this book serves as a foundation for working on your Evolution Era Harley-Davidson motorcycle. Even the owner who prefers not to work on his or her cycle will find the troubleshooting and repair sections of real value. By understanding your motorcycle's service needs, you can effectively interact with Harley-Davidson dealership personnel or an independent repair shop.

When asked by my publisher which motorcycles offered the best subject matter for a book, Harley-Davidson's Evolution V-twin models were my top choice. It is with great pleasure that I offer this tribute to an American motorcycle line that has earned worldwide respect and the recognition of millions.

1 HARLEY-DAVIDSON HISTORY: A SHARED OWNERSHIP EXPERIENCE

Harley-Davidson motorcycle owners share more than fresh air, open space, and the pleasures of cycling. In a world marketplace full of technical innovation and ever changing trends, only Harley-Davidson can offer a long, colorful history that spans the entire era of motorcycling.

Harley-Davidson owners first discover their future passion through the personal accounts of four generations of riders or by way of its sweeping history, immortalized in numerous books describing the product's evolution, the development of the Harley-Davidson Motor Company, and the racing record that surrounds Harley-Davidson. From this, they come to know the dream.

Meetings with other riders serve as the wellspring, and the legend grows. On highways and backroads, at rallies and roadhouses, a gathering at the roadside cafe, local pub, HOG Rally, Super Bike race course or a cross-country road run, owners share their wisdom, anecdotal tales and, yes, even fables. Every legend has its muse, and for Harley-Davidson, the story begins with the evolution of its V-twin engine.

FIG. 1-1. Evolution owners, like earlier Harley-Davidson riders, come from all walks of life. Their common enthusiasm for motorcycling makes every highway a celebration, and Harley-Davidson the topic of choice.

FIG. 1-2. Harley-Davidson's V-twin engine design dates to 1909. Striving for higher quality and reliability, Harley's V-twin engineering relies upon precise gear drives for the camshaft(s), oil pump and valve timing. These high standards continue from vintage L-head/pocket valve and side-valve engines to the modern Evolution engines.

FIG. 1-3. Even an offshoot of the overhead valve concept came into play in early Harley-Davidson engines. Exhaust valve was of side-valve type; an Alemite grease fitting lubricated the rocker arm.

EVOLUTION OF THE MODERN OHV V-TWIN ENGINE

By the Depression Era of the 1930s, the American landscape was a vast maze of cement and asphalt highways. Motorcycles, due largely to the engineering advancements of the Harley-Davidson Motor Company and those of competitors like Indian, offered increasingly more suitable transportation.

Long past the motorized bicycle stage and clearly capable of keeping up with expressway traffic, the heavier road motorcycles had earned a strong following. Harley-Davidson's unique V-twin engine design, notably more reliable and stronger than competitive makes, led the American field of large displacement motorcycles.

As early as 1921, Harley-Davidson had offered a 74 cubic inch twin cylinder engine in the Models 21FD and 21JD. By 1936, the Harley-Davidson engine designs included V-twins of various displacements, compression ratios and valvetrain configurations. Although depression sales of 9,812 total units were less than half those of 1928, Harley-Davidson continued to improve and develop its technology.

Birth of the Knucklehead OHV

For 1936 Harley-Davidson offered four engine sizes: 45, 61, 74 and 80 cubic inch displacement. Performance was a key sales feature, and the 74 and 80 cubic inch engines were traditional side-valve ("flathead") designs. The newest 61 cubic inch engine, found on Models 36-EL, 36-E and 36-ES motorcycles, introduced Harley-Davidson's first overhead valve (OHV) V-twin design.

The innovative E-engine soon became known among mechanics and owners as the "Knucklehead;" the closed-fist shape on the overhead valve rocker arm supports spawned this affectionate nickname. In its high compression

FIG. 1-4. Side-valve (flathead) engines of 45, 61, 74 and 80 cubic inches remained in service alongside the Knucklehead 61 cubic inch engine introduced in 1936 E-models. Shown is a vintage flathead/side-valve engine. Bike still motors to Harley-Davidson rallies.

FIG. 1-5. 1936 E-model's engine, overhead valve 61 cubic inch design, began the "Knucklehead" era. By 1941, the legendary 74 cubic inch F-model engine came on line and continued the Knucklehead design through 1947.

Special Sport solo (non-sidecar) model, the original 61 cubic inch E-engine rated a respectable 40 horsepower at 4,800 rpm. With a top compression ratio rating of 7:1, the early EL Knucklehead engine easily powered the hefty 565 pound (dry weight) motorcycle.

This overhead valve engine quickly gained improvements in the valvetrain lubrication system and other areas. By 1941, the first 74 cubic inch OHV Knucklehead F-type engine came into the product lineup. The popular, high torque side-valve 74 and 80 cubic inch engines would survive through 1948 models; however, the horsepower potential and fuel efficiency of higher revving E- and F-model OHV engines were clearly desirable.

Panhead Debuts Improved Technology

Coincidentally, Harley-Davidson's early engine displacements of 61, 74 and 80 cubic inches became OHV era mainstays. When the Panhead OHV engine emerged in 1948, that V-twin again offered two options: 61 or 74 cubic inches.

FIG. 1-6. Panhead engine served Harley-Davidson models from 1948–65. Introduced in both 61 and 74 cubic inch form, by 1953 only the legendary "74" F-model remained. These OHV engines easily powered the Hydra-Glide ('49–'57), 1958–64 Duo-Glide, and 1965 Electra-Glide model. Shown is a vintage 74 cubic inch kick-start Panhead F-engine in a mildly "chopped" pre-Electra-Glide chassis.

Panhead engines, their nickname derived from the removable valve covers that look like upside down baking pans, pioneered the use of quiet, low-maintenance hydraulic valve lifters. Compared to the earlier Knucklehead design, these engines featured a lighter valvetrain and top engine. The demand for electric starting on FL-models ended the kick start Duo-Glide era, and in 1965, all 74 cubic inch engines featured electric starting. This was also the last year for the Panhead V-twin engine.

As the European and Japanese motorcycles pressed hard into the American market, Harley-Davidson stood firmly with its designs. Rather than make Indian's fatal mistake and emulate the European vertical twin engines, Harley kept its classic V-twin layout. The 55 cubic inch Sportster XL and larger 74 cubic inch FL models held fast to Harley-Davidson's proven market niches.

Shovelhead Moves Harley-Davidson Forward

Harley-Davidson's engine design continually improved, and 1966 was a milestone year for F-models. The highly successful and reliable Panhead 74 cubic inch engine gave way to the more contemporary 74 cubic inch "Shovelhead"

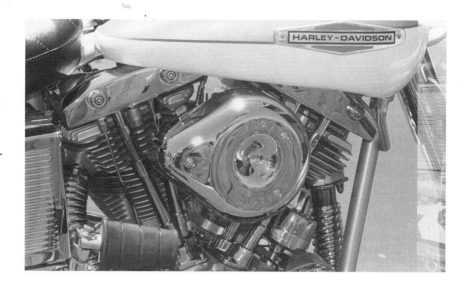

FIG. 1-7. In 1966, this new Shovelhead introduced the advanced 74 cubic inch era. The earlier Panhead 74 had served as the sole FL touring model powerplant from 1953–65. Electra-Glide's electric starting, first offered in '65 on the last Panhead engine, was clearly an asset on this higher compression, stronger Shovelhead engine.

design. The F-engine, predecessor to the Evolution designs, once again derived its nickname from the proximate shape of the valve rocker boxes.

The Evolution era 80 cubic inch FL- and FX-series engines, and also the current 883cc and 1200cc Sportster engines, each benefit from technological advances that began with the Shovelhead era. Initially, Shovelhead improvements focused on the cylinders and heads. Later, the focus turned toward modernizing the charging circuit and ignition system.

During the Shovelhead era of 1966–84, F-model V-twin engines grew from 74 to 80 cubic inches and switched from an externally mounted generator and breaker point distributor to a contemporary internal alternator and electronic ignition system. Consumer confidence in today's Evolution Era Harley-Davidson motorcycle is partly due to refinements and the notable performance gains of Shovelhead F-models.

CHASSIS DEVELOPMENTS: 1936 TO THE EVOLUTION ERA

Mid-Thirties Harley-Davidsons offered a sturdy solid tail (hardtail) frame and a classic springer style front fork suspension. The upper frame tubes sloped stylishly to the rear wheel centerline. Lower engine and transmission frame members swept up and joined these upper tubes at the rear axle.

By today's design standards, hardtail frames left the rear fender prominently above the frame. These cycles were large and weighty, yet their solo seat suggested that the operator alone would ride the cycle. For owners wanting to take along a passenger, the early Harley-Davidson sidecar gearing package (the ES chassis in early 61 cubic inch Knucklehead models) and a sidecar were the solution.

NOTE —

For collectors, chassis numbers designated "S" in 1934–52 Harley-Davidsons represent those models with a transmission that has special sidecar toting gear ratios. The S follows the year and engine letters. Example: A Model 52-FLS is a 1952 V-twin 74 cubic inch OHV road model with sidecar gears and a hand shift mechanism.

FIG. 1-8. Models with both side-valves (shown) and the Knucklehead OHV engines featured a classic hardtail frame and springer front end. Despite the lack of rear suspension, these models handled well for their era and competed readily with other large displacement cycles.

Today the combination of a true hardtail frame and a springer front end, regarded as stylistic of classic Harley-Davidson design, appears only on custom and restored bikes. While the unique "Softail" found on Evolution cycles captures the classic styling and flow of the original hardtail models, the Softail offers a fully functional and innovative rear suspension method, not the rigid rear frame of a Hydra-Glide or Springer model.

Although the Panhead engine replaced the Knucklehead in 1948, Harley-Davidson saved its major chassis design changeover for the following year. In 1949, the Hydra-Glide front forks came on line on both the 61 cubic inch (E) and 74 cubic inch (F) models, and this was a significant breakthrough in Harley-Davidson technology. Adding to the hydraulic damping, larger front brakes helped match engine performance and handling.

In the 1950s, British and German motorcycles, with refined, lighter weight chassis and higher horsepower per pound ratings, entered the U.S.

FIG. 1-9. 1958–64 Duo-Glide models (shown) carried forth the telescopic front forks introduced on 1949 Hydra-Glides. The Duo-Glide ended the hardtail rear suspension era yet continued use of Hydra-Glide's front forks and the Panhead engine, adding improved braking and other roadworthy features.

FIG. 1-10. Beautifully restored '66 Shovelhead Electra-Glide has all the attributes of a smooth, long-distance road bike: good center of gravity, a longer (more stable) wheelbase, plus the responsiveness of a high torque engine. Seen at a Bridgeport, California, summertime rally, this machine drew the attention of all Harley owners. Aside from liberal chroming, the only modification is a set of period high-rise handlebars.

FIG. 1-11. Rear swing arm on FL models first appears on Duo-Glide and earliest Electra-Glide (shown). Swing arm pivot brackets attach to rear vertical frame braces. Arm pivots smoothly on bearings. Axle shaft passes through rear of arm. A coil spring/shock absorber mounts between each leg of swing arm and an attachment point near junction of frame's rear vertical braces and backbone tubes. Design remains on Evolution cycles.

market, shifting the expectations of many American riders toward nimbler and often faster machines. Harley-Davidson attempted to meet the challenge. The Hydra-Glide's success and acceptance paved the way for the 1958 introduction of a full suspension Duo-Glide model.

The 1958–64 Duo-Glide and 1965–up Electra-Glide (electric starter) models adopted several of the proven design principles of European cycles. A lasting, significant change was the introduction of a pivoting rear swing arm with hydraulically dampened, vertical shock/coil spring assemblies mounted at each side above the swing arm. The frame had two tubes that dropped below the steering head to cradle the engine. Rearward of the engine was the down tube that on earlier models served as the seat post location.

A divorced transmission unit nestled behind the down tube. Behind the transmission, two rear vertical braces tied the engine/transmission frame cradle to two upper frame braces. These tubular upper braces originated at the down tube. The conventional swing arm effortlessly pivoted from a bracket attached to each rear frame vertical brace.

Adjusted properly, this system provided the smoothest road feel of any touring bike. The mass and wheelbase of the Harley-Davidson 74 cubic inch FL-series motorcycles also allowed room for saddlebags and other road accessories. Comfort and a large, roadworthy chassis placed these smooth running models in a class of their own.

The 1984 FXST's patented Softail rear suspension was also a milestone. Niche market demand for the classic hardtail frame inspired this design. A Softail is a swinging brace/cradle assembly that follows the aesthetic lines of the original hardtail's upper and lower frame tubes. Softail engineering provides the mix of styling plus handling that contemporary owners expect.

FIG. 1-12. Introduction of innovative softail on 1984 FXST cycles drew first distinct line between traditional FL's swing arm frame and FX/FL Softail chassis. This was also the beginning of the Evolution era, as '84 FX/ST launched first 1340cc engine.

FIG. 1-13. Highly stylized Softail frames of current Evolution era couple classic appearance with contemporary suspension and braking. Models like this Heritage Special (foreground) are in high demand among buyers, indicative of strong nostalgia for classic Harley-Davidson styling and image.

Chassis Refinements and Safety

Safety has been a continuing Harley-Davidson engineering mission. Conservative product development provides the best means for improving safety. Rather than change a motorcycle wholesale in a given model year, Harley-

Davidson's record reflects methodical, thoroughly tested improvements that steadily increase the safety of each model.

This approach has a long history. When the large displacement machines came into being in the 1920s and '30s, Harley-Davidson spent considerable time and yearly effort reducing the risks of riding a motorcycle. Attention ranged from smaller items—relocating shift levers, changing the ergonomics of manual controls and improving headlight and taillamp function—to bigger items like improving the brakes to match horsepower gains.

Customer satisfaction and Harley-Davidson's high safety standards have led to voluntary recalls and factory authorized upgrades of equipment. Reliability and safety remain key concerns. The Harley-Davidson ownership experience is often a two- or three-generation family affair, largely due to the thorough enjoyment and faith in product that owners share.

Milestone years for Harley-Davidson brake improvements were 1949 and 1972–73. The 1949 upgrade accompanied the change from a springer front fork design to the Hydra-Glide telescopic forks. For 1972, the performance level of the cycles, plus the increasing customer demand for weighty accessories on full-dressed touring models, encouraged the introduction of disc front and rear brakes on FL and FLH models. Use of disc brakes on other models quickly followed.

FIG. 1-14. Major refinement of the Seventies was Harley-Davidson's switch to hydraulically actuated disc brakes. Stopping power must match demands of contemporary horsepower, increased luggage loads and popularity of two-up riding. All Harley-Davidson Evolution cycles feature disc brakes at both wheels. FLH-series and FLTC-U model benefit from dual front disc brakes.

Popularity of the lighter weight and faster factory "choppers" expanded the use of disc brakes to FX models in 1973. These hydraulically actuated disc brakes rivaled the stopping power of import cycles.

Another milestone for Harley-Davidson was the use of one-piece cast alloy wheels and tubeless tires. In the 1970s, one of the most threatening motorcycle hazards, a tube-type tire blowout, became obsolete on most motorcycles. Although custom bikes and classic styling cues encourage the use of laced wire wheels, tubeless tires on cast alloy wheels should be regarded as a major safety advantage.

FIG. 1-15. Ultra Classic Electra Glide of the Evolution Era features disc front and rear brakes plus cast alloy wheels and tubeless tires. Despite appearance of a classic beauty, safety engineering is contemporary. Harley-Davidson has masterfully melded the best styling and safety engineering of each era.

FIG. 1-16. Use of spoke cast wheels with tubeless tires offers style and margin of safety. Final drive belts were a major advance of the Eighties, proving reliable and cost-effective to consumers.

STYLING AND MODELS: A UNIQUE OWNERSHIP CHOICE

Marlon Brando's 1954 role in the film *The Wild One* went far toward capturing the sense of alienation among young people, a trend that began in the Post-WWII period. This quest for individual expression and emphasis on the moment gained momentum as the motorcycles, youthful spirits, psychic angst and tribal behaviors depicted in the movie served as a metaphor and symbol for that generation and beyond.

Motorcyclists have always taken a slightly different route. As the open road and high horsepower became symbols of 20th Century American culture, motorcycling, with its unfettered mobility and access to open spaces came to say far more about self-expression and freedom than the Tetra-Ethyl fueled big-block V-8s that powered two-ton Detroit Muscle Cars.

Motorcycling is not just engines and chassis with impressive power-to-weight ratios. Owning and safely operating a V-twin powered Harley-David-

FIG. 1-17. A Harley-Davidson Evolution cycle is a lifestyle and source of joyful liberation. Pictured (helmets removed for photo) are Rod "Bandit" Farrace and his bride Carol on their wedding day and honeymoon at Bridgeport, California. In the midst of a large Harley-Davidson gathering, this was just one more cause for celebration!

FIG. 1-18. Chopper look now spans nearly four decades. As a statement and artform that emerged in the late Fifties and grew in the Sixties, a stripped and customized Harley ranks as the only true "chopper."

son motorcycle takes far more skill than driving a four-wheeled production car or SUV with an automatic transmission, power steering and power assisted anti-lock brakes. The cyclist sees the ride and journey as an end in itself.

As for individual expression, Harley-Davidson motorcycles have served as an art form since the early Sixties. Hardtail Knucklehead "choppers" became symbolic as mechanical sculptures and statements about our motorized culture. In defiance of the conformist four-wheeled production iron that came out of Detroit, the Harley-Davidson chopper or "hog" took the cult of individualism onto the American road.

The spreading symbolism and popularity of chopped and modified Harley-Davidson motorcycles spurred the growth of a custom parts and high performance aftermarket. So pressing became the demand for these modified motorcycles that the Harley-Davidson Motor Company soon paid attention, modeling after the stripped and lightened 74 cubic inch FLs. The undertaking received its impetus from none other than Willie G. Davidson, grandson of company founder William A. Davidson. In 1971, with AMF financial involvement in the formerly family owned business, Willie G.'s groundbreaking FX Super Glide model hit the street.

Recognizing that nearly all street choppers were hybridized crosses of aftermarket parts with various year and model Harley-Davidson components, the factory used the same formula for the FX Super Glide. This highly successful motorcycle, and all subsequent factory sporterized models, have melded the various Harley-Davidson design epochs and model types to produce lighter, sportier and, in most cases, faster bikes.

FIG. 1-19. Evolution FX Softail with Harley-Davidson aftermarket accessories lends personality to a stunning factory customized bike. Harley-Davidson's patented paint and finishing methods are a beauty to behold.

These hybrid bikes have been both popular and a radical inspiration to sales. Harley-Davidson's stable financial foundation during the Evolution Era owes much to the niche marketing of personalized, factory customized machines. With the promise of properly matched and tested components, coupled with fastidious assembly techniques and unsurpassed paint and finish work, these OEM custom bikes have earned a huge following and the assurance of exceptional resale value.

As the custom look plays a large role in vitalizing sales, the demand for full dressed road bikes also continues. A huge number of traditional cyclists look to Harley-Davidson for smooth and comfortable long-distance road bikes. They want a powerful machine capable of hauling two people and a good deal of luggage.

Early factory saddle bags (revived with the Heritage Springer FLSTS) grew into fiberglass stowage bins, while comfort for the rear passenger has become a primary aim in seat design. Although the classic sidecar option survives in the Evolution era, today most touring couples prefer straddling the motorcycle and sensing the curves, pitch and motion of the two-wheeled machine.

FIG. 1-20. Breathtakingly finished, with classic looks to the core, FLHR Road King borrows very best styling and color motifs of traditional Hydra-Glide, Duo-Glide and Electra-Glides. Add a state-of-the-art frame, front and rear disc brakes, liberal use of high tech electronics, and this 80 cubic inch/1340cc Evolution powered cycle satisfies the most discriminating interstate road riders.

K-Model and Sportster: Harley-Davidson's E-Ticket Rides

Harley-Davidson has always offered "sport solo" and competition motorcycles. A long history of winning cycles leads to the present Super Bike class dominators, the XR750 and advanced VR1000. The XR750's race breeding evolved from the earlier engineering of the K-model racing machines.

The proven side-valve 45 cubic inch Harley-Davidson engine provided a foundation for the 1952 effort to take on the British road and racing bikes. British machines were indisputably the best handling and fastest motorcycles in the world at that time. American ingenuity and the penchant for building a better hot-rod led Harley-Davidson to respond with the K-model.

In street form, K-models adopted several features found on British cycles: a rear swing arm with a vertical shock/spring at each side, a foot shifter and a hand clutch lever. Light in weight and nimbler than other Harley-Davidson sport models, these K-cycles satisfied buyers looking for a fast ride through the twists and turns of backroad America.

FIG. 1-21. 1000cc Sportster engine (shown) was guaranteed to raise pulse rates. For all-out performance in stock trim, the exploits of racing K-models, Sportsters, Buell, and H-D XR750 racing bikes are legend.

FIG. 1-22. Those who refer to the Sportster as a "lady's bike" should reconsider. This gal, obviously serious about an Evolution Sportster on display at a Reno, Nevada HOG Rally, must be a highly competent rider.... Is there something wrong with an athletic, sleek, ultra-powerful family member that has achieved status as one of the World's Best Super Bikes?

By 1954, the K-model had established a performance image. A new 55 cubic inch engine of unit construction design (engine and transmission within one casting) earned Harley-Davidson's "KH Golden Anniversary" badge. Offshoot models like the KK, with its sporty camshafts, gave these final side-valve flathead V-twins enough horsepower to occasionally run gamely against the nimbler Triumph, Norton, AJS, Matchless and BSA vertical twins.

A unique element of Harley-Davidson's racing history is the K-models of the 1952–69 era. Competing with the rapid British OHV motorcycles, these side-valve 45 cubic inch KR and KR-TT engines held their own.

Apparently, considering the American riders' sense of competition, this kind of performance was simply not enough. For the 1957 model year, Harley-Davidson would unleash a motorcycle of such lightning fast proportions that all would take notice. The original 883cc (53.9 cubic inch) overhead valve V-twin Sportster, rated a conservative forty horsepower in its 7.5:1 milder compression form, did the job. First available in XL and XLA versions, by 1958 the Sportster XLH and XLCH models began dominating the most American form of competition: quarter-mile acceleration.

The new unit construction OHV V-twin featured a high compression ratio and radical camshaft profile that quickly established the Sportster legend. This was Harley-Davidson's answer to the Fifties and Sixties era of hamburger joints and high octane street racing.

From 1958 through the Seventies, few stock production bikes of any worth could run a faster quarter mile time than an XLH or XLCH, though one British cycle, Norton's 850 Commando, gave the 883cc Sportster a close race. By contrast, Kawasaki's radical 1972–75 H-2 750cc two-stroke engine produced enough torque to approach the quarter-mile speeds of a Sportster. As I and other riders of that period found, however, just one ride on the poor handling Japanese machine was enough to convince anyone that such an attempt was perilous!

The Sportster evolved quickly, with only one design goal: rapid transit. Equipped with high lift camshafts, high compression domed pistons, and 883cc, 1000cc, 1100cc or 1200cc displacement, Sportsters have easily turned low 13-second and faster quarter mile times—in stock trim, right off the dealer's showroom floor.

Currently, the 1200cc (actually 1201cc or 73.3 cubic inches) Sportster boasts 65 horsepower at 5,200 rpm and a G-force grabbing torque of 71 ft-lbs at 4,000 rpm. At 9:1 compression, the electric starter is welcome.

The K-model and Sportster have each built impressive track records. On the racing circuit, the less nimble chassis of the K-model race bikes gave way in 1970 to the formidable Harley-Davidson XR750 model. The XR750 offers a more refined chassis, total dry weight of 290 pounds and a distinctive OHV Sportster engine design. Boasting a higher compression ratio, massive torque and horsepower approaching 100 in well-tuned form, the XR750 has made Harley-Davidson a dominant force in modern Super Bike racing.

Cal Rayborn, Jay Springsteen, Dave McClure, Gene Church, Will Roeder, Scott Zampach, Kevin Atherton, Scott Parker, and the list goes on, are among the Harley-Davidson race riders who staked their careers on the Sportster's fundamental engineering. These design features inspire the XR750, the exotic VR1000, and the current Buell cafe production machines. Could anyone argue that these racers would have achieved more track laurels on an FL or even an FX chassis? Hardly.

Racing: Legends to XR750 AMA Championships

Harley-Davidson's involvement with racing dates to the origins of the product. Recognizing the popular draw of motorcycle racing and owner identification with competitive machines, the company took an early interest in winning races and making sure that Harley-Davidson finished the more gruelling and challenging events.

Motorcycle racing has included dirt and grass tracks, ice racing, hill climbs, early style "Jack Pine" enduros, racing "on the boards" or beaches, Bonneville speed trials, TT and flat track racing, drag strip assaults and as-

FIG. 1-23. Dirt and asphalt versions of XR750 have won more AMA races in the past quarter century than any other Harley-Davidson in history. This cycle has represented the supreme American challenge among Super Bikes. Indisputably, the XR750 has earned the greatest crowd support of any racing motorcycle in the United States. (Photo courtesy of Mike Covello)

FIG. 1-24. 1000cc Sportster cafe models (XLCR) were a sensation in the late Seventies. Production XR1000 and rare roadster models (shown), offered briefly between 1983–85, were a performance hallmark. Street-legal XR1000 bike copied cues of AMA-sanctioned XR750 and XR1000 racing machines, combining a refined frame, massive horsepower, and light weight with a fork angle and suspension tuning that could run with world class high performance cycles.

phalt road racing. Harley-Davidson cycles were notably the most reliable of the early racing machines, and this went far toward cementing the public view that these cycles were both good performers and roadworthy. This tradition grew to a full-scale racing effort during the era of the K-models.

At first glance, an early K-model racer looks much like a hardtail version of the early Sportster. Lightweight telescoping front forks and a more powerful side-valve engine distinguished the K-model from its WR predecessor, a cycle that still used a springer style front fork set.

Although the KR (dirt track) and KR-TT (road racing) chassis differed in both suspension and braking design, the side-valve engine proved competitive in both classes of AMA racing until the late Sixties. When pressed to run with 750cc class British motorcycles under new AMA rulings, the dated side-valve V-twin simply could not compete in either handling or engine performance.

Harley-Davidson's answer to the British and all subsequent threats was the XR750. Capitalizing on the successful developments of the Sportster engine and chassis, the XR750 has become the foundation for the most competitive and win-oriented Harley-Davidsons in history.

In more streetable form, the Sportster "cafe racing" XLCR bikes of the late Seventies led to the phenomenal XR1000 model in 1983. This legal street hybrid, a cross between an XR750 and a cafe racer, was the crowning compliment to the XR750 race bike's record. The XR1000 was available until the introduction of the Evolution Sportster models in 1986.

Filling the void left by a race-profile XR750-caliber Sportster is the Buell cafe racer. This is the ultimate street 1200cc class, Evolution powered machine. Full fairing, a custom frame, handling to match the 71 ft-lbs torque @ 4000 rpm of the engine and a racing-bred soul, the Buell offers the kind of power and performance that cafe racers and Super Bike enthusiasts want.

Harley-Davidson racing, as real and alive today as the company's tradition of building fine road cycles, draws huge spectator participation. At Sears Point, Laguna Seca, Daytona Beach Speed Week, Bonneville Salt Flats, local drag strips and regional dirt flat tracks, Harley-Davidson owners pour out in support of America's only motorcycle icon. When the XR750 engines bark their distinctive, high torque V-twin exhaust note and aim for a checkered flag, Harley-Davidson owners smile.

The emerging VR1000 race cycle assures future victories for Harley-Davidson riders. VR1000 engines offer the most evolved form of V-twin engineering to date.

AMF: PRELUDE TO THE EVOLUTION

Although AMF has received the brunt of criticism for Harley-Davidson's slumping sales and technological growth pains in the 1970s, the incredible Evolution Era cycles owe much of their early success to the staff and manufacturing apparatus put in place during the period when AMF was the financial and manufacturing force behind the company.

AMF inherited two principle V-twin models: the FL series Electra-Glide touring bikes and a series of XL model Sportsters. At the outset of AMF's identification with the Harley-Davidson manufacturing process, Willie G. Davidson's '71 Super Glide FX design set a precedent. He mixed existing parts and engineering with those styling cues that had become popular in the custom aftermarket, thus giving that period's buyers what they wanted.

The AMF years (1971–81) helped Americans identify strongly with Harley-Davidson cycles. During the 1976 Bi-Centennial Year, successful model runs of "Liberty Edition" Electra-Glides and factory red-white-and-blue Super Glide models confirmed that Harley-Davidson knew its market.

Steps toward the Evolution success were obvious in the AMF marketing emphasis on Harley-Davidson's tradition. The 1978 introduction of the 80 cubic inch Shovelhead engine soon served as a standard for FL and FX models. Marketing positioned the heavyweight touring cycles to capture the regal

FIG. 1-25. Heritage Special Evolution model reflects marketing and design aims of AMF's 1979 Classic package. Evolution era has proven that AMF/Harley-Davidson barely tapped its sales potential. Carryover chassis and concept packages like the Classic and Heritage, FX Superglide, Fat Bob, Low Rider and Wide Glide evolved during AMF period.

tradition of the original Hydra-Glide, Duo-Glide and Electra-Glide. The Classic model of 1979 is much like the Evolution Era Heritage and other niche touring machines.

Despite the import effort to secure a share of the touring bike market, with motorcycles like Honda's Gold Wing and others, the Harley-Davidson dresser buyer remained loyal. Japanese technology, like liquid cooling, four cylinders and advanced fuel and spark systems, did appeal to many first-time touring bike buyers. Traditional American motorcyclists, however, adhered tenaciously to Milwaukee's styling motifs and engineering.

By the early 1980s, it became apparent that many American riders insisted on owning Harley-Davidson motorcycles. Buyers applauded the traditional V-twin air cooled engines and the use of Aramid fiber final belt drives rather than sophisticated liquid cooling and shaft drives offered on techy import cycles. Popular Harley-Davidson classic and sport models even flaunted traditional roller chain-and-sprocket secondary drives.

Harley-Davidson buyers have always sought the genuine article. Along with tradition and conservative engineering changes, Harley-Davidson has continually strived to improve quality. AMF and Harley-Davidson have created the most highly regarded paint and finish process in the industry. Coupled with the desire to produce more reliable motorcycles, AMF-era engineering staff and tooling provided groundwork for the Evolution engine.

When AMF returned the business to the Harley-Davidson organization in June of 1981, morale improved at Harley-Davidson's Milwaukee and York plants, within the franchised Harley-Davidson dealership network and among shareholders of AMF/Harley-Davidson stock. The re-established Harley-Davidson organization firmly pursued engine and chassis changes, took them to the marketplace and, ultimately, reaped the benefits.

THE EVOLUTION ERA

When Harley-Davidson became independent of AMF in the early 1980s, a steady market existed for niche market cycles. FX models like the Super Glide, Fat Bob, Low Glide and other factory custom bikes had experienced minor sales growth despite industry-wide complaints of decreasing motorcycle sales. Traditional FL dresser models continued to satisfy road touring owners, competing reasonably well with high tech Japanese cycles.

The more streamlined FX models, essentially Big Twin bikes with Sportster style front fork, had become a mainstay for Harley-Davidson sales. Despite the 1000cc XL Sportster's reputation for a heart-pounding ride, many buyers regarded the lightened and streamlined 80 cubic inch FXR/FXRS and FXE Super Glide cycles as the high performance option. This provided a catalyst for introducing the first Evolution engine in an FX model.

Officially, the first Evolution design engine appeared in 1984 FXST models. By 1985, all Harley-Davidson FL and FX models would use the Evo engine. A traditional 45-degree V-twin design, the first Evolution V^2 81.6 cubic

FIG. 1-26. Evolution 1340cc engine displaces 81.6 cubic inches and produced 69 horsepower @ 5000 rpm in its earliest (1984 FXST) application. 8.5:1 compression was a bump over Shovelhead engines, yet superior lubrication and cooling allowed use of 89 octane gasoline.

FIG. 1-27. Sportster 1200cc Evolution engine now approaches 70 horsepower and 71 ft-lbs torque @ 4000 rpm. This kind of power in a trim 490 pound cycle is more than sufficient for world-class performance. Nimble, cafe-framed Buell offshoot model also benefits from this power-plant. Despite enormous performance prestige, Sportster did not receive its first Evolution engine until 1986, following introduction of the 1340cc Big Twin.

inch/1340cc engine delivered a respectable 69 horsepower at 5000 rpm. Torque rated a healthy 82 ft-lbs at a relatively low and impressive 3,600 rpm.

This torque figure and low rpm lugging power held with the Harley-Davidson tradition. Still under-square at 3.498-inch bore with a 4.250-inch stroke length, the "Evo" engine's 8.5:1 compression ratio and low speed torque provides the kind of performance, cruising smoothness and economy that Harley-Davidson owners expect.

What the new Evolution 1340cc and Sportster 883cc, 1100cc and 1200cc engines offered most were roadworthiness, greater reliability and the kind of performance that could compete with other big motorcycles. The early FX Evolution models ranged in weight from 572 pounds for the FXEF, FXSB and FXWG to a maximum weight of 625 pounds for the FXSTS. The FSXT/C weighed 618 pounds.

A run of the numbers placed the lighter FX models in the eight horsepower per pound range, a respectable power-to-weight ratio by any standard. The current 1201cc Evolution Sportster engine develops a conservatively rated 65 horsepower at 5,200 rpm and 71 ft-lbs of torque at 4,000 rpm. An XLH 1200 Sportster enjoys a factory shipping weight of 490 pounds. At just over 7.5 horsepower per pound of bike weight, the 1200 Sportster remains the quickest ride in the Harley-Davidson fleet.

Evo Engine Builds On Tradition

The Evolution engine held to many of the classic Harley-Davidson features. A 45-degree four-stroke, the air cooled engine reflects a design that dates to the earliest Harley-Davidson V-twin models. The overhead valve design carries forth from the Knucklehead, Panhead and Shovelhead engines.

FIG. 1-28. Evolution V^2 engine represented a significant advance in technology. Areas of change include cylinder barrels, the head and combustion chamber design, valvetrain components and a vastly improved oiling system. 1984–up Evolution engines offer more reliability than previous designs and provide higher performance levels within the growing constraints of lower octane fuel and lower tailpipe emissions. These engines preserve best V-twin features of Shovelhead and earlier Harley-Davidson OHV technology.

FIG. 1-29. Evolution engine cut-away display at Reno HOG Rally. NEAR: 45-degree V and removable heads and cylinder barrels carry forth from earliest OHV V-twin, a Harley-Davidson hallmark. FAR: Redesigned cylinder heads improve flow and performance. Note round combustion chamber and efficient relationship of valves and valve mechanism. Intake valve (shown) is amply sized, yet fuel economy has improved due to improved mixture flow.

Cylinders, as always, are removable, and the 1340cc engine still features a separate crankcase and transmission/gearcase. The Sportster, introduced in 1957 as a V-twin unit construction crankcase/transmission design, continues its tradition of a common crankcase and transmission gearcase into the current Evolution models.

FIG. 1-30. Unit construction of Sportster Evolution engine carries forward from original 883cc 1957 model. Transmission gearcase and engine crankcase, though separate compartments, have a singular casting (shown here in cut-away display). Unitized assembly, characteristic of European and Japanese engines, offers less overall weight and room for a lighter, more compact frame.

The upper valvetrain consists of rocker assemblies, the valves, springs and retainers. These components lay in "overhead" fashion, with the valves opening downward into the improved round and domed combustion chamber. This is essentially the same OHV method used on earlier Harley-Davidson engines, although the cylinder head and overall induction flow is much better. External pushrod tubes lend one more hint of the Evo's roots.

Below the pushrods lie the roller hydraulic lifters, an efficient and quiet design carried forth from the Knucklehead, Panhead and Shovelhead eras. All engines, including the Sportster, now feature advanced roller type hydraulic lifters. This design keeps valvetrain maintenance to a minimum. A single four-lobe camshaft operates all of the valves on the 1340cc Evo engine. Sportster Evo uses four camshafts, one for each overhead valve.

The two precision connecting rods share a common crankpin on the crankshaft. This, too, is a design that has worked well on all OHV Harley-Davidson V-twin engines. The rear cylinder's rod big-end has a unique forked shape, which straddles the more conventional rod big-end of the front cylinder. Caged triple roller bearings assure long connecting rod bearing life.

Rather than a totally new engine design or concept, the focus of the Evo engine has been refinement and tuning of the classic strengths found in Harley-Davidson OHV V-twin engines. Improvements in the Evo engine's lubrication system, crankcase breathing system, ignition and induction systems set the V^2 engine aside from previous Harley-Davidson engines.

A carryover feature that best illustrates the melding of modern technology with reliable traditional engineering is the ignition system. While the ignition on FL, FH and XL Evolution engines employ the most advanced electronic

FIG. 1-31. On 1340cc engine (shown in cut-away), roller hydraulic lifters and four-lobe single camshaft make for smooth and efficient valve lift. Sportster engine uses roller hydraulic lifters with four separate, gear driven camshafts—one for each valve. Roller lifters allow for potent yet emission compliant camshaft lobe profiles. Note external pushrod tube, a carryover from earliest Harley-Davidson OHV V-twins. Pushrods link lifters to rocker arms atop cylinder head assemblies.

FIG. 1-32. NEAR: Most unique of Harley-Davidson's time-honored mechanical features is use of common crankpin and overlapping connecting rods. Rear rod is fork-shaped and straddles front rod. Triple roller caged bearing assures long service life. Design contributes to running character of V-twin. FAR: Mechanical upgrades in crankcase breathing, engine oiling and ignition represent fresh, advanced design, without sacrificing proven technology or classic appearance.

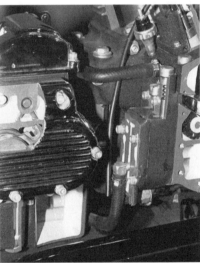

triggering methods, the electronically timed spark fires both cylinders of these V-twins simultaneously. One piston is near the peak of its compression stroke, the other at the top of its exhaust stroke. Although it might be argued that the one cylinder fires needlessly, this is the historically proven Harley-Davidson way. The gains include clean spark plug tips and extended, reliable service. Why give up a good thing?

Induction systems on the FL, FX and XL engines differ. Some engines use carburetion, others have advanced to electronic fuel injection (EFI). As emission compliance becomes a larger concern for motorcycle manufacturers, EFI will likely replace carburetion altogether.

Like the simultaneous firing of the cylinders, the FX and FL 1340cc engines still separate the engine crankcase from the transmission assembly. (We call this classical motorcycle engineering "non-unit construction.") The

FIG. 1-33. A Harley-Davidson V-twin tradition is two cylinders firing at the same time. Despite use of electronic spark triggering, this feature remains. Coil fires one cylinder at peak of its compression stroke, the other at peak of its exhaust stroke. Good way to keep spark plugs clean and ready to fire!

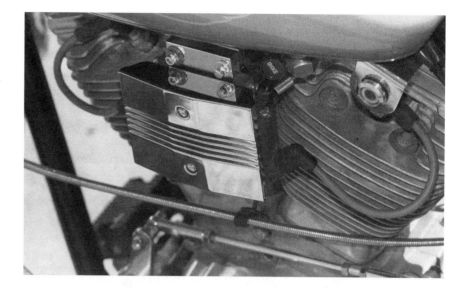

FIG. 1-34. Non-unit construction of FL and FH 1340cc Evo engine carries forth a long Harley-Davidson tradition. Transmission mounts as a complete, separate assembly, fed power through a hefty primary chain and sprockets.

Sportster engines remain unit construction designs, the transmission and engine crankcase sharing a common casting.

Evolution engine lubrication is by dry-sump method, whereby the oil supply is a remotely mounted oil tank. The oil pump sources a continuous and reliable flow of oil from the oil tank. This pump also scavenges (sucks) the draining crankcase oil and returns it to the oil tank.

This engineering again spans the entire E-, F- and XL-series OHV era. Harley-Davidson owners continue to benefit from the proven design. Dry sump lubrication is generally more costly and commonly found in high horsepower automotive racing engines that face radical G-force changes. It is much to Harley-Davidson's credit that Evolution engines continue to use gear driven dry sump oil systems.

FIG. 1-35. Continually pressurized dry sump lubrication system and strategic finning of engine cylinders have advanced both reliability and overall cooling of Evolution engines. Large, remote mounted oil tank and carefully re-engineered oil flow have Harley-Davidson engineers and owners convinced that surface-to-air and oil cooling provide a viable alternative to liquid cooling systems.

Continuing the Heritage

The FL-, FX- and XL-series Evolution models offer the entire range of modern road use motorcycles. At a HOG Rally, Sturgis or Daytona Beach Speed Week, streets are lined with every kind of Harley-Davidson motorcycle. Owners, regardless of their cycles' model type or level of refinement, find camaraderie and a common purpose. I know FL, FH and XL owners from every walk of life, and all share a common conviction when it comes to motorcycling: Harley-Davidson means a long tradition, worth waiting for.

There really is only one Harley-Davidson. Whether your ride is an FLSTC Heritage Softail Classic or FLSTN Special (each with their modern chassis and stunning classic styling), an FLHR Road King touring machine of the first order, the FLTC-U Ultra Classic Tour Glide in full factory dress, an awesomely beautiful and classically elegant Heritage Springer FLSTS, a stylized FLSTF Fat Boy, or a lightning fast XLH Sportster 1200 in dazzling two-tone color scheme, the Harley-Davidson motorcycle knows no limits or boundaries. These cycles magically span the past, present and even our image of the future. Harley-Davidson's line of Evolution motorcycles is, in fact, the dream come true....

Harley-Davidson's overall promise, and subsequent success story, has been a commitment to its heritage and continued valuing of the ownership experience. For this reason, Harley-Davidson engineering and styling will always grow in step with owner expectations. Historically, this has meant incremental changes, conservative trends and continual appreciation for the motto, "If it ain't broken, don't fix it!"

Harley-Davidson adheres to three model profiles: FL and FX "Big-Twins" and the XL Sportsters. Add to this the racy cafe Buell. The distinct lineup permits endless expression of personality among a loyal Harley-Davidson customer base. Continual product improvement, without radical changes, means that today's expectant buyer will find fulfillment when the time comes to take possession of a new machine.

2 BUYING AN EVOLUTION ERA MOTORCYCLE

Harley-Davidson's Evolution Era began with the 1984 FX/ST. Since that time a wide range of models, including anniversary and classic editions that offer special color and trim schemes, have given buyers a wide choice of motorcycles. For Harley-Davidson, a stable market, continued consumer demand and brisk sales have taken the guesswork out of what sells.

WHICH MODEL FOR YOU?

The choice for Evolution buyers centers on picking the right style and type of motorcycle. Facing a wide array of models and niche specialty bikes, the buyer of a new or pre-owned Harley-Davidson motorcycle needs to understand the basic design and intended use of each model line.

HOG-ese 101: Harley-Davidson Nomenclature and Model Differentiation

For the neophyte, a conversation about Evolution motorcycle models sounds like a nightmarish game of *Scrabble*. Every letter draw brings either a handful of consonants, like F, X, L, C, D, W, G, H, S, R, T and U, or the same two vowels, E or U.

Identifying Harley-Davidson's Evolution models is not that difficult. By

FIG. 2-1. For Harley-David-son motorcycle buyers, the news just gets better. Evolution models have been virtually devoid of lemons, creating a viable market for pre-owned cycles and less consumer wariness about buying an earlier Evo model.

learning the sequence in which letters appear, then understanding what each letter and its position mean, you can break the code and become more fluent in HOG-ese. Let's begin with some time-honored Harley-Davidson basics.

In the earliest years of the company, Harley-Davidson identified each model with a number or numbers, sometimes followed by a letter. From 1916 forward, a motorcycle's year of production appeared in the model description, followed by letters that noted exactly which chassis, engine and special equipment the cycle featured.

For example, the first year of the Knucklehead OHV 61 cubic inch motorcycle was 1936, and the Knucklehead engine was known as the "E" engine. Therefore, a 1936 Knucklehead powered motorcycle was a Model 36-E. The model name often had other letters attached, like an "L" or "S," which stood for Special Sport solo (L) or Sidecar gears (S). Therefore, a 1936 Harley-Davidson Model 36-EL was a Special Sport solo chassis with the new 61 cubic inch OHV (soon nicknamed Knucklehead) engine.

This identification scheme followed the 61 cubic inch E engine through its last usage in 1952. In 1941, the models 41-FL and 41-F introduced the legendary Harley-Davidson model "F" engine, a 74 cubic inch Knucklehead design. This F engine designation survived as the engine code letter in the Knucklehead (1941–47), Panhead (1948–65), Shovelhead (1966–84) and even the current Evolution eras. Even when the 74 cubic inch engine grew to 80 cubic inches in the late 1970s, the F model designation stayed with these Big Twin machines.

For the Sportster, introduced in 1957, the engine designation "XL" applies. Sportster identification codes begin with the model year, followed by XL, then additional letters to describe particular equipment. For example, a "Model 83-XLS" is the rarer 1983 Sportster 61 cubic inch model called the "Roadster Custom Sport." This performance machine with "S" as the last identification letter has an unusual (for a Sportster!) Fat Bob gas tank and cast wheels. (See Fig. 1-24.)

FIG. 2-2. XLH Sportster 883 Hugger: Same features as base XLH 883 but slightly shorter at 87.25 inches (due to fork rake difference). Lower saddle height by nearly an inch, and lowest ground clearance in Harley-Davidson V-twin fleet at 4.5 inches. Low and sleek, designed for a fast one-up ride. (Photo courtesy of Harley-Davidson)

In the Evolution Era, Harley-Davidson's letter codes get busy. For engine designations, only the F (1340cc Big Twin) and XL (883cc, 1100cc and 1200cc) letters apply, which makes the first part of the identification process simple. The next letter in the Big Twin F-model code, however, leads into the mire of niche models.

FIG. 2-3. XLH Sportster 1200: Fastest stock production bike built in the United States. Great looks...classic peanut tank shown here on '93 model, but latest style offers a 3.2 gallon tank good for 150 mile range at a rated 57 mpg on the highway—providing, of course, that you don't find an especially curvy road through a mountain pass. Not for the faint of heart or those who like cruise control. I find 1200 Sportster irresistible—unless they build a Sportster Deluxe with the 1200 engine.... (Photo courtesy of Harley-Davidson)

For simplicity's sake, view the second letter of an F-model identification code as a description of the cycle's front fork style. There are three fork styles. The traditional telescoping L-type fork comes from the road touring era that began with the 1949 Hydra-Glide models. (Pre-Hydra-Glides had factory springer front ends, and some springer models had designations like EL or FL, so let's begin this history lesson at 1949.)

This broad telescoping front fork style is popular today on all Harley-Davidson Big Twin models that use "FL-" as their first two identification letters. So, whether you have a full-dressed touring cycle or a Fat Boy factory custom job, you have the classic Hydra-Glide looking front fork.

"X" as either the first or second letter in the model code (X as in Sportsters or FX- as in Big Twin models) means your front fork style is the sleeker telescoping type introduced on the original Sportster. When the 1971 Super Glide hung a Sportster type front fork on an F-engine (Big Twin) chassis, the Model 71-FX was born. From that time forward, every Big Twin chassis equipped with a Sportster style front fork uses the model identification FX.

The only additional usage of the FX designation is the FXSTF Springer Softail front fork. Why Harley-Davidson did not assign a new second letter to describe the Springer and FLSTS Heritage Springer is not clear. A likely reason is that the FXSTS and FXSTB models also use the Softail rear suspension, which places these cycles among another distinct class of Big Twin F-models.

Moving to the third letter of the identification code, you will find more specific engine and/or chassis details. For the Evolution era Sportsters (1986–onward), all models have held the "XLH" designation, followed by their engine size (883, 1100 or 1200) and a package name like "Liberty," "Anniversary," "Deluxe" or "Hugger." Simple.

On the Big Twin FL- and FX-models, the third letter acquires more meaning. On FL- model cycles, the third letter may be an "H" or "T." If so, you have a traditional touring motorcycle in your sights. (H is for Electra Glide; T stands for Tour Glide.) This is an 80 cubic-inch F-powered cycle with a classic Hydra-Glide/Duo-Glide looking front fork and a conventional rear swing arm with vertically mounted shock absorbers. Simply, you have a motorcycle that resembles the classic fully dressed Duo-Glide (1958–64) and Electra Glide (1965–up) road machines that made long distance touring possible.

The classic hardtail look of modern Softail frames appears on both custom and classically styled Big Twin F-models. There are FLST and FXST motorcycles. By now you should figure, this means that one has the Softail rear suspension with the Hydra-Glide/Duo-Glide looking front fork (FLST-). The other features a Sportster style front fork with the Softail rear suspension (FXST-).

FIG. 2-4. FLHS Electra Glide Sport (shown) and later FLHR Road King: True FL ride and chassis quality in a highly stylized road look that stirs up lots of memories— and will make many more. Nice way for two-up to see the country. (Photo courtesy of Harley-Davidson)

FIG. 2-5. FXSTS Springer Softail: Classic custom street look with simulated appearance of hardtail. Mixed tire types, lots of engineering in patented factory Springer front end, with classic cues of a period chopper, right down to laced wheels and an unmatchable custom paint job. Tasteful chrome, and streetable. (Photo courtesy of Harley-Davidson)

FIG. 2-6. FXRS (shown) and later FXDS Dyna Low Rider Convertible: Nice blend of nostalgia and light protection from a removable windshield. Just the right chassis dimensions for a safe ride at any highway speed limit. Ride two-up comfortably on cast wheels and tubeless tires, easily stripped down for the sleeker street look. Well appointed and priced right. Among my top picks of the 1340cc class Evolution bikes. (Photo courtesy of Harley-Davidson)

FIG. 2-7. FLSTF Fat Boy: This one gets my attention and vote. Aside from stealing looks from an incredible period in Harley-Davidson's motoring history, modern nuances make this a practical ride as well. Hard to have best of all worlds, but in this case, Fat Boy pulls it off. A remarkably stunning piece of roadworthy machinery. (Photo courtesy of Harley-Davidson)

Use of a letter "D" in the third position (FXD-) refers to the Dyna style chassis. This, essentially, is a touring chassis with conventional rear swing arm, vertical rear shock absorbers and a Sportster style (FX-) front fork.

Dyna models (Dyna Wide Glide model FXDWG, Dyna Low Rider model FXDL, Dyna Super Glide model FXD, Dyna Convertible model FXDS-CONV, etc.) feature a lower chassis profile and a wide-stance raked front fork. Dyna's factory stripped and mildly "chopped" look grew from the popular Super Glide style bikes of the Seventies. Super Glide and Dyna frame designs evolved from the hefty touring chassis, stripped of bulky hardware, sans the huge fiberglass saddle bags and massive seat, and fitted with a Sportster type front fork.

Mixing styles, chassis features and fork designs has created a wide range of Harley-Davidson Big Twin models. These cycles provide a colorful collage of engineering innovation and classical styling. Among my favorite models is the FLSTF "Fat Boy."

A Cycle For Your Riding Pleasure

When selecting your motorcycle, I have one piece of advice that you should value most: *Make certain that the machine you choose will match your riding environment.* On countless occasions, buyers select a motorcycle on the basis of styling appeal only, soon finding that their riding experience suffers greatly for this choice.

I stayed briefly at Ouray, Colorado, during the summer of 1995. A number of Harley-Davidson riders from the Plains States spent the night at my motel, and we talked over cups of coffee in the parking lot.

Each of the cycles were Evolution models. They ranged from a Sportster 1200, Dyna Wide Glide, Fat Boy and Dyna Convertible to a Springer Softail and a new Ultra Classic Electra Glide 30th Anniversary Edition with an EFI induction system. We discussed their riding experience and perceptions of each other's motorcycles.

The highway from Durango, Colorado, to Ouray climbs over Molas Pass at 10,900 feet and Red Mountain Pass at 11,008 feet. One of the most scenic and enjoyable motorcycle rides in the Western United States, the route provides exceptional challenges as well. Approaching Red Mountain Pass and dropping into Ouray requires both hands on the handlebars, with a 25 mph speed limit in sections and sheer drop-offs along the canyon side of the road.

Fork rake angle and trail, center-of-gravity, ground clearance and leaning angles all play out on a road like Highway 550. High altitude challenges the carburetion or EFI system to its limits. In terms of safety, handling and performance, the road serves as an ample test. These owners shared impressions about each motorcycle's suitability to this riding environment.

The Sportster 1200 rider, one-up on the cycle, said that the engine ran flawlessly and performance at high altitudes diminished only slightly. Braking, acceleration and overall handling felt safe and sure. His only complaint was the vibration from 71 ft-lbs of torque transferring directly to the cycle's frame without cushioning. Still, he was very happy with his ride.

An FXDWG Dyna Wide Glide has a 32-degree front fork rake as opposed to the Sportster's 29.6-degrees. Laced wheels and a MH90-21 front tire with

FIG. 2-8. FXDWG Dyna Wide Glide: Sportier than Dyna Convertible with a set of laced wheels and fork raking that makes for a slightly lower version of the "Easy Rider" era's Ape Hangers. (Photo courtesy of Harley-Davidson)

a 130/90HB-16 at the rear make for a really nice street and boulevard cruiser, but the run into Ouray left this rider with a distinct impression: The cycle handled okay on the straights and sweeping curves, but on the posted 25 mph off-camber turns, the feeling was tense and demanded his full attention.

The Fat Boy owner said that his riding style is nice and easy. His bike was smooth and stable at posted speeds. He commended the riding comfort of this low saddled model. Its large front fork set, Softail and solid match of beefy front and rear (MT90B/16) tires made the bike feel good at highway speeds.

For the FXDS-Conv Dyna Convertible rider and companion, the ride was nothing but fun. Handling and riding comfort proved superior, and the 28-degree rake and relatively short 4.1-inch trail of the front forks kept the Dyna Convertible on the tail of the Sportster through every corner. The owner felt confident that this was the right choice for highway and multi-purpose use and was very happy with his package.

The Springer Softail and Ultra Classic Electra-Glide were at opposite ends of the spectrum. An FXSTS Springer Softail features a 21-inch front wheel, 32-degree front fork rake with 5.25-inches of trail, 5.59 inches of ground clearance and a lean angle of 28/29-degrees (right/left). The FLHTC-I Electra Glide touring cycle boasts 16-inch wheels, 26-degrees of front fork rake with 6.16-inches of trail, 5.12 inches of ground clearance and a lean angle of 31/30-degrees.

As expected, the Springer Softail owner had a supreme white-knuckle experience on the curvy 25 mph zone, slowing to meet the posted limit and avoid the fearful sense that he would high-side the cycle. Having enjoyed a

FIG. 2-9. Harley-Davidson engineering is tops. Extensive research and development on both Softail rear suspension and Springer front end have earned U.S. patents and trademarks. These laurels, however, do not mean that either the Softail or Springer front end is right for every rider. You must take responsibility for choosing a model that matches both your riding style and road conditions. *Weigh this decision carefully.*

wonderful cruise along the interstate stretches and those milder, sweeping curves of Highway 550, this rider's confidence fell when he encountered the nerve-wracking drop into Ouray from Red Mountain Pass.

The Ultra Classic Electra Glide owner simply smiled through all of these anecdotes. This was his fourth Harley, and he was the most experienced road rider of the bunch. An FL's ride quality, predictable handling and smooth performance were this touring rider's choice.

We talked about his first Harley-Davidson, a '61 Duo-Glide, followed by a Panhead Electra-Glide, then a previous Evolution FLHTC Electra-Glide that had carburetion. The only distinction noted by this veteran highway rider was the smoother power and high altitude gains of the Sequential Port Fuel Injection on his '95 model. He was happy with the engineering breakthrough and planned to keep his collectible 30th Anniversary cycle for a very long time.

FIG. 2-10. There will always be FLH riders, touring aficionados who want to cruise the open road unfettered. These machines, complemented by a long list of Genuine Harley-Davidson accessories, can make small chores out of big road maps. But remember, a dresser or cycle with a large array of aftermarket add-on accessories will require more preliminary work during routine servicing. Think about added labor costs involved with repairs and maintenance.

These owner comments emphasize some important considerations around choosing the right cycle. I have nothing but concern for the buyer who mistakenly acquires a hot looking boulevard cruiser or chopper style cycle, then has to endure the difficult handling quirks of such a design on a tight and curvy mountain road.

If your riding environment is primarily the open road, occasional rides over scenic two-lane mountain passes and lots of miles per day, look toward the proven suspension and engineering of FL and FLH models. Those who run sprints on sweeping interstates and curvy switchbacks might consider a Sportster or Buell. For a much happier and safer investment, match your next motorcycle to your favorite riding routes.

FX Versus FL Models

Prior to the Super Glides of the early Seventies, there were only two choices when buying a Harley-Davidson road machine: an FL-series highway touring motorcycle and the Sportster. The Super Glide and subsequent FX models changed that forever.

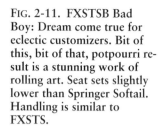

FIG. 2-11. FXSTSB Bad Boy: Dream come true for eclectic customizers. Bit of this, bit of that, potpourri result is a stunning work of rolling art. Seat sets slightly lower than Springer Softail. Handling is similar to FXSTS.

The original FX models strived for the mild custom street bike look of the period. The recipe was basic: 1) Strip away the bulky saddle bags, massive spring-loaded touring seat and ornate accessories of the traditional FL chassis, 2) keep the FL's proven 74 cubic inch Shovelhead engine and divorced transmission, 3) pirate a sleek front fork assembly from the XL Harley-Davidson Sportster model, and 4) increase the front rim and tire diameter.

Although primitive by today's FX engineering standards, early FXs offered a particular buying group the bolder, more aggressive custom look. Some argue that the first FX package delivered nimbler handling as well. Regardless, today's Evolution FL and FX cycles with Sportster style forks have ground-up engineering to achieve a balance between good looks, safer handling, function and reliability.

Evolution FL models maintain the more traditional Hydra-Glide/Duo-Glide/Electra Glide style telescoping front forks. You will find these distinc-

FIG. 2-12. Mimicking pre-1958 hardtail FL models, patented Softail looks like frame tubes dropping from seat to rear axle centerline. Difference, however, is that rear swing arm/cradle assembly is a live suspension member. Two nitrogen pressurized shock absorber/coil spring assemblies control and dampen movement at each side of swinging cradle. Intentionally, these shocks are not visible from either side of cycle.

tively larger, classic looking forks on models with both the Softail and conventional swinging arm rear suspension. Likewise, FX models with the Sportster style front forks may have either the Softail or conventional swinging arm rear suspension.

Now you can identify the chassis differences between a FX, FL, Softail and conventional swing arm model. Choosing the right motorcycle should focus on styling, road handling ability and features that will suit your riding environment. Although this sounds easy, selecting from the array of factory stylized cycles requires careful consideration.

Agile Sportster or Cafe Buell

For the Evolution Sportster buyer, the choice is largely around engine size, transmission type and modest differences in styling. The Evolution Sportster's styling remains a classic, drawing on the quick and nimble attributes and image of the original design.

FIG. 2-13. Sportster's traditional rigid-mount engine provides rider "at oneness." Road changes and throttle demands translate as visceral experience. Former British bike riders find the Sportster attractive, especially cycles like this mildly modified Evolution Era model. For a vibration free ride, consider an FX or FL model with elastomer motor mounts.

Refinements like disc brakes and belt final drive go far toward improving stopping power and lowering maintenance requirements. Alloy cast wheels and tubeless tires, available on the no-frills base 883 XLH, 883 Hugger and XLH 1200 models add to the safety and looks of these models.

Since 1957, this model has featured a taut frame, unit construction V-twin engine/gearbox, quick access clutch and transmission controls, and responsive swing arm rear suspension with lighter telescopic front forks. Add the high durability of an Evolution engine, and the Sportster becomes a fast, reliable ride that handles well.

For handling purists who want an American ride, consider the Buell. Like Sportsters, the XR750, XR1000 or latest VR1000 racing cycles, unit construction and pragmatic cafe styling sets Buells apart. The chassis wraps around a 1200cc engine for a low center-of-gravity. Aerodynamics prove superb. Optimal handling and race-bred suspension elevate the Harley-Davidson V-twin engine to new heights.

But be cautious: Ultra-fast, with racing handling characteristics, the Buell is not for the inexperienced rider. Operating this cycle requires ongoing alert-

FIG. 2-14. Sportster offers stronger highway image. Both XLH 883 Deluxe and XLH Sportster 1200 boast two-up seating. 883 Deluxe (shown) captures traditional look with wire laced wheels and distinctive peanut fuel tank.

FIG. 2-15. Buell, a privately developed motorcycle intent on surpassing best features of legendary XLCR and XR1000 models, has emerged as most refined Sportster-powered model to date. Frame, tank, rider position, front forks, wheels, tire combination and 1200cc Evolution engine place Buell in step with World's most potent superbikes. Harley-Davidson dealers now offer Buell with full-warranty and repair services.

ness and attunement to advanced riding technique. For cruising the boulevard two-up, a Sportster XLH 883 Deluxe or 1200 will do nicely for most riders. For aggressive one-up road rallies and assaulting curvy two-lane mountain passes, the Buell excels—plan on plenty of rest between riding stints, and stay in shape.

Fig. 2-16. Close look at Buell reveals Grade 8 aircraft quality U.S. hardware, shimmering at every chassis attachment point. Product is American ingenuity throughout, boasting traditional Harley-Davidson 45-degree air-and-oil cooled V-twin power. Handling is superb, while reliability keeps pace with awesome power-to-weight ratio.

Fig. 2-17. If laying over the tank and athletically chasing white lines is your kind of hourly pleasure, consider a Buell.

Buying A Pre-owned Motorcycle

The huge popularity of Harley-Davidson Evolution motorcycles means a waiting list for new cycles. Meanwhile, the field of used Evolution bikes grows larger, and there are many reasons to consider a pre-owned cycle.

Engineering advancements make all of the Evolution bikes worthy. However, in instances where particular components have received upgrades on later models, you would be smart to buy the earlier model at a discount price that leaves room for necessary improvements.

FIG. 2-18. Your Harley-Davidson dealer will prove cooperative and helpful in sharing information about particular year models. Parts and service personnel know which upgrades may be necessary, or recommended, to enhance reliability of a given pre-owned Evolution cycle.

FIG. 2-19. One practical place to learn about models is a HOG (Harley Owners Group) Rally. Many newcomers to the Harley experience attend a HOG Rally before getting into a buying mood. In Chapter 3, I share information about the HOG program, a valuable and fun resource for new and experienced Harley-Davidson owners—and their families.

Once you have determined the chassis and style of motorcycle that will meet your needs, consult your local dealer. Ask about the more desirable year models and why you should avoid, or allow for upgrades on, other years of the model(s) that hold your interest.

As a rule, later Evolution cycles seldom require upgrades. There are exceptions, however; situations like particular engines prone to cylinder base gasket and rocker box gasket leaks. (Your local dealer can help identify affected models.) Here, you need to know the cost of the retrofit gaskets, and also installation labor charges, before negotiating the price of such a machine.

Considering the cost of new cycles, and the long waiting list for particular models, you might find a pre-owned model that more than satisfies your needs. Among the advantages of a pre-owned purchase, cost plays the largest role. There are many low mileage Evolution cycles for sale, often with just the right ownership history.

Another plus with pre-owned motorcycles is that they offer a track record of value. Note the resale pricing trends, and consider special edition or commemorative models that tend to hold or gain collectible value. Typically, such cycles depreciate at a normal rate for several years, then they begin to show either an appreciation in value or a much slower rate of depreciation when collectible interest increases. Besides, it's always a plus to have a limited edition or one-off machine.

Pre-owned Motorcycles and Upgrades

Although the Evolution generation of Harley-Davidsons is relatively young, there have been changes and upgrades along the way. None of the Evolution cycles should be considered "lemons," although design improvements may make some later components more reliable.

Problems generally occur with "first year" applications of new technology. Items like a new gearbox or gearset, a chassis and suspension system changeover or the use of redesigned electronic components can either be a valuable upgrade or a testbed. Some "improvements" have a learning curve, so the first year model of a given design change is often worth asking questions about.

Aside from Harley-Davidson's own technological shifts, there are also those changes mandated by outside forces. One such example is the compulsory switch from asbestos content to non-asbestos gaskets, which left many manufacturers with a dilemma.

Harley-Davidson has used several replacement and supercedure gasket designs in an effort to eliminate engine oil seepage. The latest generation of print-a-seal style gaskets for rocker boxes and cylinder bases, plus the use of improved cylinder studs with Loctite on threads (replacing older rolled thread studs), go far toward curing this nuisance problem.

The dealer can help you determine whether any factory warranties or recalls apply to a particular pre-owned cycle. By asking these questions, you will also learn whether there is a safety or reliability concern that applies to a prospective motorcycle. You can also find out whether Harley-Davidson will assume responsibility for the cost of repairing or upgrading the motorcycle if you decide to buy it. If not, the cost is yours.

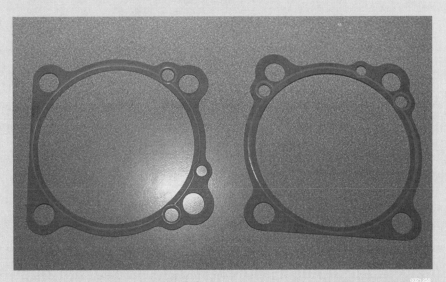

When considering a pre-owned Evolution cycle, watch for signs of cylinder base and rocker box oil seepage. Shown here are upgrade/supercedure cylinder head gaskets. If current owner of a model with leak prone gaskets has not upgraded these pieces, consult your local dealer about labor and parts costs for such repairs. Negotiate the price based upon these considerations.

Once you have confidence that a given model will satisfy your riding style and goals, gain as much knowledge and insight about the particular models in question. Again, your local dealer's parts and service personnel can quickly bring you up the learning curve. Asking impartial owners (not the seller of the bike) about the model can also be useful.

When you have narrowed the field to a particular model or models, and their respective "better years," you can begin your search in earnest. Now the question is one of finding a motorcycle in good condition, at a fair price with a good and documented history.

If the seller is a private party, ask about service and maintenance records. A reputable dealer may also furnish a documented history of the cycle if the service department has performed routine maintenance, warranty or repair work on the machine.

The documented history of a cycle's maintenance is of vital value. A concerned owner will keep records that show routine service on the motorcycle. This says a lot about the condition and treatment the cycle has received. When looking at a pre-owned motorcycle, ask the owner if he or she has service records to share.

In looking at a pre-owned cycle, value its documented history, odometer mileage, signs of good care, overall condition and any extra features or accessories. Again, do your homework, and consider any upgrades that might be necessary—and their potential cost.

Assessing A Pre-owned Machine

I enjoy buying pre-owned machines. Although some buyers get a severe case of anxiety over the prospect of getting "stung," several safeguards can increase your confidence when searching for, and examining, a pre-owned motorcycle.

When you find the right motorcycle and the price is in line for the year and model, it's time for a thorough inspection of the bike. If this is not an area in which you feel competent, read on. I'll take you through a "professional" look at a pre-owned motorcycle. You can then determine whether to have a Harley-Davidson dealership or the motorcycle mechanic of your choice make the inspection.

In these illustrations and comments, we'll do a pre-purchase inspection of Harley-Davidson motorcycles. These steps can help you confirm whether a pre-owned cycle is a quality, roadworthy machine or the worn and damaged financial black hole that we all fear.

Remember, this is a pre-purchase inspection. If the seller has reservations about subjecting the cycle to this kind of scrutiny, you either have a problem motorcycle on hand or may need to involve the owner in the process.

Some owners do not want their cycle "messed with." Discuss your goals and willingness to take the cycle to an authorized Harley-Davidson dealership or mutually acceptable shop for the inspection. If the shop is an independent facility only known to the seller, ask the shop owner to let you observe the inspection steps. Be familiar with the procedures outlined here.

FIG. 2-20. The engine and gearcase is of primary concern when buying a motorcycle. Check the engine's outside appearance and look for oil seepage around rocker boxes and cylinder base gaskets. Make sure the engine has run long enough in your presence to seep oil. A freshly cleaned engine will not show signs of leaks.

FIG. 2-21. Oil consumption is difficult to determine by looking at a cycle. Check the tailpipe for oily soot, and make sure you know the difference between oil and a rich fuel mixture. Oil is black and has a greasy feel, while a rich mixture leaves a dark grey or black carbon-like powdery crust. Light brown to light grey, depending upon altitude of operation, is normal.

FIG. 2-22. Pull the two spark plugs and look closely at their tips. Check color and texture of firing residue. Signs of oil are always bad, indicating worn valve guides or piston rings. Dark brown, grey or black soot indicates poor spark or tuning, incomplete combustion (possibility of low compression) or a rich fuel mixture. Pinpoint cause before discounting dark plugs as "it just needs a minor tune-up."

FIG. 2-23. Compression test proves useful. Follow factory recommendations for acceptable compression pressures and variations. Compression gauge needle should jump up immediately on first cranking strokes and reach recommended compression. A slow rise and less than normal compression suggest ring wear. Nearly no rise usually means a burnt valve(s). (Head gasket leakage can mimic this.) To pinpoint location of compression loss, move to a leakdown test.

FIG. 2-24. I have used leakdown testers for twenty-five years. They pinpoint the exact area(s) where compression loss occurs and provide a good sense of actual condition of cylinders, pistons and rings, castings (cracks, porosity, warpage and distortion), head gaskets and valves. In the tune-up chapter, I share details on how to perform and assess a leakdown test.

FIG. 2-25. Oil consumption is not always a piston ring and cylinder barrel problem. If the engine uses oil and the leakdown or compression tests cannot find trouble, consider worn valve guides, an overfilled oil system, a restricted oil passage, leaking cylinder base or rocker box gasket(s) or a porous cylinder barrel, head or case casting. Here, cut-away display helps illustrate relationship between valves, rocker box and oil consumption.

FIG. 2-26. Abnormal engine noises must be isolated. Some engines come from the factory with very slight valvetrain gear noise, but be sure to separate this kind of sound from a rod knock, primary drive noise or abnormal transmission bearing and gearset sounds. A stethoscope helps isolate noise and pinpoint areas of concern.

FIG. 2-27. Check color, smell and condition of oil in the engine, primary chaincase and gearbox. Feel oil for abrasive contamination and examine tank and oil for metallic debris. If the shop can drain the engine oil tank and system, or better yet, remove the filter for dissection and inspection for metal contamination, all the better. On primary case, small amounts of nylon adjuster shoe material in the drain oil is normal.

FIG. 2-28. Ride the bike and note how clutch feels during take-off and on changing gears. Normal and complete separation of plates makes for smooth shifts and easy take-up of clutch. Slippage is always a bad sign. An obvious acrid (burnt) odor or fried friction material in primary case oil is a sign of a toasted clutch. Minor adjustment seldom provides a cure. If cycle exhibits clutch slip, chatter or other wear symptoms, allow for cost of a major clutch overhaul.

FIG. 2-29. Listen for whining in primary drive and gearcase while engine idles and during a road test. Note odometer mileage reading and determine whether the cycle sounds normal for this mileage. Ride cycle with engine and gearbox fully warmed up. Make sure shifts remain smooth and gearbox stays relatively quiet.

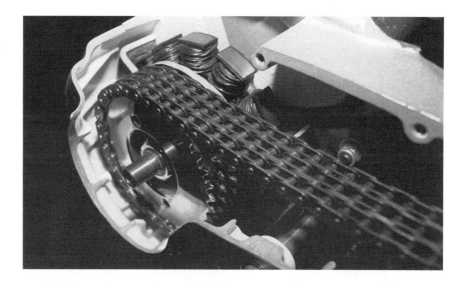

FIG. 2-30. Some costly yet barely perceptible problems occur around the final drive. Chrome sloughs from belt drive sprockets. Chain sprockets wear and peen over at their tooth crowns. Belts fatigue, and chains stretch. Service chapters show how to measure this wear, perform adjustments, and install new chains, sprockets, or belts.

FIG. 2-31. A quick sign of chain or belt wear is the slack adjustment at rear axle. If slack adjuster take-up looks extreme, closely inspect the chain or belt, and also the sprockets. If wear is obvious, determine the cost of replacing these items.

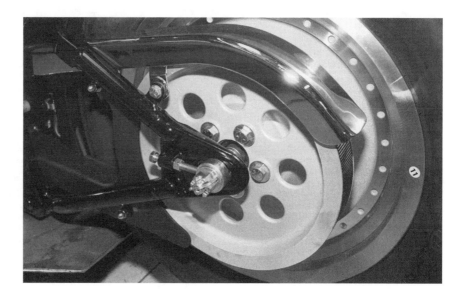

FIG. 2-32. NEAR: Wheel or frame damage—indicating if the motorcycle has been down or in a collision—may be difficult to identify. A Harley dealership can make a thorough inspection, measuring frame and suspension alignment. FAR: On laced wheels, spoke nipples and rim condition give clues to damage. Nipples should have somewhat even number of spoke threads showing. With cycle on a frame hoist/stand and wheels free of ground, you can measure rim runout.

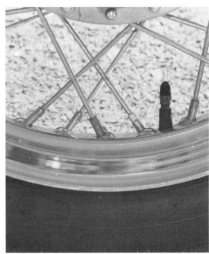

FIG. 2-33. Sportster and Buell unit construction engine/transmission assemblies require special service procedures. Labor times vary between unit and non-unit transmission repairs. Determine any problems here and get a flat-rate estimate of labor time from the local Harley dealership's service department. The shop knows common gear and bearing wear points.

FIG. 2-34. Variety of factory "custom" Evo models reduces need for aftermarket changes. Screamin' Eagle and Genuine Harley-Davidson accessories represent factory approved method of modification. While there are many non-factory accessories that work well, I lean toward showroom stock models or those lightly accented with tasteful accessories. Avoid any motorcycle with changes that could adversely affect handling, safety or possible warranty protection.

FIG. 2-35. Inspecting brakes, steering head bearings and swing arm requires lifting front and rear tires free of floor. Frame bushings, steering head bearings, shock absorbers and front fork leg assemblies each require attention during a pre-purchase inspection. Labor costs for inspection pay off.

FIG. 2-36. Engine mount brackets on Sportsters are rigid part of frame and must be free of cracks and repairs. FX and FL engines mount in elastomer rubber to reduce vibration. Inspect motor mounts for fatigue and oil damage.

FIG. 2-37. On wheel bearings, brake rotors, brake pads, and hydraulic brake components, look for loose or grating bearings, rotors with signs of heat scoring or wear grooves, excessive brake pad wear and leaking master cylinders, brake hoses, brake lines or calipers. These items indicate how the previous owner rode the cycle and the kind of maintenance schedule followed.

FIG. 2-38. Make sure all gauges, lights and the charging circuit work properly. Listen to the starter motor and note whether the battery charges at an idle with lights on. You can check generator output and battery condition with an inexpensive voltmeter. (See Wiring and Electrical chapter.) If cycle has aftermarket electrical accessories, make sure wiring looks professional, intact, free of splices and of original quality. Wiring indicates the caliber of work performed on a cycle.

FIG. 2-39. Placing a value on aftermarket accessories and customizing, including paint and striping, is difficult. Unless pieces are of top quality, recognized for their continued value, and universally regarded as an asset, *don't pay extra for them!* Dealer installed Genuine Harley-Davidson and Screamin' Eagle pieces offer distinct value. For non-factory accessories, be careful.

BUYING A NEW EVOLUTION MOTORCYCLE

If a new motorcycle fits your budget, and you have the patience to wait for delivery of a popular cycle, the time is right. New cycles have the most advanced technology and upscale components. Continued research finds better materials, assembly techniques and design strategies. If sales and inflation trends continue, a new Harley-Davidson motorcycle should hold its value for many years. Most owners of '84 and newer Evolution bikes have found their cycle's value remains constant. Inflation aside, it's awfully gratifying to find that your late-'80s or early '90s cycle can resell for its original purchase price!

If you decide to buy a new Evolution motorcycle, consider this a wise investment. Take care of your new motorcycle, as outlined in the subsequent chapters of this book, and your Harley-Davidson will return exceptional value. Whether you buy a new or pre-owned model, welcome to the ranks of enthusiastic and committed owners!

3

RIDING YOUR
HARLEY-DAVIDSON

There is something unique, even magical, about riding a motorcycle. Whether your first highway ride or the familiar sensations kindled by years of seat time, motorcycling forges an enduring, unspoken bond between rider and machine.

Why you ride motorcycles becomes clear every time you click the shift lever into first gear. As your right hand coaxes the throttle, and your left hand smoothly releases the clutch lever, the eager pull forward of an Evolution cycle sends a succinct message to your central nervous system: It's time to ride!

When everything goes right, without risk of bodily injury or accidental damage to your valuable cycle, open road motorcycling is the most enjoyable motoring experience. The goal, clearly, is to be in control of your motorcycle and safely operate the machine under the widest variety of situations and riding conditions.

Your enjoyment of an Evolution motorcycle begins with understanding its design, correct operating procedures and engineering. Know your bike's features, controls, and the adjustments that will ease your riding experience.

FIG. 3-1. A safe, trouble-free ride on a Harley-Davidson motorcycle ranks high among life's better moments.

ORIENTATION TO YOUR MOTORCYCLE

Today, many buyers of Harley-Davidson Evolution cycles are first time motorcyclists. This phenomena reflects a major demographic shift. Baby Boomers, who perhaps wanted Harley-Davidsons in the Sixties or Seventies, were either discouraged from riding a motorcycle at that time or could not afford one. Those days are past for many!

Every form of recreation has its price, however. Sobering statistically, more than half of all annual motorcycle collisions occur within the first six months of ownership. Familiarity with the motorcycle's features and controls proves vital to safety and preserving your cycle.

FIG. 3-2. Now reaching their middle years, many Boomers have emerged as financially able and culturally stressed out. Motorcycles symbolize freedom and offer a well earned recreational release. While Harley-Davidson motorcycles have always attracted knowledgeable, more experienced riders, they are more powerful and heavier than the typical "first cycle." An FX, FL or XL can pose a challenge for the first-time rider.

If you lack familiarity with motorcycling or a newly purchased Harley-Davidson, resist the temptation to jump on your bike and roar away. With the excitement and intensity of the buying experience, many riders do not take the time to become familiar with the cycle. Likelihood of accidents and damage to the cycle is very high at this point. Do not allow others to pressure you into doing something reckless before you are fully familiar with the controls and proper riding techniques.

Set aside time to look your motorcycle over. You should have the owner's manual that accompanies each new model. This booklet has useful information covering the manual switches, fuel petcock/shut-off lever, choke control or enrichener (carbureted models), clutch and brake levers, brake pedal and transmission shifter lever. Know which way the shifter moves and the location of each gear position. Become familiar with the ignition switch, turn-signal switch, speedometer and odometer, light switches and the horn button. When orienting yourself to each switch, take time to locate and practice operating the device. Be able to reach the switch or control without looking at it.

One of the most important switches on the motorcycle is the engine cutoff or "kill switch." New riders often find the controls confusing, and one of the most common mistakes is to twist open the throttle and not have the where-

FIG. 3-3. A new buyer (or very lucky raffle winner!) should consider trailering the cycle home before taking full stock of its features. If you lack riding skill or have no exposure to a Harley-David-son, the first hours spent with the machine are crucial to your safety and the preserva-tion of the motorcycle.

withal to shut the throttle down and pull in the clutch lever. Many of us have witnessed first time operators shift into gear, release the clutch lever, twist open the throttle, then panic and drop their feet to the ground while still grip-ping the open throttle. *Know the location of the kill switch.* In an emergency, or if you forget the operating procedures, this cutoff switch can prevent se-vere bodily injury and damage to your valuable motorcycle.

Without the engine running, go through the motions of a simulated ride. Visualize yourself riding while you pull in the clutch lever, depress the shifter to engage the transmission's first gear, then ease the throttle back slightly as you release the clutch gently. Sense the force of the gear shifter, clutch lever, front brake lever, rear brake pedal and throttle.

FIG. 3-4. Cars and trucks do not have a hand lever clutch or hand twisted throttle. Adept drivers of four-wheeled vehicles may find a motorcycle completely alien. For safety's sake, especially while learning to operate your cycle, *know the location of the kill switch and how to use it.*

FIG. 3-5. Before riding the cycle, a safety check is smart. Whether the motorcycle is new or pre-owned, you need to check tire pressures. Always use the best gauge within your budget, as your safety depends on tire pressure. Check pressure "cold," after the cycle has set for several hours in a shady area.

FIG. 3-6. Using a clean rag or shop towel, check oil levels for the engine, primary case and transmission gearcase. (Consult your owner's manual or dealer about proper fill levels for your particular machine.) Check brake master cylinders at their sight windows; you do not have to remove the caps. Become familiar with each of these fluid checks, as you will perform them frequently.

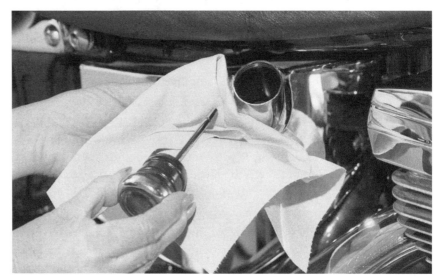

FIG. 3-7. Look the bike over carefully, paying attention to rims and tires, cable housings and cable ends, plus the visible hardware that holds together the engine, chassis, transmission, steering/handlebar assembly and forks. Check your headlight (high and low beam), taillight and turn signals. Your safety depends upon properly working lights and turn signals that other drivers can see.

FIG. 3-8. On Evolution cycles, the brake lights work from the front brake lever or rear brake pedal. Make sure brake lamp comes on correctly. The light should activate when the lever moves slightly, before actual engagement of brakes. (Consult your Harley-Davidson factory service manual for brake light switch details.)

FIG. 3-9. For city operation and initial riding experience, back off the throttle tensioner screw far enough to eliminate any drag. When you release the hand throttle, it should close quickly and without hesitation.

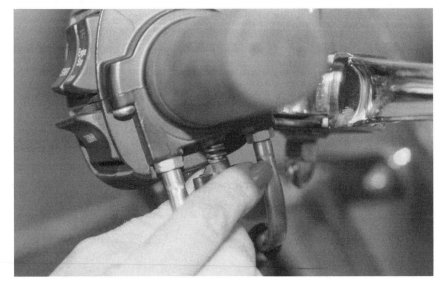

The throttle handle and clutch lever should move freely and snap back when released. Harley-Davidson models have a friction adjusting screw on the hand throttle assembly. This adjuster applies pressure to the hand throttle, allowing the operator some relief from holding the throttle open on long rides. *Never ride in town or traffic with tension set on the hand throttle.*

A deserted parking lot makes a good location for your first ride. This run is an orientation to controls, not a ride that requires your neighbors' attention, stares of the kids at the car wash, or any passersby. For now, you have only one agenda: Learn to handle each of your motorcycle's controls without having to think about their location. Save the parade lap for when you know how to operate the machine safely and can make an impression.

While sitting in the saddle, check the mirrors. Make sure their heads are secure and that the settings will hold. Clean the mirrors if necessary. Apply the front brake gradually and note how much force it takes to keep the cycle

FIG. 3-10. A deserted parking lot is the best place to practice steering transitions. Expect the DMV to test your skill at these maneuvers with a "figure-8" or similar riding course. Smooth transitions are a simple yet significant indicator of your ability to steer a cycle under all operating conditions.

from rolling. Do the same with the rear brake pedal. Brakes should have a firm feel, not mushy or rubbery. Make this test a habit, your ongoing assurance that the brakes perform adequately before you operate the motorcycle.

First Start-up of the Engine

Since Evolution cycles feature electric starting, you have only the choke system to think about when bringing the engine to life. Become familiar with the location of the choke or enrichener knob. Learn how your engine starts best, which choke settings and durations work best at various altitudes, and how to operate the choke effectively.

NOTE —
If, for any reason, you "bump start" an Evolution cycle engine that has an evaporative emissions control system, you must first press the starter button to activate the solenoid-operated butterfly valve. Riders failing to do this will discover that the valve does not open. Symptoms of a closed valve include a slow top speed and very poor acceleration.

Turn on the fuel petcock. (Some later Evolution cycles have a vacuum operated petcock shut-off.) Pull the choke or enrichener knob to "on" mode, following the Harley-Davidson guidelines in the owner's manual. I like to minimize the time that the choke stays on. In colder climates, turning the throttle a few times will squirt extra fuel through the accelerator pump and make starting easier. With the knob out and shifter in neutral, crank the engine until it starts.

After the brief initial warm-up, if the temperature is below 50° F, a constant velocity (C.V.) carburetor should run for five minutes (approximately three miles) with the enrichener knob pulled out fully. Follow this with a few minutes, or miles, with the knob pushed in halfway. When warmed thoroughly, you can push the knob in all the way. If still cold, try leaving the knob at halfway for a bit longer, until the engine can idle stably.

When temperatures are warmer, or if your Evolution cycle has an earlier non-C.V. carburetor, you will need to experiment with the choke or enrichment settings. Enrichment has two objectives: 1) The engine should respond fairly smoothly when you open the throttle, and 2) idle should be stable, neither too slow nor "blubbery" and unstable.

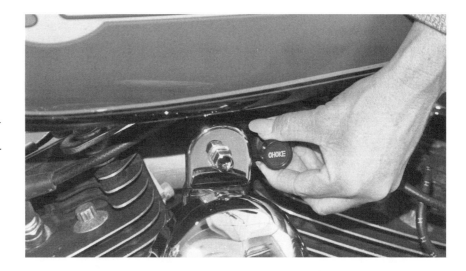

FIG. 3-11. Although experience may show otherwise, Harley-Davidson emphasizes that warm-up should be 30 seconds or less. This short warm-up, even in very cold weather, complies with stringent emissions requirements. If you follow this recommendation, finding the right enrichment or choke knob setting becomes a crucial part of your first few miles of riding.

FIG. 3-12. Changes in altitude and temperature require different choke requirements. When you ride from Chicago to Denver, or Los Angeles to Reno, expect to alter your regular starting and warm-up procedures. Always make certain that air filter is clean for adequate flow. This will also affect starting and enrichment response.

Finding the most sensible choke or enrichener knob settings is one more step toward becoming familiar with your Harley-Davidson. Remember, too much choke will foul spark plugs, wash upper cylinder walls with fuel (leading to premature ring wear), and build up carbon (which can cause pre-ignition). Too little use of the choke creates a lean backfire condition and unstable running, which could impair safe riding.

BECOMING A CONFIDENT RIDER

My exposure to motorized cycles has been a long one, beginning with Briggs & Stratton powered mini-bikes, a Cushman scooter, Japanese motorbikes and Italian scooters. The act of balancing a cycle and mastering the sensations associated with motorized two-wheeling came naturally, long before I ever operated a high horsepower motorcycle. This was a distinct advantage that I cannot overstate. Those of us who rode motorized cycles at a very young age, learning their feel and the language of road sensations, were fortunate. Surely that is the time when our minds form easy partnerships with our motor re-flexes—a time when we react with far less hesitation.

By seventeen, I had fearlessly straddled and ridden several Japanese high-way bikes, a BSA Thunderbolt 650 and a Harley-Davidson Duo-Glide. Of that period, the worst handling bike of the bunch was Suzuki's X-6 Hustler, which took me rapidly up the rider's learning curve. The bike, lent to me by its boastful owner, stubbornly refused to negotiate the fast sweeping corner north of Minden, Nevada—leaving me squarely at odds with an oncoming 18-wheeler.

As the front wheel tramped and wobbled, I instinctively braked for an in-stant, then counter-steered without braking. The speeding cycle swerved across the opposing lane and left the pavement at the opposite side of the road—all in one spontaneous maneuver. The cycle stayed upright, coming to a stop on a smoothly graded fresh dirt pad. According to my friend and witness, Brent Howerton, the whole scene looked like I had planned it. Brent had been struggling to catch me on a Yamaha 250cc highway bike. Tempted to duplicate my maneuver, he told me there was not enough time or space to follow.

My training grounds were sprints through each of the Sierra passes, runs across straight line desert highways (with no posted speed limits), scrambles up the Virginia City truck route and cruises on the interstates and freeways. Each venue provided a few more credits in Advanced Riding.

Riding on dirt is an excellent training ground for learning to steer, brake, clutch, shift and throttle a motorcycle. Devoid of traffic, a designated dirt trail offers a place to safely practice slow-speed steering, counter-steering (see later side-bar), and how to throttle properly while avoiding trouble.

Today there are myriad schools, motorcycle safety training programs and books written to the subject of asphalt riding. Experts like Keith Code (author of *Twist of the Wrist* and *The Soft Science of Road Racing Motorcycles,* and founder of the Superbike School—see appendix) introduce enthusiasts to the mindset and objectives of professional road racers. You can minimize risk to yourself, passengers and your valuable motorcycle by attending an appropri-ate riding school.

FIG. 3-13. Some come to road motorcycling from oth-er cycling backgrounds. My friend, Steve Shaw, raced large displacement motocross bikes for years, never looking at street bikes. Steve's wife Peggy and her father, Harry Murphy, introduced him to Harley-Davidsons. They now own *three* Evolution models—a FX, FL and a Buell!

FIG. 3-14. A dirt motorcycle is a sensible way to keep your reflexes sharp. At home, we have Honda XR200R and XR350 enduro motorcycles. In wintertime, when road touring is impractical, my son Jacob (shown) and I dress warmly, put on safety gear and ride these dirt cycles. This keeps our senses primed and provides good physical conditioning.

FIG. 3-15. Consider the cost of today's motorcycles, insurance and medical costs. Your life and the life of passengers have incalculable value. You owe yourself and companions your very best riding skills. The path begins with learning safe riding techniques.

Throttle and Shifting Tips

Sitting in the saddle, your arms should have a slight bend as your left hand grips the left handlebar grip and right hand reaches the throttle. Make sure you can easily turn the handlebars. Your right hand should drop naturally onto the throttle grip.

Twisting the throttle should require a downward effort, with the throttle fully releasing as you let off tension. Do not hold your hand too high on the throttle, or you will find the throttle jerking and tending to "open itself" as the cycle thrusts forward. When you reach forward for the front brake lever, the throttle grip should fall back effortlessly to its idle position.

While moving up through the gears is natural for those with driving experience, downshifting and smooth compression braking on a motorcycle require some practice. For this reason, the deserted parking lot makes a good place to perfect your shifting technique.

Slowing down smoothly requires three functions: 1) rolling back on the throttle, 2) applying the front and rear brakes in a uniform and smooth manner, and 3) sensing the speed change points and downshifting to the next lower gear. As you downshift, release the clutch lever in a fluid motion.

If your timing is correct and road speed matches the gear change, you should feel a very slight braking effect, almost like a "boost" on your braking effort, yet without any jerkiness or the sense that the rear wheel is binding or locking. This finesse develops with practice.

FIG. 3-16. Riding a cycle differs somewhat from an automobile or truck. Compression braking, control and being in the right gear at the right time require constant upshifting and downshifting. First gear is at the bottom of the shift changes. For safety's sake, be back in first gear by the time your cycle reaches a complete stop.

There are two symptoms to avoid: 1) no compression braking and 2) too much engine braking, in the worst case causing rear tire skid. In mastering the proper use of gears and compression braking, it helps to monitor your gear change points on the way up through the gears as you accelerate. These upshift points can serve as markers for when to downshift as you come to a smooth stop with both brakes applied.

Use Both Front and Rear Brakes

The old bicycle adage, "never apply the front brakes alone" can apply with motorcycles. You should apply both of your motorcycle's brakes simultaneously. The front brake, when used properly and in conjunction with the rear brake, accounts for the majority (75–85%) of your braking effort in a hard stop. Learn to use your front brake effectively, with a steady "squeezing" effort on the lever. Do not hesitate when safe to use the front brake.

The only time when using the front brake can be a hazard is on loose, slick or steeply angled traction surfaces. A good example is when you leave a paved road and enter a graded dirt road. As you negotiate the corner, applying too much front brake could cause front wheel skidding and loss of control. A motorcycle can quickly go down if the front wheel locks while the bike has committed to such a corner. Use the front brake very cautiously, or not at all, on steep banking corners or when the stable asphalt road gives way to an oil slick or gravel covered surface.

We determine a motorcycle's necessary braking effort by the amount of mass, vehicle speed and road surface conditions. Add to this the design of the cycle, its tire diameters and profiles, plus fork rake angle and trail, and you find that different motorcycles, or a change in load, can create unique braking dynamics. The best riders address these changing dynamics by first identifying the stopping characteristics of their motorcycle. From my experience and that of others, you should sense a fluid motion as the cycle brakes properly. Visualize the front brake hand lever and rear brake pedal as they *squeeze* the brake pads against the rotors with a steady, increasingly firmer clamping force.

Develop a feel for smooth and controlled stops. Feedback signals include how the steering responds, how much the cycle pitches forward (hard front brake application), dragging or skidding of the rear end (heavy rear brake application), and the extremes: violent diving of front forks from severe overuse of front brakes or skidding of the front or rear tires from too-hard braking.

The amount of front fork dive is a good indicator of smooth braking. Hard braking at 60 mph requires far more hand-lever effort than a similar stop at 20 mph. If you apply the same kind of hand lever effort for both situations, you will find the front forks compressing too much on the 20 mph stop. On your cycle, learn what degree of movement corresponds to controlled, steady braking. Practice on a safe, straight stretch of road without traffic. Ride alone and use caution.

NOTE —
Some adjustment of the front fork resistance is possible by changing fork oil viscosity. See service and chassis performance sections for details.

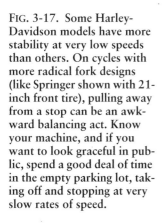

FIG. 3-17. Some Harley-Davidson models have more stability at very low speeds than others. On cycles with more radical fork designs (like Springer shown with 21-inch front tire), pulling away from a stop can be an awkward balancing act. Know your machine, and if you want to look graceful in public, spend a good deal of time in the empty parking lot, taking off and stopping at very slow rates of speed.

Counter-Steering

There are three distinct ways of turning a motorcycle. At crawl speeds, for example in a parking lot, you turn the front wheel in the direction of your turn. At higher speeds, you can initiate a turn by leaning towards the direction you want to go. Or you can use a counter-steering technique. To counter-steer, you actually push the handlebar, slightly, on the side where you want to turn. (Example: You want to turn left, push slightly at the left handgrip. For a right turn, push the right grip.)

Counter-steering at first seems counter-intuitive. Pushing on the right handgrip, for instance, turns the front wheel slightly to the left, which you might expect would initiate a left turn. But instead, the cycle turns right. This is because you are making the cycle lean, without leaning your body.

Counter-steering is most effective when you need to swerve to avoid a hazard or a potential accident.

Expect an immediate response from the cycle. Turn the handlebar slightly in the opposite direction you want to steer when you need to quickly stand the bike up or swerve into another lane. This maneuver requires practice and prudence.

Practice counter-steering without traffic around. Use extreme caution. Move the handlebar ever so slightly in each direction and note the feel of the cycle as you focus your attention and eyes on the point where you intend to end up. Repeat the movement in the opposite direction. Do this over and over again, until you can perform a counter-steer and swerve without thought or hesitation.

Counter-steering is a highly effective move that changes the entire dynamic of turning. If you are only accustomed to leaning into curves, it will take practice and mental conditioning to accept and master counter-steering.

Improving Your Balance

As you start off with your motorcycle, you will find that the cycle becomes steadier with speed. Typically, a cycle like your Harley-Davidson will achieve stability between 3-5 mph. This is a valuable dynamic of motorcycles. Gyroscopic effect of rotating wheels and tires contributes to stable movement of the bike. Coincidentally, the effective vehicle weight on the road decreases as speed increases.

By practicing your stops and starts, the balancing act will improve your neuro-muscular reaction time and movements. Unlike an auto or truck, where you sit in a fixed position and turn a wheel to make the vehicle steer, riding a cycle means shifting your weight, locating your legs and torso properly, moving the handlebars when necessary and leaning correctly as you apply throttle and assume a stable riding mode.

These movements can take place simultaneously. For the experienced rider, motorcycling becomes an instinctive, neurological/muscular response. Proper conditioning develops the right patterns. The best place to start, since these reactions will apply to all riding situations, is at slow operating speeds.

Strive to become *one with the machine*. I cannot emphasize this enough. Motorcycling is an activity that requires full-body participation, mental alertness and constant readiness. Accidents and risk occur when any of these elements fall short.

Steering With Your Eyes and Body

Every capable rider discovers that body posture and line of sight determine your control of a motorcycle. There is a distinct pattern for approaching each corner. Begin by slowing down: Roll off the throttle, and if safety dictates, apply both brakes *before* you reach the corner. Line of sight and body posture determine your location on the road. First look at the turn, then allow your eyes to follow the curve to your chosen exit point. All schools of cycling recommend that you *turn your head but not your shoulders*. Your head and eye position should align your vision with the horizon.

Regular turning requires a leaning effort. Once you master counter-steering, you can consciously force a lean by pushing the handlebar slightly at the side where you want to turn. Whether you use counter-steering or a smooth and natural leaning posture to negotiate a normal corner, you must know how to lean your cycle effectively. The degree your cycle leans will determine both the turning angle and the bike's location on the pavement.

Remember, when cornering on the road, you need to lean or counter-steer more to turn more. Make sure, however, that your road speed is appropriate for the angle of lean you demand of your motorcycle. Extreme oversteering can drop your cycle to the pavement. Wise judgement develops only from riding experience, so be cautious and prudent until you master the dynamics of cornering your motorcycle.

Remember, too, that when you need to slow-turn in a parking lot, the dynamics change entirely. A crucial difference is that instead of leaning with the cycle, you stay upright. This strategy shifts as speed increases. You must master the transition between near standstill steering and the normal leaning or counter-steering techniques that apply on the road. Balance during these transitions proves even more challenging with a passenger on board.

"Rolling on" (opening) the throttle as you lean into a turn will stabilize the cycle and help your cornering effort. Downhill turns can be hazardous, as you cannot roll the throttle open. Statistically, nearly 80% of all motorcycle accidents occur on downhill turns. Use caution.

FIG. 3-18. A cardinal error is deceleration while in a turn. This upsets steering and handling. You find yourself in this situation when you have miscalculated the corner—one more reason to constantly read the road ahead. Once you have safely entered a turn, you can "roll on" throttle to maintain stability. Increase speed when safe and suitable.

Safely Joining Traffic

Once you have mastered the controls and slow speed operation of your cycle, you can prepare for traffic. Before entering the road and traffic, make sure you can be seen. When I had my motorcycle repair shop years ago, cycling customers and friends would complain constantly that auto and truck drivers were trying to kill them. Aside from the legal implications of such a prospect, there was a half-truth to the remark.

WARNING —
Although the use of a helmet has been a source of controversy, there is no moral, political or rational reason not to wear one. There are reams of statistical proof that helmets help save lives and prevent brain injuries. Helmets also provide a place for better faceshield protection, which can prevent flying road debris from causing eye injury or even death.

Try estimating the speed of a bird or aircraft flying directly toward where you stand. A motorcyclist, in broad daylight, presents the same kind of visual effect for approaching motorists. The classic accident is an auto or truck driver who turns "right in front of the motorcycle." I find that this is usually the result of poor distance judgement (bird in flight analogy), complicated by a cycle that may be traveling faster than anticipated or with the headlight off.

You have too little surface area for many motorists to judge your approaching distance. To decrease this risk, wear a bright and reflective helmet, bright clothing and gloves. Orange, yellow and green vests or jackets make the best choice. Reflective surfaces at the sides of a brightly colored helmet can reduce risk of getting hit from the side.

Harley-Davidson makes good use of turn signal lamps on Evolution cycles. These bright safety devices should be part of every turn and lane change. Make use of your turn signals an automatic response whenever you ride.

During daylight hours, when your taillamp is on with the headlight, your brake light may be hard to detect. Before making a stop or slowing down from higher speeds, pump the brakes gently to produce a flashing rear brake light. (Keep brake pedal pressure below the point that you activate the brakes.) Day or night, motorists will be more likely to see a flashing brake light.

Use your mirrors. At all times, know what's coming from behind and each side. Always glance to the side before changing lanes to be certain there is not a vehicle in your "blind spot." (Despite your open air riding position, motorcycles are not exempt from blind spots.) Ride cautiously, and stay alert when in multi-lane traffic: A motorcycle is often in another motorist's blind spot.

FIG. 3-19. During daytime, double your visibility to oncoming motorists by running with your headlight on. States have made this a mandatory part of riding, and there's good reason. Take advantage of this safety measure.

FIG. 3-20. NEAR: Under certain lighting conditions, other motorists will see turn signals more readily than they will see you. Always use your turn signals for turns, and switch them off immediately after the maneuver. FAR: Know the horn button intimately, and use it to indicate your motorcycle's position or your next move. I use my horn as a warning device, not to vent frustration.

My accident-free record has been the result of defensive riding. Early on, rather than blame others for "trying to kill me," I accepted the fact that they often could not see me or had a vague sense for how fast my motorcycle was approaching. Riding defensively means *expecting the worst* from other motorists. Much of the time, you'll find that you made the right call.

Night riding means dressing in a bright helmet and clothes that pick up headlight reflection. Slow down. Allow more distance between cars and cycles. Pay attention to the movement of car headlights, as they give clues to bumps and obstacles in the road. Read distance more carefully, and use your high beams whenever legally possible.

> **WARNING —**
> *Although legal in many states and fashionable, several cycles riding in a tight cluster at night constitute a supreme hazard! You have less response room for avoiding obstacles or an erratic, drunk driver. An accident could drop all of your cycles to the pavement in an instant.*

If at all possible, keep from locking up the front brake or skidding with either wheel when stopping on a curve. Unless you intentionally want to let the cycle go out from under your body as you escape the machine, maintain maximum traction as you slow the cycle down. Skidding while leaning on an angle will radically reduce control.

Riding through curves can be exhilarating. The mixture of excess speed and a curve, however, will cause more adrenaline flow than any other riding condition. This is where many motorcyclists have accidents.

Experienced riders often begin a curve at the outside to allow for a larger turning sweep and radius. Progressing through the turn, they move toward the inside of the curve, then begin their exit in a wide sweep outward. This is a fluid and singular movement, not choppy or wiggly. There are numerous exceptions and reasons to modify this approach. A conservative rider, facing a heavily trafficked route, might hold a middle of the lane line through a corner. This keeps the cycle away from oncoming traffic with enough room to maneuver if an obstacle arises.

FIG. 3-21. For emergency stops, night or day, front brakes provide 75-85% or more of the stopping power. Apply both brakes evenly, smoothly and with steady, firm pressure. To stop on a curve, reduce throttle and come to a balanced stop by increasing braking effort as the cycle slows. Knowledge of counter-steering techniques can assist when making panic stops or stopping under irregular conditions.

FIG. 3-22. NEAR: Riding the center of a lane requires a road surface free of potential hazards. Especially on urban freeways, riding center of a lane can be hazardous. A long dry spell followed by rain can coat this section with a slick film of oily water. Determine safest line when you encounter slick pavement. FAR: Watch your lane and the road shoulder for loose gravel. Avoid icy spots if at all possible.

Road Hazards and Other Precautions

Swerving to miss an object in the road or car requires skill at counter-steering. A controlled swerve requires 1) turning the handlebars in the direction you want to turn, 2) holding on tightly with feet firmly on the pegs and legs squeezing the fuel tank, and 3) looking and leaning in the direction you want to swerve. Always remember the relationship between line of sight and your location on the road. Swerve before braking, or swerve after braking—*never perform a counter-steer swerve while braking.*

If you have no room to swerve to avoid an obstacle in the road, try to minimize the impact. The general safety recommendation is to slow down and stay straight as you approach the obstacle. Approach at a 90° angle if possible. With feet firmly planted on the pegs, lift your weight from the seat to reduce the jarring and risk of getting tossed from the motorcycle.

Slick and irregular surfaces can be hazardous. Crossing grooves in the road at the wrong angle is a nightmare in action. When you have to ride on a slick roadway, slow down. Stay light on the throttle and brakes, and do not make fast moves or changes. "Float" over unexpected slick spots at the straightest possible angle. Allow the thrust of the cycle to propel you forward. Keep upright and straight.

There's nothing more nerve wracking than crossing a road berm edge or grooves from a railroad track. Again, the ideal angle of approach is 90°. The most dangerous and risky approach is anywhere near parallel to the obstacle. Riding in a single track, a two-wheeled motorcycle has extreme difficulty climbing out of deep grooves or crossing pavement ledges.

Of necessity, I have successfully ridden road motorcycles on packed snow and slush. If you must do this, ride slowly. Use an extremely light touch with the brakes, throttle, and steering. Wheel lockup can occur instantly on ice with road type tires, as there is little friction between the road and tire. A locked wheel, especially at the front, can cause your cycle to skid or slide out and fall—instantly.

FIG. 3-23. A technique learned in motocrossing and enduro riding is to apply brakes hard before an obstacle or ravine. This will compress the front fork. Just as you reach the obstacle, release brakes, which will cause fork legs to rebound. This lightens weight on the front wheel, reducing jarring while maintaining better control.

An unavoidable slick spot (bridge surface, ice, snow or a chemical/oil spill) may appear unexpectedly. Slow down as much as possible before the slick stretch, and line up with the danger area as straight as the road will permit. As you approach the slick area, release both brakes, stay upright and "float" across the section—don't make sudden moves or throttle changes.

Oil presents a supreme hazard to motorcycles. Watch for oil on the road. If you find the pavement is oily, stay in tire tracks on the high side of the lane. When you stop at a gas station or area where trucks and cars park, avoid putting your boot down on oil. You may slip and land on the ground, followed by your valuable Harley-Davidson cycle!

Some hazards are simply unavoidable. One, in particular, is dog syndrome. You inevitably will find yourself on a quiet street or country lane when someone's mean spirited, unleashed dog mistakes your Harley-Davidson for a king size bicycle and rider.

Slow down and shift to the appropriate gear before you reach the animal. Don't try to kick the dog, as this could cause swerving or loss of control. (Kicking at the dog could also offer the animal just what it wants—a leg to bite!) Accelerate as you pass the dog, and stay on track.

As another concern, consider how you leave the highway and park safely. Signal *first* to let other drivers know your intent. Check your mirrors, and glance to your left side. Slow enough for handling the change to soft dirt or shoulder material, then leave the pavement and get well off the road.

When you park, whether on or off pavement, be careful. I once parked my cycle on its centerstand when the asphalt was summer hot. Two hours later, one of my co-workers called me with a shrill yell. The beautiful cycle lay on its side, gas oozing from the fuel cap. There was an impression where the pavement gave way beneath the cycle's centerstand. Fortunately, the only damage was a cracked mirror.

Two-up Riding

If you plan two-up riding with a passenger, make sure your cycle has an appropriate rear seat and foot pegs. The shock absorbers may need adjustment to compensate for the added weight, especially if you tote luggage. (See your Harley-Davidson owner's manual and other chapters of this book for details on adjusting the shock absorbers.) If you intend to ride any distance, you'll

Riding and Mechanical Troubles

Whether or not you plan well and take care of your motorcycle, mechanical problems do occur on the road. Proper maintenance will prevent many kinds of troubles, but be prepared. You or one of the other cyclists in your riding group may have trouble.

1) Tire leak or blowout: This can happen to anyone, although more often with tube type tires. Once you sense the problem and which tire is going flat, keep your bike as straight as possible. Gently apply the brake at the wheel without a leaking tire. As the cycle slows to a near stop, work your way to the roadside. By the time you stop safely, you may be lucky and find the tire still holding a slight amount of air.

2) Throttle stuck open: This is treacherous. If opening and closing the throttle doesn't slow the engine, hit the kill switch—now. Pull in the clutch lever at exactly the same time to prevent the rear tire from skidding. Apply the brakes uniformly to get the cycle stopped and off the road as quickly and safely as possible.

3) Wheel wobble: This unique motorcycle anomaly can range from slight shaking of the front forks to a highly dangerous, full-scale tank slapper! Release the throttle smoothly and crouch low and forward to shift weight onto the front fork. Keep a snug grip on the handlebars until the wobble stops, then apply the brakes gradually and get off the road. Inspect the front wheel and tire, fork, your cargo and/or passenger weight distribution, steering head bearings and other obvious prospects. If you cannot determine the problem, *don't ride the cycle until a qualified technician examines and repairs the bike.*

4) Secondary chain or belt breakage: On a well maintained cycle, this should not occur, but when it does, chain breakage is worse. A broken chain can jam in the primary sprocket or around the rear sprocket and frame. The most dangerous consequence is abrupt rear wheel lockup.

5) Broken primary chain or seized engine: Either of these bleak prospects could instantly lock up the rear wheel. If you sense the engine seizing (very hot and slowing rapidly), back off the throttle, pull in the clutch lever, and let the engine die as you coast as safely as possible to the roadside and stop.

FIG. 3-24. Statistically, motor vehicle accidents are most likely to occur within a few miles of home. Don't take a chance. Wear leathers and a safe helmet whenever you ride. For Harley-Davidson riding apparel, traditional colors are black and orange. Don't hesitate to play up the orange when flying your H-D colors! Being safe in traffic begins with being visible.

need to adjust your mirrors and even the headlamp. The passenger has responsibilities, too, and you may need to explain these concerns.

Ask your passenger to get on and slide as far forward as safety allows. The passenger has no handlebars to hold, so your waist or hips become grips. Prepare the passenger for the tug and movement of the machine. They should not hold too tightly when you need slack, like during takeoff. Coach the passenger to lean into turns as you do and help you balance the machine.

Strongly warn the passenger about dangers associated with mufflers and hot exhaust pipes. One of the most common injuries for motorcyclists is a muffler burn on the leg. These kinds of injuries are avoidable, especially through the use of protective riding apparel.

Leathers offer far more than a good appearance when you ride. You can prevent both burns and "road rash" by properly protecting yourself. Some of the most dangerous and inappropriate articles of clothing for riding a motorcycle are shorts, tank tops and light tennis shoes or thongs. This dress code is a severe injury looking for a place to happen.

Rider Education Resources: AMA, MSF and the "HOG"

There are many ways to learn motorcycling. In most states, an active AMA or Motorcycle Safety Foundation (MSF) instruction program offers riding schools. Consult your Harley-Davidson dealership, DMV office or the local AMA or MSF chapter for information on these schools.

Beginner and advanced rider courses are available, and I would encourage anyone to take a Motorcycle Safety Foundation (MSF) course. The many techniques and proper riding habits shared in this chapter came either through experience or exposure to MSF instructional programs. Do yourself a favor. Take an MSF course.

FIG. 3-25. Western Regional HOG Rally at Reno, Nevada, provided an excellent opportunity for riders to assemble. Camaraderie is infectious. Harley-Davidson and HOG create a helpful learning environment at these rallies.

FIG. 3-26. What other motorcycle manufacturer provides an opportunity for owners to test ride *every new model available*? This was no run around the parking lot, either. At Reno HOG Rally, new demo cycles went out for a 17-mile tour! Some riders rode every bike available. Harley-Davidson has confidence in its products and a willingness to share information.

An outstanding resource for the newcomer or veteran Harley-Davidson owner is the "HOG" (Harley Owner's Group). At a regional HOG Rally, you can learn about the technical features of Harley-Davidson motorcycles and take an MSF classroom course. You can even test ride the full range of new models (licensed and experienced riders only, please!).

Technical seminars, conducted by factory speakers and training personnel, discuss new developments and recommended upgrades. Harley-Davidson respects the intelligence, loyalty and financial commitment of its customers. HOG Rally seminars offer a frank exchange of information and a chance for owners to share concerns.

4

BASIC SERVICE
AND LUBRICATION

Harley-Davidson Evolution cycles are well built, precision machines. With proper maintenance, your cycle will start and run flawlessly, providing years of trouble-free service. Your motorcycle requires routine minor tune-ups, periodic oil changes, lubrication and thorough inspections.

Although many of today's owners prefer taking their Harley-Davidson cycle to a dealer for service, you can perform most routine work on your cycle. If you do your own service work, you will build a better understanding of the machine and become more skilled at troubleshooting problems and making emergency field repairs.

Despite my busy schedule and long working hours, I set aside time for servicing my own cars, trucks and motorcycles. I enjoy mechanics, and my aims are those of a professional technician—as yours should be.

To make sure that my standards match Harley-Davidson's expectations, I invest in factory service manuals. There is only one way to do the job right, and factory engineers know their products' needs. *Get the factory service*

FIG. 4-1. When you need to know a service procedure or how a component functions, you will find the genuine Harley-Davidson factory service manual valuable. This is an official and accurate reference for your motorcycle. To perform safe, reliable repairs, use these guidelines.

manual that covers your particular Evolution model, and review relevant sections of the book before performing each service task. I have genuine Harley-Davidson manuals and factory reprints that cover 1917 to the present. These service guidebooks, despite changes in our language, are each an easy read and highly useful. Harley-Davidson provides a valuable resource.

TOOLS TO SERVICE YOUR CYCLE

An Evolution motorcycle represents a large investment. Your cycle, riding apparel and accessories deserve good care. When you perform your own service work, make sure your work setting matches the value of your motorcycle.

Few of us have a shop facility that rivals the local Harley dealership. An inadequate shop and poor tools will make service work difficult. Restrict service work to the capacity of your shop and tools. Otherwise, you may damage your valuable cycle or accessories, or worse yet, your own body. Fortunately, Harley-Davidson work does not require as many specialized tools as some vehicles. In particular, less complex emissions and induction systems allow easier service.

Like other motor vehicles, Harley-Davidson parts are expensive. Losing parts will stop your work and send you rushing to the dealership. Some parts have special order status and take time to obtain. Each part has its place.

Before starting service work, label clean coffee cans or similar nonbreakable containers to hold nuts, bolts and lock washers. Parts illustrations in unit repair sections of your factory service manual are helpful. Especially on a pre-owned Evolution motorcycle that might have suffered from mediocre repairs, account for each part.

If you lift your cycle, keep the frame steady. Never place a jack under brake pipes/hoses, exhaust system parts or running boards. Consult your service manual for proper lifting procedures. When you are unsure about cycle lift points, talk with your local dealership's service department.

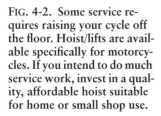

FIG. 4-2. Some service requires raising your cycle off the floor. Hoist/lifts are available specifically for motorcycles. If you intend to do much service work, invest in a quality, affordable hoist suitable for home or small shop use.

FIG. 4-3. For heavy lifting, ask a robust friend or relative for assistance. Personal injury is less likely when hydraulic force, like this hoist, takes the place of brute strength. Wrestling with parts can lead to broken components and severe bodily injury. This is unnecessary and avoidable.

Filling Your Toolbox

Your Harley-Davidson motorcycle garage requires a good assortment of wrenches and tools. Most Harley-Davidson hardware fits traditional U.S. thread and wrench sizes, however, metric tools will also be necessary when working on your Evolution motorcycle.

Your hand tools should include U.S. and metric open and box ended wrenches plus U.S. and metric sockets of 1/4"-, 3/8"- and 1/2"-square drive. You will also need specialty sockets for spark plugs and other service details.

Many jobs call for a hydraulic press. If a press is beyond your budget, sublet your heavy bearing, gear or bushing work to your Harley-Davidson dealer. Attempts to improvise with a hammer are dangerous and usually result in damaged parts.

Some repairs require highly specialized tools. Harley-Davidson service manuals itemize these tools and describe their use. Although endorsed and often sold through Harley-Davidson dealerships, Kent-Moore (address in the Appendix) makes most of these tools.

Precise Measurements

Professional motorcycle service requires precise adjustments and measurements. A dial indicator and magnetic stand are valuable tools. Shimming bearings, checking shaft end float, adjusting backlash of gears, setting bearing endplay and other chores require use of a dial indicator.

A magnetic stand or a gooseneck holding fixture will help with awkward dial indicator measurements. You will also need a precision micrometer(s) for measuring shaft diameters and checking the thickness of shims, rotors and bearings.

Harley-Davidson service work demands a wide range of torque wrenches: 1/4" drive inch-pound, 3/8" drive inch/foot-pound, 1/2" square drive foot-pound, and even a heavy duty 3/4"-square drive type for certain brake caliper fasteners, primary fasteners, and other high torque hardware. To do this kind of work, invest in quality torque wrenches, and have a tool specialist calibrate your torque wrenches periodically.

FIG. 4-4. A dial indicator and magnetic stand can aid in adjusting wheel bearing end play and runout on shafts. You can also detect camshaft lobe wear with a dial indicator.

FIG. 4-5. Torque wrenches come in a variety of sizes. This assortment serves final tightening needs from fork leg nuts to ultra-sensitive alloy case screws.

Nitty Gritty Tools

Your hand tools should include a hacksaw, a set of chisels, punches and drifts (both hard steel and malleable brass), Allen hex wrenches, and a set of Torx-type drivers. Motorcycle accessories may also use Phillips head or other types of screw drivers. Seal and bearing cup driver sets are optional; careful improvising often works satisfactorily.

> **WARNING —**
> *Wear safety goggles whenever you work with air impact tools, sharp cutting tools, hammers, drivers, chisels or punches.*

Fuel Line and Brake Work Tools

For brake tubing nuts and fuel pipe fittings, a flare nut wrench set is mandatory. (Open end wrenches will damage compression and flare nuts.) Your Harley-Davidson Evolution cycle has hydraulically actuated disc brakes. If you intend to perform brake work, invest in quality brake tools.

Disc brake work requires pad/caliper piston tools and a micrometer for checking disc and rotor thickness/variance. You need special hones for master cylinder and disc caliper rebuilding, and a clamp to retract the caliper piston when installing new pads. (See brake work section of this book for details.) A bleeder hose prevents fluid contamination during brake bleeding.

Air Tools for Speed and Efficiency

Air wrenches are a major timesaver. A wide range of pneumatic tools quickly tame difficult repair jobs. In addition, air impact wrenches can enhance the quality of some repairs. This is especially true when working with high torque settings or if subassemblies suffer from semi-seized hardware.

FIG. 4-6. Air wrenches and other pneumatic tools save time and ease repair work, especially when removing and installing brake calipers, transmission and primary drive nuts and other fasteners that have high torque settings.

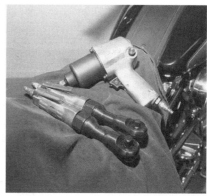

CAUTION —
Always use specially hardened impact sockets with air impact tools.

When you use an air impact tool for the removal and installation of high torque fasteners, you can eliminate the awkward use of a breaker bar. Save your knuckle tissue, and avoid the risk of slipping with a breaker bar and scarring your cycle's gorgeous—and spendy—paint finish.

WARNING —
Never use air guns for final torque settings. Bring torque to just below final setting, and use a torque wrench for final torque recommended by Harley-Davidson. On your cycle, there are many expensive parts that could become damaged by overtightening nuts, bolts and other fasteners.

Engine Overhaul Tools

Engine overhaul requires far more tools than a valve spring compressor, cylinder hone and ring compressor. For an out-of-frame rebuild of an Evolution engine, you would sublet the re-boring of barrels, any crankshaft assembly work, valve grinding, fitting piston pins, installing precision bearings and other machine shop procedures.

Before you rebuild your Harley-Davidson Evo engine, consider tool costs. How often will you perform this task? Shop mechanics invest constantly in expensive specialty tools to achieve professional results.

Tune-up and Electrical Tools

From a service standpoint, the electronic distributor has reduced maintenance. Electronic ignition eliminates the need to gap points or set dwell. Instead, troubleshooting now consists of ohmmeter and voltage tests. Here, a precision digital-type volt/ohmmeter is a must item for your tool set. It is an ideal companion for your electrical troubleshooting and tune-up work, offering quick, concise diagnosis of everything from shorts and open circuits to testing alternator current and battery voltage.

Round out your tune-up tools with a vacuum gauge, float height gauge, needle/seat driver, assorted screw drivers, proper size Allen wrenches and Torx sockets.

FIG. 4-7. Electronic ignitions have reduced service requirements. Harley-Davidson's high energy electronic ignition is accessible and serviceable. For these ignitions, the primary troubleshooting tool is a digital volt-ohmmeter. Access to module requires special riveting method. (See tune-up section of this book or your service manual.)

FIG. 4-8. Special ratchets and sockets serve specific needs, in this case the safe removal of spark plugs. Note swivel head on ratchet. Socket has rubber insert to protect plug's porcelain. Be careful when threading spark plugs into alloy spark plug threads. Always start by light finger touch.

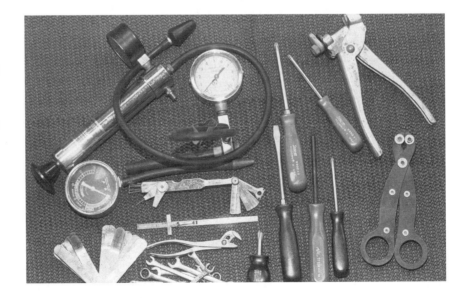

FIG. 4-9. Carburetor tuning requires float height gauge, needle/seat removal tool and a complete assortment of quality screwdrivers (clutch head, straight slot, Phillips and Torx). You need ignition wrenches for electrical repairs.

FIG. 4-10. Continuity tester is helpful; however, a volt-ohmmeter (shown) works far better than any test lamp. *Never* use pinpoint testers that puncture wire insulation. They damage insulation, weaken wire and leave circuits susceptible to shorts.

FIG. 4-11. Harley-Davidson starter systems allow hookup of a remote starter switch for quickly aligning timing marks or checking compression.

FIG. 4-12. Induction ammeters, although not as accurate as more expensive test equipment, provide quick view of starter current draw or alternator output. Held over starter cable or charge wire, meter reads magnetic field as amperage flow. (Make certain that magnetic interference from adjacent wires does not influence readings.)

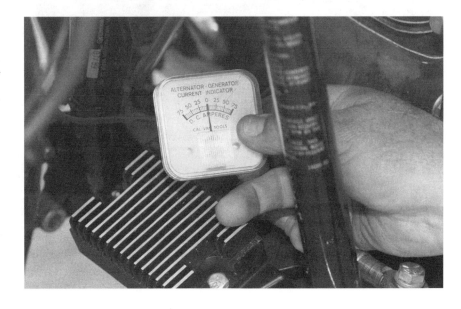

FIG. 4-13. Battery maintenance, a critical need for your
motorcycle, requires tools for
cleaning cable terminals and
posts. A battery hydrometer
test is useful when you suspect a dead cell, while sim-
pler voltmeter tests answer
most battery and charge system questions. (See electrical
service section of book for
more details.)

FIG. 4-14. A quality hand
vacuum pump/pressure
gauge is valuable. Emission
control devices and the Evo's
'V.O.E.S.' switch can be tested easily with a vacuum
pump.

FIG. 4-15. Fuel pressure affects performance on Electronic Fuel Injection systems.
Harley-Davidson's Sequen-
tial (Port) Fuel Injection requires fuel pressure tester and
other diagnostic tools to pinpoint trouble.

Compression Test Versus Cylinder Leakdown

Although the compression gauge registers cranking compression (a quick reference for overall engine condition), a more reliable test is cylinder leakdown percentages. The leakdown tester pressurizes a cylinder through the spark plug hole, with the piston at top-dead-center (TDC) of its compression stroke (both valves closed). If the valves, rings, head gasket or cylinder castings cannot seal normally, the tester will indicate the volume or percentage of this leak.

The advantage of a leakdown test is two-fold. First, the piston rests at TDC, the point of greatest cylinder wear (maximum taper). With parts immobile, leakage and piston ring blowby show up readily. It is not uncommon for an engine to display "normal" cranking compression yet have 30% or higher leakdown due to poor ring seal! 8–10% cylinder leakage means your engine is in like-new shape. Secondly, the leakdown tester pinpoints the leak. If an intake valve leaks, air blows back through the carburetor or EFI throttle body. A leaking exhaust valve sends an audible signal out the tailpipe. Piston ring wear telegraphs through the crankcase breather and ventilation system.

If a leakdown tester is unavailable or more costly than your budget allows, a suitable substitute is a K-D Tool air-hold fitting designed for changing valve springs. Screw the fitting into a spark plug hole. With the piston at TDC on its compression stroke, adjust air line pressure to a point between 60 and 80 psi. Attach the air hose coupler to the fitting. Listen for high volume airflow to pinpoint where leakage occurs.

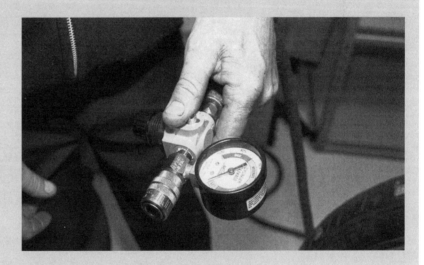

A leakdown tester exceeds all other methods of evaluating engine seal. This gauge is capable of pinpointing worn valves, defective piston rings, a blown head gasket or casting cracks. You need compressed air to operate tester.

Timing Light

The timing light has remained an important element of ignition tuning, as normal wear to camshaft timing gears still requires periodic tests of spark timing. The best timing light has a built-in advance readout, which allows testing the electronic spark advance's function.

Better timing lights are inductive variety. Here you hook the connector/clamp to the insulation of a spark plug cable without disconnecting the cable from the spark plug.

Soft Tools

Conventional composition gaskets leak from the effects of heat (embrittlement), shrinkage or inability to fill minute gaps and voids—like a valve cover with a few thousandths of an inch of gasket gap. Such a leak could spill the entire tankful of oil along a remote highway in Nebraska! Aging, fatigue, vibration and oxidation can affect neoprene, rubber, cork and, yes, even metal gaskets.

FIG. 4-16. A timing light (shown) and volt-ohmmeter help with tuning and trouble-shooting. Volt-ohmmeter has become an important electronic and electrical trouble-shooting tool. Some tasks require more precise digital volt-ohmmeter.

FIG. 4-17. Timing lights with built-in advance use the engine as a test stand for spinning the ignition rotor safely to 1000–1250 rpm (2000–2500 crankshaft rpm). Timing light's advance mechanism allows zeroing timing to factory TDC mark or any other degree setting within the timing light's range. My Snap-On light (shown) allows accurate readout of ignition's full spark advance range.

FIG. 4-18. Products like liquid thread locker and special sealants (called chemical "soft tools" in the automotive and motorcycle trade) have become common OEM features on Harley-Davidson cycles. Keep these items on your workbench. Smaller packages will fit your on-the-road saddlebag toolbox.

FIG. 4-19. Alongside a lonely highway in an emergency, Ultra Blue can create a temporary gasket for stopping an oil leak. Small tubes of Ultra Blue and its counterparts, Ultra Black and Ultra Copper, make smart companions for your saddlebag tool kit.

Your Harley-Davidson dealership and aftermarket suppliers offer sealants and chemical "soft tools" that meet OEM guidelines for your cycle. Harley-Davidson factory service manuals describe these rubber bonders, thread locking liquids and gasket forming materials. Do not substitute other products.

RTV silicone sealants are unlike conventional gaskets and sealants. Rather than deteriorate when exposed to corrosive oils, products like Permatex/Loctite's Ultra Blue or Ultra Black become more flexible, pliant and oil resistant. During engine or transmission assembly, use the silicone and threadlocking products that Harley-Davidson recommends in your factory service manual.

For exhaust system joints and flanges, follow Harley-Davidson's recommendations. The wrong type of silicone or other sealants on an exhaust system will lead to leaks.

> **CAUTION —**
> *Factory warranties on emission hardware will not cover an oxygen sensor damaged by the use of high-volatility RTV sealant. SFI/EFI and exhaust feedback emission and fuel devices use oxygen sensors. Never use a non-automotive silicone sealant, like bathtub caulk, on engine or geartrain parts.*

Harley-Davidson recommends specific sealants to provide proper fitup of parts. Some assemblies require an anaerobic sealer that will cure in the absence of air. Print-a-seal type gaskets provide a quality mixture of composition and silicone-based sealant properties. Harley-Davidson uses print-a-seal gaskets on engine and gearcase assemblies.

> **CAUTION —**
> *Do not use RTV/silicone sealants to replace OEM engine and gearcase gaskets. Some Harley-Davidson cut gaskets double as selective fit spacers. Without proper clearances, internal moving parts will fail. Unless otherwise specified in your factory service manual, do not use RTV sealants in combination with selective fit gaskets.*

Neoprene-lipped seals serve well on most shaft surfaces. The outer jacket of shaft seals at engine covers or the transmission case can be coated lightly with automotive RTV silicone or other recommended sealants before driving the seal into place. Although coating the outer jacket of a seal will not prevent the lip portion from failing, you can reduce the likelihood of housing bore-to-seal seepage.

Once you become familiar with the properties and proper uses of sealants and adhesives, they prove as handy as a screwdriver or wrench. Your Harley-Davidson service manual will describe where and how to use these products.

Sourcing Harley-Davidson Parts and Lubricants

All of your parts needs can be met by the local Harley-Davidson dealership. I would recommend using Genuine Harley-Davidson parts in every OEM repair, restoration and service procedure that you perform.

There are many experts within the aftermarket who know Harley-Davidson product thoroughly. I respect these individuals and manufacturers for their wisdom, commitment and effort to build greater performance or stamina into Harley-Davidson motorcycles.

In the performance upgrade and accessories chapters of this book, I refer to aftermarket products. For routine service needs and maintaining your cycle to a high standard, however, I recommend that you use genuine Harley-Davidson parts over all others.

When it comes to lubrication needs, your dealer offers a full line of genuine Harley-Davidson lubricants. Although experience has taught me to value some aftermarket filters, oils and grease products, I turn to Harley-Davidson for routine service parts and lubricants.

At a HOG Rally, where factory-level instructors conduct technical seminars, owners learn that Harley-Davidson's oil and grease products *meet the specific needs of the Evolution motorcycle*. While I strongly advocate the use of a quality synthetic oil in liquid-cooled engines, Harley-Davidson's technical experts have convinced me that Harley-Davidson Motor Oil will surpass all other products in protecting the Evolution V^2.

FIG. 4-20. There are some instances where aftermarket parts may work as well as Genuine Harley-Davidson parts; however, Harley-Davidson has the best sense for the design features and limitations of its products, and your dealer will warrant the product. Some aftermarket air filters rank well. K&N has always provided a quality alternative to OEM air filtration. For routine service of a stock cycle, however, a Genuine Harley-Davidson air filter will offer the kind of protection and service life that most owners want.

FIG. 4-21. For oil filtration, I use only Harley-Davidson filters. Pressure ratings are crucial to adequate oil flow, and Harley-Davidson regards oil filter development as a part of engine design. With factory-engineered filters, your engine will receive maximum filtration without restrictions in flow. Considering the cost of an oil filter, this is cheap insurance.

An air cooled motorcycle engine and its emission requirements differ from those of a liquid-cooled automotive type engine. High cylinder operating temperatures require exceptional heat protection that the oil must provide. Automotive motor oils, whether synthetic or conventional type, cannot use certain additives. Here, Harley-Davidson has an advantage: the ability to formulate a special blend additive package, higher in protective zinc, that is legal for motorcycle use and offers better engine protection than any currently approved automotive oil.

For this reason, I choose Genuine Harley-Davidson Motor Oil and other Harley-Davidson lubricants. Readily available at your local dealership, fully compliant with any warranty requirements, and specially blended to serve your motorcycle, these oils, greases, special brake fluids and protective chemicals are your wisest choice.

DO-IT-YOURSELF SERVICE

Your Evolution motorcycle and its V^2 engine make a valuable machine. Some owners prefer taking their cycle to the local Harley-Davidson dealership for any kind of service work. You can, however, find that basic service is not difficult and provides useful insight into the workings of your motorcycle.

Various service and repair operations require different skill levels. In other chapters of this book, I will share details on how to perform more involved service, repairs and troubleshooting procedures.

My purpose with the service chapters of this book is to help you "think like a professional mechanic." Lubrication and detailing can be a useful means of orientation. You will quickly acquire skills at handling tools properly, working close to the heart of your Harley-Davidson and taking an increasingly greater role in the maintenance and preservation of a fine motorcycle.

Unfortunately, we cannot work together in a classroom setting. Instead, we'll do the next best thing, and I'll walk you through basic service procedures using photos and comments. The backdrop for most of these photos is

Reno Harley-Davidson, so you can witness a professional mechanic/technician performing these steps.

For now, our goal is fundamental service that you can readily perform. If you like this kind of work and want to move to the next level of skill as a Harley-Davidson home mechanic, later chapters of this book will cover more in-depth repairs and service.

You may decide to simply use this information to provide a better understanding of the repair process. If so, at the end of the basic service sections, I share tips on interacting positively with your Harley-Davidson dealership's service department or an independent shop. Learning the service procedures in this book can, at the very least, increase your communication skills with professional mechanics and service personnel.

Lubrication Service

Performing your own periodic lubrication and service work begins at the first 500 miles on your new motorcycle. Your Harley-Davidson dealership spent a good deal of time doing "pre-delivery" service and inspection of the cycle, however, the first 500 miles make up the run-in of engine, transmission, clutch and other vital components.

Consult your Harley-Davidson operator's handbook and factory service manual for information on when to service various points on your Evolution motorcycle. Use the chart in your service manual as a guideline for proper maintenance intervals. The chart explains which items need checking, adjustment or replacement. This format is necessary for your cycle's warranty to stay in effect.

Routine service invariably includes oil changes. At engine oil and filter change points, select a Harley-Davidson motor oil that suits the climate and riding environment. Although typical oil changes are at the first 500 miles and every 5,000 miles thereafter, change oil more frequently on a cycle driven under cold weather, dust or hard operating conditions.

To minimize risk of introducing harmful debris into your engine, thoroughly wash and dry the engine case, oil tank, oil drain lines and oil filter area before removing the oil filter or drain plug.

FIG. 4-22. Oil must be fully warmed before changing. Once oil is hot, you can remove the oil tank drain plug from the tank or drain hose. Wear heat and oil resistant gloves to prevent burning your hands during this procedure. (Engine shown is not hot.) Oil will drain faster if you remove the tank's fill cap.

FIG. 4-23. 1340cc engines have a tappet filter screen located near rear tappet guide on the engine case. You can carefully remove this screen and clean the filter. (I use carburetor spray cleaner and blow the part thoroughly clean and dry before reinstalling it.) As a safety precaution, replace the O-ring on re-installation of tappet filter. Stock up on OEM type O-rings if you intend to perform oil changes.

FIG. 4-24. While oil drains, remove oil filter. If not overtightened, a strong hand grip should free filter. (You may need a special filter wrench, #HD-96221-80 or equivalent, to loosen a tight filter.) Use a glove as insulation against hot filter and oil. Wipe filter stand with a clean and lint-free shop rag or cloth.

FIG. 4-25. When wiping oil filter stand and removing oil tank fill cap, use care and avoid contaminating the oil system.

FIG. 4-26. Take a small amount of clean engine oil and coat surface of new filter. Pour some fresh oil (approximately four ounces) into the filter, and let the oil settle into the filter core. Rub a film of fresh oil on gasket surface.

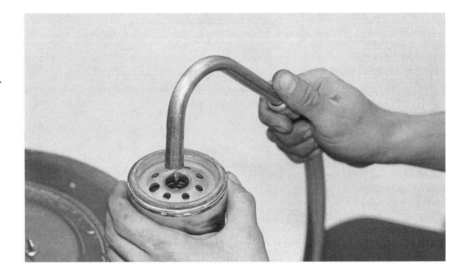

FIG. 4-27. *Start threads carefully*, and hand tighten filter. In most cases, one-half turn after gasket contacts filter stand is plenty; however, *make sure the filter feels snug.* Always check for leaks after starting engine. Leakage from a loose oil filter can cause severe engine damage (or at least an oily mess).

FIG. 4-28. Clean and inspect drain plug gaskets or O-rings. If these seals show wear, replace with new gasket of same type and size. Stock new drain plug gaskets or O-rings if you plan to perform your own lube and oil change services. Be cautious when threading drain plug or tightening Corbin hose clamp. Tighten all hardware securely, to specifications.

FIG. 4-29. Pour fresh oil carefully and avoid spilling by using a spout can or funnel. After filling the oil tank with its specified amount of oil (minus the amount you put in the new oil filter), replace cap. Start engine. While running engine at an idle, watch oil light. Light should cancel quickly and not come back on if engine speed is at 1000 rpm or higher. Check for oil leaks around filter and drain plug. Shut off engine, let it set for several minutes, then recheck oil level on dipstick with your motorcycle standing upright. Make sure oil reaches FULL mark. Add oil as needed.

Miscellaneous Items

Cable lubrication is a crucial part of motorcycle maintenance. Today's cables require less attention than years ago, however, they do need periodic inspection, lubrication and adjustment. Cable fraying or signs of cable housing damage mean time to replace cables. See later chapters of this book for cable replacement plus clutch and throttle cable adjustment.

On models with speedometer or tachometer cables, periodic attention is necessary. Using genuine Harley-Davidson graphite lubricant or equivalent will assure longer cable life and service. Remove cable from within its housing, clean with a suitable solvent and air blow dry. Coat cable with fresh graphite lube and reinstall in housing.

Front fork oil is an important part of your cycle's suspension and handling. Periodically, this oil needs changing, and in some instances, a viscosity change can improve your cycle's ride or safety. See later chapters of this book for information on changing fork oil and other suspension service.

FIG. 4-30. Your safety depends upon a throttle that responds as it should. Periodically disassemble hand throttle control assembly. Clean, air blow dry and apply graphite to the housing and sliding parts. Inspect throttle cable ends carefully and make sure cable is in good shape. Replace throttle cable if worn.

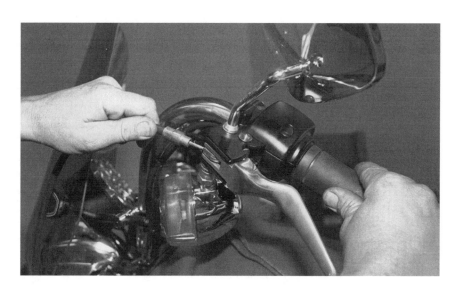

FIG. 4-31. Check fluid levels of front and rear hydraulic brake master cylinders. Avoid contamination and damage to your braking system. Clean debris away from master cylinder caps and clean your hands before removing caps to inspect or add brake fluid. Make sure bike is upright when checking fluid. Follow factory service specifications for proper brake fluid for your model motorcycle. Typically, Evolution cycles require D.O.T. 5 fluid.

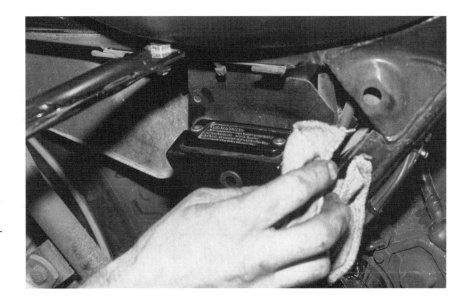

FIG. 4-32. Brake pad inspection and rear brake pedal adjustment are periodic demands. See brake service chapter of this book for details on adjusting your motorcycle's rear brake pedal, inspecting pads and rotors, and performing brake work.

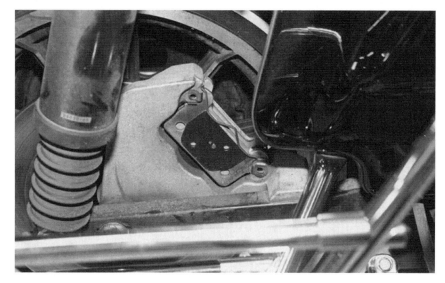

Air Filter Service

Foam air cleaner elements offer long service. When exposed to high dust levels, however, filters become clogged. Check your foam air filter frequently, especially after riding through a dusty region. In high dust situations, disregard normal service interval, and clean air filter if you cannot see light through matrix layers.

When planning a long trip through dusty country, consider cleaning the air filter at your earliest stop. It takes nothing more than hot, soapy water and a dab of proper oil. (*Only use oil on foam elements that require oil.*) A clogged filter will reduce fuel economy and performance. Carbon buildup and internal engine damage can result from long-term neglect. Even on an overnight trip, if necessary, take time to clean the air filter.

Fig. 4-33. In extreme cases, clean air filter element immediately. If you are uncertain whether air cleaner will flow enough air, perform a simple field test. Remove filter and aim it toward bright sunlight or a flashlight. (Keep away from heat or flame—air cleaner element contains flammable fuel fumes!) Light should be uniformly visible over full surface of filter.

Fig. 4-34. Some Evolution air filters require cleaning and oiling. Others require cleaning only. On models with oiled filters (shown) remove air filter cover and shake foam element loose from wire mesh core.

Fig. 4-35. This style Harley-Davidson washable air filter does not require oiling. Simply clean in hot soapy water. (Soak for a while if necessary.) Rinse, air blow dry at very low pressure. Install in reverse order of assembly. Always inspect air filter mounting gaskets for damage. Your engine must seal thoroughly between carburetor or EFI throttle body, air cleaner and air cleaner cover.

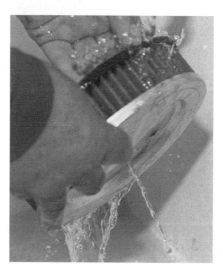

Primary Drive and Transmission Lubrication

Your cycle must be safely upright when you refill the primary chaincase. Unless you have invested in a cycle lift, this will likely require a second person to hold the cycle upright. Use fresh H-D Primary Chaincase lubricant #99887-84 or current specified lubricant for your motorcycle.

Before removing inspection plates or fill/drain plugs, clean the surrounding area. Always keep debris and abrasive contaminants away from the engine or gearcase openings. These are expensive items, responsible for taking your motorcycle across long and lonely ribbons of highway. Cleanliness during service helps assure reliability.

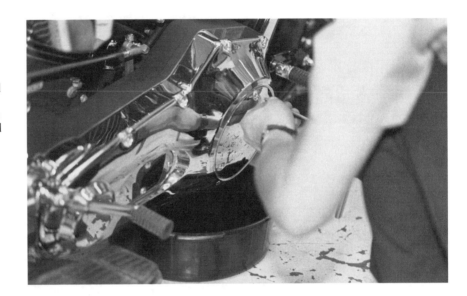

FIG. 4-36. 1340cc engines (F-series) require primary chaincase oil changes. With your cycle safely upright and warmed up, you can drain the primary chaincase. Place a drain pan beneath case, and remove drain plug located beneath the primary cover.

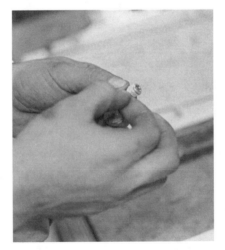 

FIG. 4-37. Remove clutch cover. When you have thoroughly drained oil, clean plug and inspect the seal. (Replace if worn.) Install drain plug using Teflon tape or liquid on drain plug threads during installation.

FIG. 4-38. With cycle upright, you will fill primary to lower edge of clutch inspection cover on '89 and earlier models. 1990-up cycles require fill to bottom edge of clutch diaphragm spring. To find this diaphragm spring, measure 2-3/4-inches from clutch adjusting screw centerline, downward toward lower edge of inspection cover opening.

FIG. 4-39. If worn, install a new O-ring for the clutch cover. Harley-Davidson recommends replacing cover screw plastic seals, so make sure you have these new parts on hand. At 500 miles and each subsequent 5,000 miles, plan on changing this oil. There's lots of heat and load on the primary chain and sprockets. Periodic oil changes will maximize service life of these vital parts.

FIG. 4-40. On XL Sportster engines, the primary chain and transmission share common lubricant. Again, fill and fluid inspection is at clutch cover. After warming up engine and transmission, place a drain pan beneath transmission drain plug, which is located beneath primary chaincase. Wearing a heat and oil resistant service glove, loosen and remove plug. Drain lubricant.

FIG. 4-41. Clean drain plug thoroughly, including removal of metal particles from magnet. Install clean plug and tighten carefully to specifications found in your service manual. Remove clutch inspection cover screws with a suitable driver (typically a Torx type).

FIG. 4-42. Hold XL cycle upright and fill primary/transmission units through clutch inspection cover opening. XL engines take approximately 32 fluid ounces of Harley-Davidson Sport-Trans Fluid. Verify your cycle's fluid capacity, which should bring oil to level of clutch spring diaphragm when filled. Pour slowly, allowing oil to move throughout primary and gearsets.

FIG. 4-43. Inspect "quad-ring" on primary/clutch inspection cover. Replace this seal and screw washers if you see any signs of wear. Install cover and secure each screw. I tighten these screws in cross pattern, stepping from light tension to proper, fully tightened tension.

FIG. 4-44. On F-series 1340cc Evolution engine, transmission is a fully self-contained assembly and requires its own lubricant. There is a dipstick/fill hole and a drain plug beneath case. Drain and refill with Harley-Davidson Transmission Lubricant specified for your cycle.

FIG. 4-45. Typical fill capacity for four-speed separate gearbox is one pint; five-speeds take 1.5 pint. *Always confirm fluid capacity for your cycle before filling gearcase or engine.* Cycle must be upright when checking fill level at dipstick (below starter motor) or inspection point.

Secondary Chain and Belt Maintenance

Secondary chain or belt inspection and adjustment are tasks you can perform. Knowing proper adjustment method can be handy if you find yourself on the road with a slightly loose secondary drive belt or chain. Measure chain or belt deflection. Have proper deflection limits committed to memory or in your saddlebag log book. You will find these specifications in a factory service manual for your specific motorcycle. The engine should be completely cool before checking belt tension. Set transmission shifter into neutral. Remove any cargo and set cycle on its side ("jiffy") stand. Inspect the belt or chain and sprockets carefully for signs of damage or fatigue. On models with chains, maintain the chain with Harley-Davidson Chain Spray or Chain Lube Plus.

FIG. 4-46. Perform routine rear chain lubrication after a run, when chain is hot. Wipe chain thoroughly with rag. Spray lube onto chain according to instructions. (Place newspaper behind and under chain to catch overspray and runoff!) Allow lube to soak into hot chain for at least an hour, then wipe off all excess with a rag before riding.

FIG. 4-47. You may need to remove chain and clean it thoroughly. This requires careful removal of master link and chain. Soak chain in solvent or kerosene, and clean with parts cleaning brush. Hold chain against old rags as you air blow it dry with compressed air. Lubricate with Harley-Davidson Chain Lube.

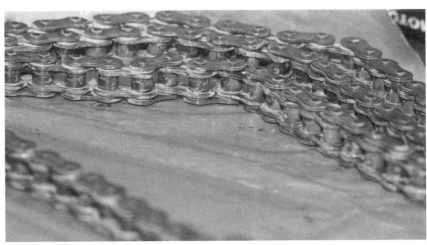

FIG. 4-48. Although a simple technique, installing master link properly is crucial to your safety and the cycle's reliability. Easiest way to perform this task is to place chain with opening at top run. Link comes through from back of chain. Install sideplate at face of chain. Install spring clip with closed end facing toward engine. Make sure spring clip seats in link pin grooves.

NOTE —
Correctly installed, master link spring clip's closed end will rest against the pulling pin of master link. With master link on top run of chain, open end of spring clip always trails away from direction of pull.

FIG. 4-49. Cleaners like Simple Green and some of Amway's products work well at cleaning a secondary drive belt. Goal is to remove oily road film, dirt and oxidized material. This can eliminate nuisance noises like "chirping" under deceleration. Do not use a cleaner that contains a mineral base or petroleum distillates (either of which would harm rubber). Belts do not require lubricant, although I find that treatment with 303 Protectant helps reduce oxidation.

Adjusting Secondary (Final) Drive Belt or Chain

Once clean and lubed (chains only), chain or belt can be adjusted. Determine midway point between primary and secondary sprockets. You will measure deflection of belt/chain at midpoint.

FIG. 4-50. Before checking tension, rotate chain to at least four equal positions to determine stretch. Degree of variance is good indicator of chain or belt stretch. If chain will stretch 3/4ths of a sprocket tooth space, it's time for a new one. Find tightest point. This is where you will test deflection.

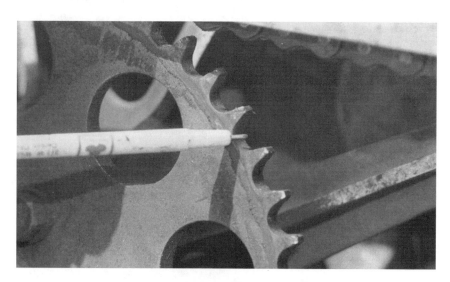

FIG. 4-51. For chain secondary drives, use a straight edge ruler. Note height of chain link pin midway between sprockets. Lift lower run of chain with a pencil. When you have removed all slack, note new height of same chain link pin. This change in measurement is the deflection of your chain. Compare this figure with specification in your Harley-Davidson factory service manual.

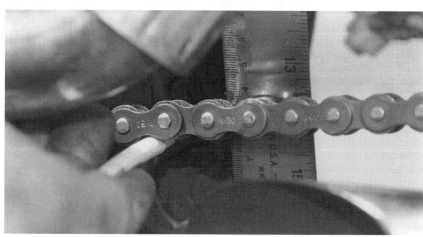

FIG. 4-52. For belt adjustment, Harley-Davidson's own Belt Tension Gauge (#HD-35381) is handy. Apply 10 pounds pressure at secondary belt midpoint. Rotate rear tire to get a measurement at several sections of belt. (If there is a wide variance, check for belt and/or sprocket wear.) At tightest point, you can take measurements. Compare this amount of deflection to specifications found in your factory service manual.

FIG. 4-53. Belt tooth fracture will occur when belt is too loose. Cracking can indicate belt too tight. Belts are tough, with 13 Aramid fibers. Road debris damage up to two fibers is considered okay by factory standards.

FIG. 4-54. To adjust a secondary (final) drive chain or belt, you will need to remove axle nut's cotter pin, if so equipped. (Some models use a special nut with lock washer.) Loosen axle nut a few turns. At rear of each swing arm leg, locate adjuster.

Fig. 4-55. If you have confidence that axle/swing arm and frame alignment is correct, you can carefully turn adjuster nuts exactly same number of flats, in clockwise fashion, to tighten chain or belt. This will keep axle alignment. Check chain deflection as you tighten nuts equally. Stop when deflection is correct.

Fig. 4-56. If you overtighten chain or belt by mistake, loosen adjuster nuts evenly. Tap on rear of tire at midline to drive out adjuster slack and assure that equal tension applies at each adjuster nut. When belt or chain deflection is correct, verify that axle is true with frame. Tighten and torque axle shaft nut to specification found in Harley-Davidson service manual. *Always install a new cotter pin.*

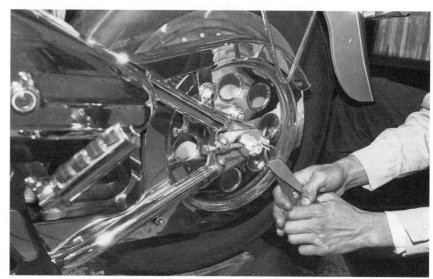

Fig. 4-57. If you suspect that axle shaft is not true with frame, take measurements. Measure between swing arm pivot centerline and rear axle shaft centerline. If measurements match at each side of swing arm, axle is true with swing arm pivot. If cycle's frame and rear swing arm are straight, rear axle is in alignment. (See suspension section of this book for more details on frame and swing arm alignment.)

Battery and Electrical Maintenance

FIG. 4-58. Carefully remove battery. Using protective gloves and goggles to prevent bodily injury, clean battery case and cable ends with a solution of warm water and baking soda. You can dip corroding cable ends into this solution and gently brush with an old paint brush. Avoid splashing solution on your clothes, body or your motorcycle's finish. Rinse cable ends with clean stream of water.

FIG. 4-59. You can clean the outside of battery with baking soda/water solution. (Do not get baking soda inside battery cells, or permanent battery damage will occur.) Once you wash solution away and dry battery case with old disposable rags, you can remove battery caps from each cell and inspect fluid levels. Add distilled water as necessary.

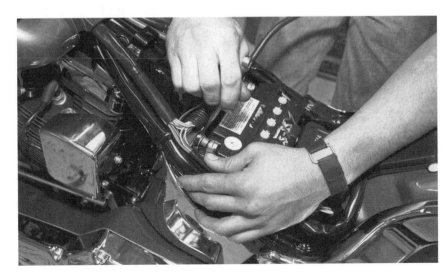

FIG. 4-60. If cells are extremely low on electrolyte, suspect a defective battery. Never add electrolyte (sulfuric acid solution) to a used battery. After safely adding distilled water and trickle charging the battery, let battery set for awhile, then test cells with a hydrometer for specific gravity. Compare these findings with requirements described in your factory service manual before reinstalling battery.

Assigning Work To A Shop

For many owners, courting a second career as a motorcycle mechanic is impractical. Some find no appeal in hands-on mechanical work. Or perhaps your life-style is too busy, or work space too small, for servicing your own cycle. Sometimes the cost of special tools or the tasks required with a certain repair job range beyond your capacity. Chasing parts and tying up your cycle for an unreasonable period could be costly and stressful.

FIG. 4-61. An engine assembly overhaul requires special tools and skills. Unless you would enjoy a career at motorcycle mechanics, consider subletting these types of jobs to your local dealer or other specialist.

A cost effective repair takes tools and your valuable time into account. Even the most competent mechanic will find that a unit repair overhaul of a V-twin Evolution V^2 engine requires a high skill level, extra care and many specialized and expensive tools.

Sending such jobs to a specialist can save considerable time and help assure quality workmanship. You'll save in the long run by setting the "challenge" aside and simply recognizing that you would be better off assigning the work elsewhere.

When you can recognize and describe troubles, you make a better customer. The service writer/estimator has a much easier job of interacting with both you and the assigned mechanic. Your Harley-Davidson service manual can verify whether a particular service or repair is likely for the kind of trouble you have experienced.

Having worked from repair orders within automotive and truck dealership environments, I suggest you approach the service department with diplomacy. In a culture that reveres consumerism yet wants to ostracize sales people, there is a strained relationship, sometimes even mistrust, between customers and service writers who "sell service."

Surveys often reveal that American consumers mistrust repair facilities, believing that shops "take them for every dime possible." Surely, this happens with unscrupulous shops or those service operations that set profit above all other considerations. The current trend, however, is toward improved customer relations, especially at the franchised Harley-Davidson dealerships. You can help play a role in this change.

Your best safeguard is information, becoming a well-informed consumer who has a sense for the task at hand and reasonable costs. In fairness, remember that the shop staff has experience at troubleshooting and repairs.

If you insist that a certain repair be done, you will pay whether that is the problem or not. Both labor and parts will be charged, regardless of the outcome. When in doubt about a possible problem, you are wiser to pay for further diagnostic work and an opinion from the professional mechanic.

Unless a problem is obvious, request thorough diagnostic procedures. Harley-Davidson dealership diagnostic equipment and other advanced tools can quickly troubleshoot and diagnose electronic and electrical problems. If a service facility like your local Harley-Davidson dealership has such equipment, you can radically reduce the risk of engine or powertrain mis-diagnosis and unnecessary repair work. Money spent here is spent wisely.

As an informed consumer, you can save unnecessary expense. If you can listen to reasonable suggestions while avoiding a sales pitch, you will also be a welcome and respected customer at the local dealership or independent service facility.

FIG. 4-62. Harley-Davidson places importance on customer satisfaction. Ethical transactions at dealership service departments are encouraged, often through incentives for achieving a high Customer Satisfaction Index (CSI) rating. Customers are poled about service quality and ethics. As a vehicle manufacturer, Harley-Davidson ranks exceptionally high in customer satisfaction.

Remember that the adage "too much knowledge is dangerous" applies. When you glean insight from this book or your Harley-Davidson factory service manual, don't become overbearing with your wisdom. An ethical mechanic or service writer will happily share information and engage in dialog. Such an exchange is valuable, as there are many diagnostic gaps that only a professional mechanic's experience can overcome.

When you find a shop or dealership that you like, respect the professional mechanic/technician and an ethical service management staff. They can help keep your Evolution motorcycle running in the most expedient manner.

5

ENGINE TUNE-UP AND
ELECTRICAL SERVICE

You can easily perform minor tune-up chores on your Evolution V^2 engine. The inductive discharge ignition system requires nothing more than verifying advance spark timing and observing timing function. Periodic spark plug changes and air filter service (described in Chapter 4) round out the routine.

Fuel system maintenance consists of cleaning or replacing the fuel supply valve's filter/strainer, setting curb idle speed, checking the choke/enrichener function, and setting fast idle speed. Jets and idle mixture on all Evolution Era carburetors have been set by Harley-Davidson at the factory. For Federal and most State emissions compliance, the manufacturer recommends that you do not modify the carburetor or try to change its factory jetting and fuel circuits.

IGNITION TUNE-UP

If you can operate a timing light and change a spark plug carefully on an alloy cylinder head, you can tune your Evo engine! At the first 500 miles and each 5,000 miles thereafter, tuning begins with changing the spark plugs.

FIG. 5-1. Read old spark plugs for proper firing, correct fuel mixture and signs of weak compression or ignition. (See Chapter 2 for further details.) Harley-Davidson's service manuals recommend "white, yellow or light tan to rusty brown powdery deposits" as a sign of good engine operation. A glazed looking light brown is a sign of severe overheating.

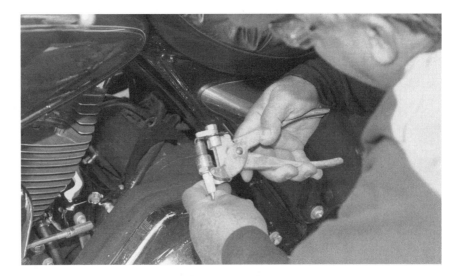

FIG. 5-2. Always check spark plug gaps before installing new plugs. Use a wire type gauge for measuring gap, and only bend ground strap to set gap. *(Warning: Do not put pressure on center electrode, porcelain or ceramic sections of spark plug.)* Properly set, wire gauge should pull through spark gap with a light tugging effort. While convenient plug gapping tool (shown) is suitable for conventional spark plugs, *use only a wire gauge tool on platinum type spark plugs.*

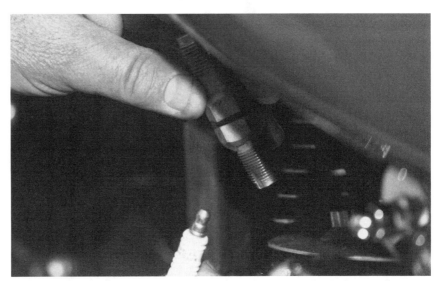

FIG. 5-3. Examine spark plug threads in cylinder head. If not clean, Harley-Davidson recommends softening deposits with a penetrant oil and chasing threads. If you use a thread chaser, *do not cut metal from cylinder head threads.* Be sure that chaser is square with threads and use extreme caution here. If possible, keep debris from entering cylinders. Crank engine with plugs removed to expel any debris before installing fresh spark plugs.

FIG. 5-4. Thread spark plugs carefully and by hand until seated against head. Clean plug threads should enter cylinder head with an easy start and no resistance. Torque with a torque wrench to factory specs found in service or operator's manual for your cycle (range from 11 to 28 ft/lbs depending upon year and model). If no torque wrench is available, seat plugs firmly with your fingers, then tighten plugs 1/4-turn further.

Checking and Setting Spark Timing

Harley-Davidson Evolution engines feature high energy ignitions with an electronic module that eliminates the need for breaker points. These electronic "inductive discharge" ignition systems have no need for a vacuum or centrifugal spark advance mechanism, as the module provides proper spark timing advance electronically. The electronic ignition's rotor drives off the camshaft, and the sensor plate mounts in a stationary manner. Once proper spark timing is set, no parts move other than the rotor.

FIG. 5-5. Vacuum switch sends signal to module (retrofit Screamin' Eagle performance unit shown here). This causes spark timing curve to change. Signal triggers one of two optimal spark timing curves to meet various engine loads and throttle positions. Vacuum Operated Electric Switch (V.O.E.S.) sources its vacuum signal at carburetor.

To check spark timing, I use a timing light with built-in advance. (See Chapter 4 for details.) This enables testing of the full range of spark advance in both of the V.O.E.S. modes.

> **CAUTION —**
> *Make certain V.O.E.S. is hooked up and operational when performing a timing check and adjustment. Failure to do so could overly advance timing and damage the engine. Consult your factory service manual for V.O.E.S. testing procedures and vacuum hose routing for your motorcycle.*

If your cycle is not equipped with a tachometer, you may need a tachometer test instrument to accurately determine engine speed when testing spark advance. The range of rpm is usually sufficient enough, however, to run the engine safely to this speed by ear. You will note that advanced timing degrees cannot be exceeded, and if you rev the engine slightly higher, the timing light will still indicate "Advanced" mark.

FIG. 5-6. You can remove timing inspection plug at engine case and insert a plastic viewing plug, available from your dealer. This is part #HD-96295-65, followed by a suffix letter for your particular model. Screw plug into engine case and take care not to hit flywheel.

FIG. 5-7. Consult your factory service manual for flywheel identification marks that indicate front and rear cylinders on your Evo engine. These marks signify TDC (top-dead-center) and full spark advance positions of the flywheel. Marks are visible through inspection hole.

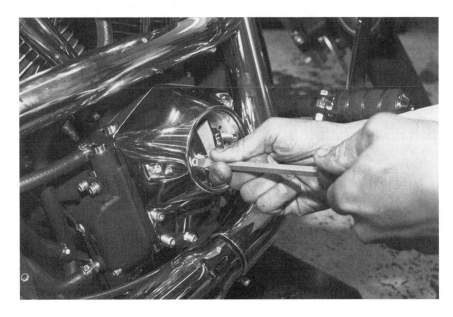

FIG. 5-8. If your timing sensor plate has been moved in an emergency field fix situation, you can make a temporary timing adjustment by installing the plate and centering screws in sensor plate slots. This will allow short-term operation of the motorcycle, just long enough to find a suitable timing light for setting spark timing to factory specifications.

FIG. 5-9. Verify spark timing at rpm specified for your motorcycle's engine. Run your engine to the specified rpm range. A standard induction timing light (or an advance light set at "0"-degrees) should show advanced timing reference mark in center of timing inspection hole. If not, adjust timing until this occurs.

FIG. 5-10. Adjust spark timing by carefully removing outer and inner covers over sensor plate. Outer cover with rivets requires drilling into rivets with appropriate drill bit. (Most models require a 3/8" drill bit, but verify drill bit size in your factory service manual.) Use extreme care and remove rivet heads only. Do not damage gearcase cover! Loosen inner cover screws and detach cover and gasket.

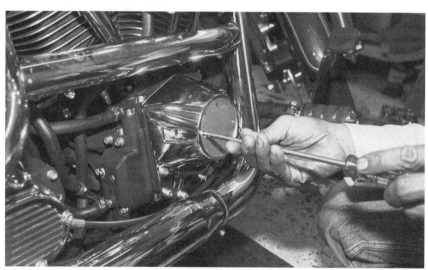

FIG. 5-11. Loosen sensor plate screws, just enough to rotate plate. Move plate slightly (one direction will retard timing, opposite direction will advance spark timing). Secure plate screws and again raise rpm to specification found in your factory service manual. When mark aligns properly at this rpm, advanced timing is correct.

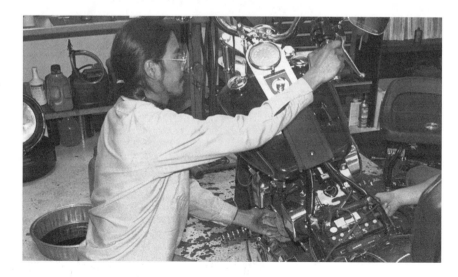

FIG. 5-12. Replace gasket if there are any signs of wear. Tighten inner cover screws snugly (15–30 inch/pounds, same as sensor plate screws). You need a rivet gun and special Harley-Davidson rivets, Part #8699, for outer cover. A rivet gun is inexpensive, but learn to use it before installing outer ignition cover.

WARNING —
Always use Harley-Davidson gearcase cover rivets. Use of conventional type rivets can lead to stud end of rivet falling into the engine case when you drill rivets to remove cover.

CARBURETOR TUNE-UP

There have been two types of Evolution carburetors, both of side-draft (horizontal air flow) design. Earlier models use a traditional slide-valve type arrangement, where the throttle cable is connected to a slide in the carburetor. Opening the slide lets in more air and fuel. Fuel is gravity fed to the carb by a needle-and-seat fuel inlet operated by a float. An accelerator pump circuit squirts fuel when you open the throttle, and a choke valve is used for cold starting. In addition to the cable controlled cold start choke circuit, these carburetors offer idle, mid-range, high speed and acceleration fuel circuits. This is a fundamental and proven carburetor design, similar in function to traditional Harley-Davidson types.

FIG. 5-13. Early Evolution models use a traditional type carburetor. The throttle cable is directly connected to a slide in the carburetor throat. Slide controls air intake and fuel flow through main jet.

FIG. 5-14. On later Constant Velocity (C.V.) carbs, throttle cable is connected to a butterfly valve in carb throat. When you open throttle, incoming air lifts slide and needle in main jet fuel circuit. This makes air/fuel flow transitions smoother than with non-C.V. carburetors.

Later Evolution motorcycles feature a distinctive "constant-velocity" type carburetor. This constant velocity (C.V.) carburetor is in some ways similar to a classic concentric design carburetor with its throttle slide and main jet needle, but the Harley-Davidson C.V. carburetor uses engine vacuum to lift the piston/slide and jet needle.

When you open the throttle on a C.V. carburetor, the throttle cable directly opens a throttle valve within the carburetor's throat. The throttle plate rotates open, and a vacuum diaphragm, a balance spring and atmospheric pressure each work together to smoothly move the piston-and-needle assembly upward. Fuel flows in increasing volume as the slide lifts and air velocity/volume increases.

Engine vacuum and varying rates of air flow through the throat of the carburetor (governed by the amount of throttle you apply and the position of the vacuum piston's venturi slide) determine the amount of air/fuel mixture that will enter your engine's cylinders. The vacuum piston's slide changes the venturi shape at different throttle settings and under the full range of engine loads. This variably shaped venturi offers the most efficient air flow velocity and volume at each throttle position. Simultaneously, specific fuel circuits within the carburetor supply proper amounts of fuel for idle, mid-range and high speed running conditions.

C.V. carburetors also use a needle-and-seat float system for fuel delivery to the carb, and a cable controlled (manual) choke system, called the "enrichener." Unlike a common choke valve at the carburetor's intake, the enrichener is a valve within the carburetor that opens a fuel passageway for cold starting enrichment of the fuel mixture. There is the enrichment circuit for cold starts, an idle and low speed circuit, the mid-range slide positions and fuel flow circuit, high speed vacuum piston/slide positions, and a mechanical (linkage) operated accelerator pump diaphragm system. This is why you can twist open the hand throttle of a C.V. carburetor without the engine running and pump fuel into the venturi area of the carburetor.

Both carburetor types are emission era designs, and emission laws restrict owners and mechanics from altering fuel flow circuits. Jets are pre-set at the

FIG. 5-15. For earlier non-C.V. Evolution carburetors a high altitude (over 4000 feet above sea level) kit is available from your Harley-Davidson dealership. This kit can only be used at these elevations. A lean mixture condition will occur below 4000 feet elevation, causing poor running and risk of severe damage to your cycle's engine.

FIG. 5-16. C.V.-type carburetors compensate for altitude changes. When atmospheric pressure changes with altitude, the engine's capacity to produce vacuum also changes. Since the C.V. carburetor's fuel flow relies on vacuum, this decrease in available manifold and "ported" vacuum at higher altitudes will effectively lean out the fuel mixtures. A C.V. carburetor eliminates need to "re-jet" or temporarily "kit" the carburetor for higher altitude operation.

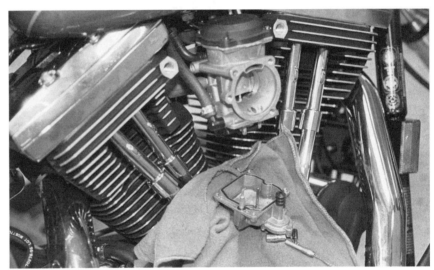

factory, although the earlier carburetor types can be fitted with legal "high altitude kits" available for operating the cycle above 4000 feet elevation.

Carburetor Adjustments

There are only three adjustments that you can legally make to your carburetor: cold idle speed, warm idle speed and setting the float's height. Cold idle speed setting begins with making sure the choke or enrichment cable is adjusted correctly.

The factory specifications describe how to adjust the two idle speed settings for your particular model. Follow these factory specifications and make sure that throttle and choke or enrichener cable adjustments are correct before setting idle speeds.

You will also find float adjustment details and specifications for your model in a Harley-Davidson service manual. Enter this specification in the chart entitled "Routine Tuning Data for My Evolution Motorcycle" (Fig. 5-20). Take this information on the road.

FIG. 5-17. Choke valve (non-C.V. carburetors) must open fully with choke knob pushed to its off position. In your Harley-Davidson factory service manual, you will find procedures for replacing and adjusting choke or enricher cables. Before adjusting fast idle (cold start "choke on" or fuel enricher mode) or warm (curb) idle speed, make sure cable works freely and that adjustment is correct.

FIG. 5-18. When adjusting float on non-C.V. carburetors, suspend float vertically (as shown here) and measure space between bowl mounting flange and base of float. Use dial-caliper (preferred method) or a square metal straightedge to measure this distance. Lip/flange at needle is adjustment point. To adjust float, bend lip/flange *without pressing float against needle*. Too much pressure on needle will distort measurements and could damage needle and seat.

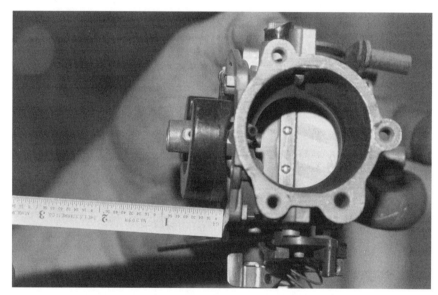

FIG. 5-19. When adjusting float on C.V. carburetor, stand carb on its manifold end, then tilt body 15 to 20 degrees before measuring float height, as shown here. Beyond 20-degree tilt, the needle's pin return spring will collapse from float weight and distort reading.

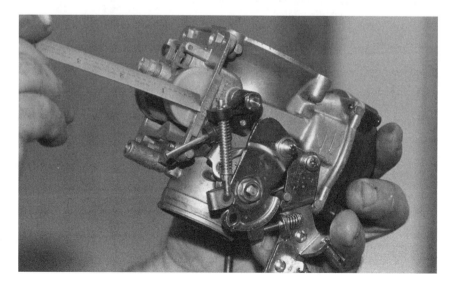

If your carburetor requires an overhaul or other repairs, the Harley-Davidson service manual offers useful and easy to follow troubleshooting and repair guidelines. When you travel, carry this book and the factory service manual in your saddlebags. You could readily overhaul a carburetor behind a barn in South Dakota—using proper tools and these two books for guidelines.

Routine Tuning Data For My Evolution Motorcycle

Next Air Cleaner Service (Mileage Or Interval)		
Next Oil Change and Full Service Of Motorcycle (Mileage Or Interval)		
Engine Oil Type and Viscosity:	Cold Months	Hot Months
Front Fork Oil Type and Viscosity:	Normal Use	Optional Use
Next Spark Plug Change (Mileage Or Interval):		
Spark Plug Type Normal Heat Range:		
Spark Plug Gap Width:		
Optional Spark Plug Heat Ranges:	Cold Weather	Hot Weather
Symbol For "TDC" Timing Mark:	Front Cylinder	Rear Cylinder
Symbol For Full Spark Advance Mark:	Front Cylinder	Rear Cylinder
Total Spark Advance @ Rpm:		
Maximum Degrees Of Spark Advance	_____ -degrees @ _____ RPM	
Choke Or Enrichener (Fast) Idle RPM		
Engine (Warmed) Curb Idle RPM		

FIG. 5-20. For your routine service work, use this checklist/reference chart. Write in this book or photocopy some quick reference charts for your shop and saddlebag tool kit. This is useful data for servicing your motorcycle on the road. Use your Harley-Davidson factory service manual to fill in blanks. Commit this information to memory.

YOUR ELECTRICAL SYSTEM

Motorcycle maintenance includes the electrical system and wiring. Repair work and routine service frequently require renewal of wiring and changing connectors. Often, the frame-up restoration of an older motorcycle requires wiring from scratch.

FIG. 5-21. Your Evolution cycle has well-formed wire harnesses with quality wire. Wire insulation is plastic, which can deteriorate over long periods of time, but insulating tape and plastic looms protect most of these wires from exposure to the elements and oxidation. In harsh climates or around corrosive salt air settings, your cycle's wiring and insulation need careful scrutiny.

A successful wiring job can be gratifying. I remember my first job as a truck fleet mechanic. My employer bought a two-ton capacity stake truck. The vehicle came really cheap, via a U.S. Government surplus source, as someone had cut every wire behind the instrument/dash panel and left the truck paralyzed! My first task was to re-wire the entire chassis and engine electrical system. Armed with a wiring schematic from the local truck dealership, I chose the proper wire gauge for each circuit and carefully began routing the scores of new wires.

When I finished and turned the key, the engine started—and the lights, turn signals, wipers, accessories and all instrument gauges worked, too! In fact, everything operated safely, as I had routed all circuits through an OEM fuse panel for reliable service.

Your Harley-Davidson works dependably when the lights glow brightly, the turn signals flash, the starter spins briskly, spark plugs fire crisply and on time, the alternator charges and, in the case of SFI engines, the pressurized injectors pulsate properly. Understanding the dynamics of your cycle's electrical system can enhance your troubleshooting skill, a vital asset on the road.

Electrical System Overview

Evolution cycles all use a 12-volt wet storage battery to supply current. Nearly all of these motorcycles use an electric starter. The exceptions are the few four-speed FX-series Evolution cycles with kick starters.

The starter motor and its function are similar in principle to popular automotive designs, with a piggyback solenoid and gear reduction between the armature shaft and drive gear. This piggyback solenoid type starter system assigns the starting operation to a start button at the handlebars. When you push the start button, a relay closes and sends current to the solenoid unit mounted atop the starter motor. This engages the starter drive and also delivers current to the starter motor. Solenoid activation begins when low amperage current flows from the key switch's start pole to the solenoid. As magnetism moves the solenoid plunger, the drive gear engages and higher amperage current flows to the starter motor.

FIG. 5-22. As the starter draws more amperage than any other item in the electrical system, the battery's hot (positive) lead cable attaches directly to the solenoid switch to minimize resistance. Harley-Davidson uses a 12-volt negative-to-ground electrical scheme.

Harley-Davidson starter motors have remained conventional and reliable field coil/pole shoe "series wound" armature types—despite the industrywide push toward the use of permanent magnet motors. Series wound motors are easily serviceable.

Evolution alternators are of high output design for a motorcycle application. Considering lighting, starting and accessories demands of touring bikes, the maximum output of 19–23 amps is essential. Typically, these alternators will reach 10 amps output by 1,000 rpm. This assures adequate lighting at an engine idle.

Alternator and Charging System

Although alternator designs have evolved since the 1960s, their operation remains much the same. A wire lead with 12-volt current feeds the alternator's external regulator. Through transistor and diode switching, current reaches a field coil. While the engine cranks, a high field current is generated to increase available voltage. This is the pre-charging mode.

FIG. 5-23. Lighting, turn signals and a starter motor draw on the bench of 90 amps maximum at free speed (on some models, with stall loads of 300–400 amps!) mean that battery and charge circuit for an Evolution cycle must be ample. Battery ratings of 19-plus ampere-hours are essential. Your battery must be in top condition to perform well under these kinds of loads.

Once the engine starts, the alternator's rotor spins at speed with alternating current produced within the stator winding. Basically, the stator sends AC current to a rectifier bridge and diodes, which convert the AC current to usable 12-volt DC current for recharging the battery and keeping lights bright. Diodes also prevent battery current from draining at the alternator.

The battery (BAT) pole on the alternator/regulator can perform two roles: 1) act as a route for charging current returning to the battery, and 2) serve as a monitoring source for the battery's state of charge plus electrical loads on the system. During normal operation, all amperage drains on the battery send a voltage reading to the alternator's regulator. This voltage determines battery drain and required volts to hold the current flow stable and recharge the battery at a rate determined by its state of charge.

Headlights or any other electrical demand will drop voltage readings at the battery when the engine is not running—or if the engine speed is too low to compensate for the voltage drain of accessories and devices.

The alternator maintains full battery voltage under a range of loads. When your cycle's battery has a low state of charge, the alternator returns high amperage current to the battery. Although this current flowing to and from the battery is actually a quantity of *amperage*, the battery and regulator interpret the flow in terms of *voltage*.

Charging a 12-volt battery requires meeting a range of voltages at various temperatures. At very low temperatures, for example, the regulator may test at 14.9–15.9 volts of current. The same regulator at 80° F may operate between 13.9 and 14.6 volts, while 140° F ambient temperature produces 13.3–13.9 volts. Above 140° F, the same regulator may offer 13.6 volts.

Since a fully charged battery reads approximately 12.6 volts, the charging circuit must at least maintain that voltage. This requires enough current flow to recharge the battery plus the amperage necessary to operate the entire range of electrical accessories and lights while the engine is running. How odd that 13.5 or more volts serve the charging needs of a 12-volt electrical system!

FIG. 5-24. Your Harley-Davidson's alternator and regulator require no periodic service. Voltage regulator (shown) is external to alternator and not adjustable. When voltage tests indicate problems with the battery, alternator or regulator, your factory service manual outlines troubleshooting and repair/overhaul procedures to follow.

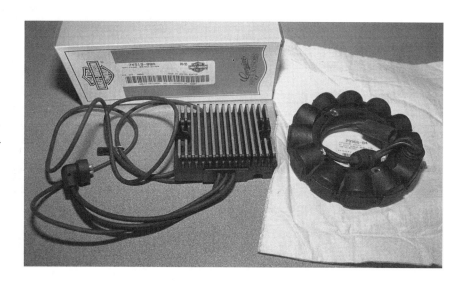

Battery condition and state of charge are very important to your motorcycle's performance. While the engine cranks, a 12-volt battery may momentarily read 9 or 10 volts. At times, a very cold engine can draw this kind of heavy load. All Evolution motorcycles need a quality battery in premium condition. The new generation of high cold cranking amperage (CCA) batteries exceeds older OEM requirements by a good margin. (For details on battery service, see lubrication service chapter.)

The Lights

Motorcycle lighting is basic, with current simply flowing through switches, fuses/relays, then to headlights, tail lamps, turn and brake lights, warning lights and interior lamps.

Look at your wiring schematic in the Harley-Davidson service manual for your model, and trace out your lighting wires. Know how they route, and inspect wires for good connections, safe routing and integrity. In preparation for an emergency field situation, be able to identify lighting switches, wiring circuits and light relays. To avoid shorts and unreliable service, your cycle's lighting system requires safe routing of wire, correct wire sizes and secure connections. Periodically check these items and lamp sockets for solid contact. You need your lights to work—not only for your visibility, but also to assure that you remain visible to other motorists.

Other Circuits

Factory and aftermarket accessories pose a challenge. Sound systems, add-on lighting, auxiliary CB radios and other additions to your cycle's electrical system demand careful consideration. Where should components source their current supply? What wire gauges are suitable? How do you route wires safely? (You'll find information about these issues in the accessory chapter.)

Your cycle's electrical system follows the layout illustrated in the factory service manual. In general, motorcycle electrical systems have easy to identify wiring circuits and components. Your Harley-Davidson dealer can supply replacement parts—from relays and bulbs to full wiring harness sections.

FIG. 5-25. For cycles equipped with add-on electrical accessories, the charging system cannot keep up with battery drain at an idle. Today's motorcycle alternators can meet most idle charging requirements. If you add electrical accessories, however, be certain to note their amperage draw. Some accessories draw too much amperage at an engine idle, placing strain on the battery.

FIG. 5-26. Some models, especially touring bikes, have more complex wiring, switches and accessories. Evolution Era motorcycles use electronic modules and "computer age" components. These systems depend on constant voltage levels, perfect wire connections and secure grounds.

FIG. 5-27. Touring bikes with trailer light connections demand more than a test lamp check. You can detect insufficient current flow or resistance at a ground lead with your volt-ohmmeter.

Relays

Evolution motorcycle electrical systems employ relays. For example, smaller gauge wiring from the starter button activates a relay, causing current to flow from a higher amperage (heavier wire gauge) battery source lead to the starter. The main advantage of relays is that minor amounts of current can control major current flow. Although circuits like the horn and starter motor draw larger amperage (a measurement of electrical resistance), they can use lighter wiring over several sections of wire routing. Relays are a practical, safe way to perform mechanical tasks. You can use low amperage over long spans of light wire to activate the relay/switch. When the relay contacts close, they allow heavy current to flow through heavier gage cable over a shorter distance.

Relays have two basic designs, each with a different function. The *electrothermal* relay receives and delivers current via a bi-metallic contact set. After the contacts heat to a given point, the switch opens, stopping current flow. As the contacts cool down, the switch closes. The traditional turn signal "flasher" is this type of relay.

The starter, on the other hand, is an *electro-magnetic* relay, activated by low amperage current. When contacts close on a Harley-Davidson electro-magnetic starter relay/solenoid, higher amperage current flows to the starter motor and the plunger moves the pinion gear into engagement with the drive teeth of the clutch ring gear. The starter motor then spins the engine through the primary drive.

Troubleshooting Your Electrical System

Of all my electrical testing equipment, one of the most valued tools is a combination volt-ohmmeter. The ohmmeter can read circuit continuity levels and ohms resistance. A voltmeter reads the actual voltage available at a given circuit. Adjusted for alternating current (AC) or direct current (DC), a voltmeter can measure line voltage between any two points. For motorcycle troubleshooting, these tools provide a wealth of useful information.

Ohms, a measurement of electrical resistance, follow the engineering formula: 1 ohm = 1/siemens = 1 volt/ampere. Simply, each ohm is an increment of resistance to current flow. Conductive liquids or solids (such as electrical wiring) serve as mediums through which we measure ohms resistance.

Aside from testing alternator/regulator diodes or components in a fuel injection or electronic ignition system, most electrical troubleshooting centers around continuity of current flow and availability of voltage. The ohms setting on a volt-ohmmeter will quickly satisfy a wide range of these continuity checks, helping you find shorts and partially or fully open circuits.

For light use and rough troubleshooting, an inexpensive analog volt-ohmmeter can perform a wide range of useful tests and still fit neatly into your saddlebag tool kit. For testing EFI/SFI and other precise electronic components, however, you need a precise digital readout volt-ohmmeter.

WARNING —
Never create electrical sparks at or near the battery. A hot or defective battery emits explosive gases.

FIG. 5-28. Grounds are as important as hot sources. Ohmmeters take the guesswork out of testing your motorcycle's engine, chassis/frame and body grounds.

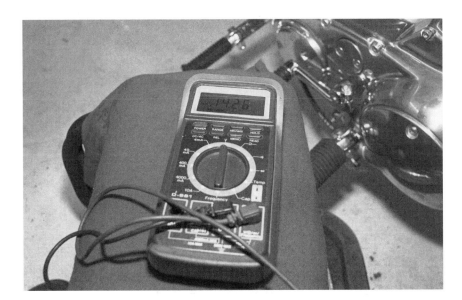

CAUTION —
Connect or disconnect multiple connectors and test leads only with the ignition off. Switch the multimeter functions or measurement ranges only with the test leads disconnected.

CAUTION —
Around sensitive electronic components, do not use a continuity/test lamp with an incandescent bulb to test circuits. Use only an LED (light emitting diode) test lamp. Do not use an analog (swing-needle) volt-ohmmeter to check circuit resistance or continuity on electronic (solid state) components. Use only a high quality digital multi-meter with a high input impedance rating (at least 10 megohms).

CAUTION —
When using an analog (swing needle) voltmeter, be careful not to reverse the test leads. Reversing polarity may damage the meter.

Four things are required for current to flow in any electrical circuit: a voltage source, wires or connections to transport the voltage, a consumer or device that uses the electricity, and a connection to ground. For trouble-free operation, the ground connections, including the battery ground cable and the body ground strap, must remain clean and free from corrosion. Most problems can be found using only a multi-meter (volt/ohm/amp meter) to check for voltage supply, for breaks in the wiring (infinite resistance/no continuity and such), or for a path to ground that completes the circuit.

Your Harley-Davidson's "D.C." electric current follows a logical flow, always moving from the voltage source (+) toward ground (–). Keeping this in mind, you can locate electrical faults through a process of elimination. When troubleshooting a complex circuit, separate the circuit into smaller parts. The general tests outlined here may be helpful in finding electrical problems. This information is even more valuable when used in conjunction with OEM wiring diagrams found in the factory service manual for your model cycle.

Testing for Voltage and Ground

The most useful and fundamental electrical troubleshooting technique is checking for voltage and ground. Grounds are critical, and vibration often causes loose connections. Powder-coat surfaces can also make grounding difficult. Spend time tracing resistance and voltage drops at ground circuits.

A voltmeter or a simple test light should be used for this test. For example, if the tail lamp does not work, checking for voltage at the bulb socket will determine if the circuit is functioning correctly or if the bulb itself is faulty.

To check for battery voltage using a test light, connect the test light wire to a clean, unpainted metal part of the cycle or a known good ground. Use the pointed end of the light to probe the hot lead of the connector or socket. *Do not stick pointed probe end through wire insulation. This could permanently damage the wire or insulation.*

To check for continuity to ground, connect the test light wire to the positive (+) battery post or a battery source. Now use the pointed end of the light to probe the connector's ground lead or the bulb's socket wall if that is the ground source. The test lamp should light up.

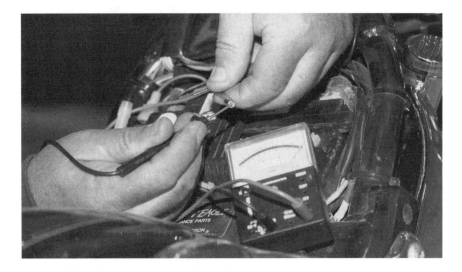

FIG. 5-29. To check for voltage using a voltmeter, set meter to DCV and the correct scale. On 12-volt Harley-Davidson systems, connect negative (-) test lead to negative (-) battery terminal or a known good ground. Touch positive (+) test lead to the positive wire or socket/connector that you want to test.

FIG. 5-30. On a 12-volt negative ground system test for proper ground, connect positive (+) test lead to a positive (+) battery voltage source. (For a positive battery source, select a terminal junction point safely away from battery to avoid risk of making sparks near battery.) Touch the negative (-) test lead to wire leading to ground. Meter should read actual battery voltage.

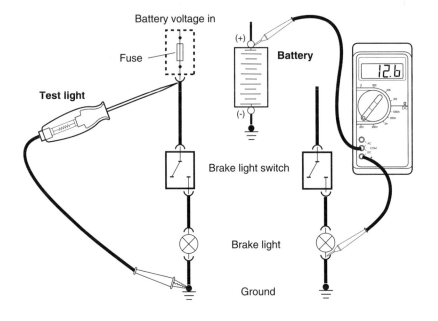

FIG. 5-31. Using a test light (near) and voltmeter (far) to test for voltage in a circuit.

A test light only determines if voltage or a ground is present. It does not determine how much voltage or the quality of the path to ground. If the voltage reading is important, such as when you test a battery or need a precise reading of a circuit's voltage, use a digital voltmeter. To check the condition of a ground connection, check for voltage drop on the suspected connection as described at "Short Circuit Test."

Continuity Test

The continuity test can be used to check a circuit or switch. Because most automotive circuits are designed to have little or no resistance, a circuit or part of a circuit can be easily checked for faults using an ohmmeter or a self-powered test light. An open circuit or a circuit with high resistance will not allow current to flow. A circuit with little or no resistance allows current to flow easily.

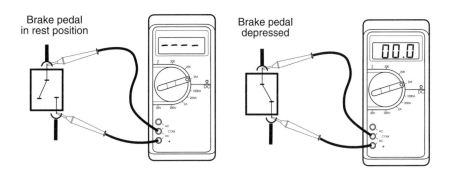

FIG. 5-32. This is a brake light switch being tested for continuity. With the brake pedal in a resting position (switch open), the test reveals no continuity. With brake pedal depressed (switch closed), there is continuity.

When checking continuity, keep the ignition off. On circuits that are powered at all times, disconnect the battery's negative (-) cable. Using the wiring diagram found in your factory service manual, a continuity test can easily find faulty connections, defective wires, bad switches, defective relays, and malfunctioning engine sensors.

Short Circuit Test

A "short circuit" is simply a circuit that takes a shorter path than intended. The most common short that causes problems is a short to ground where the insulation on a hot lead wire wears away, and the metal wire becomes exposed. If the exposed wire is live (positive battery voltage on a 12-volt Harley-Davidson negative ground system), either a fuse will blow or the circuit may become damaged.

> *CAUTION —*
> *On circuits protected with large fuses or relay breakers (25 amp and greater), the wires or circuit components may be damaged before the fuse blows. Always check for damage before replacing fuses or relays in this rating range. Always use replacement fuses of the factory recommended rating.*

Shorts to ground can be located with a voltmeter, a test light, or an ohmmeter. However, these shorted circuits are often difficult to locate. Therefore, it is important that you use the factory wiring diagram when troubleshooting your motorcycle's electrical system.

Short circuits can be found using a logical approach based on the path that current follows. To check for a short circuit to ground, remove the blown fuse

FIG. 5-33. Volt-ohmmeter being used to check for short circuit to ground. NEAR: Test for short using battery power. FAR: Continuity/ohm test for a short.

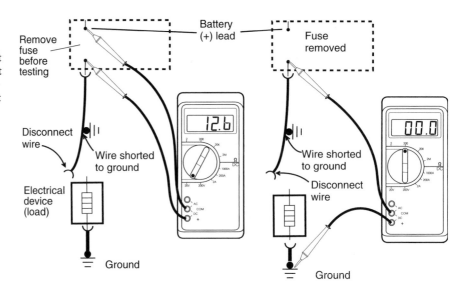

or breaker from the circuit and disconnect the cables from the battery. (For safety's sake, always disconnect negative battery cable first. When installing a 12-volt negative (–) ground battery, always secure the positive (+) cable first, then the negative ground cable.)

With cables detached from the battery, disconnect the harness connector from the circuit's device/load or "consumer." Using a self-powered test light or an ohmmeter, connect one test lead to the load side fuse/relay terminal (terminal leading to the circuit) and the other test lead to ground.

A short circuit can also be located using a test light or a voltmeter. Connect the instrument's test leads across the fuse/relay terminals (with fuse or relay removed) and turn the circuit on. If necessary, check the factory wiring diagram in your service manual to determine under which circumstances the circuit should read live.

Working from the wire harness nearest to the fuse/relay junction, probe junctions and terminals with one lead of tester (other lead attached at fuse/relay terminal). Move or wiggle the wires while observing the test light or your meter. Continue to move down the harness until the test light blinks or the meter reading fluctuates. This will pinpoint the location of the short.

Visually inspect the wire harness at this point for any defects. If no defects are visible, carefully slice open the harness cover or the wire insulation for further inspection. Make sure that you find the trouble. Repair the defects to OEM standards. Some wire sections can be replaced or properly spliced. On critical voltage circuits like an SFI system, however, you will need a complete new harness to ensure circuit integrity and the quality of connections. Consult your Harley-Davidson service manual for recommendations on repairing a particular electrical circuit.

Voltage Drop Test

The wires, connectors, and switches that carry current have very low resistance so that current can flow with a minimum loss of voltage. A voltage drop results from higher than normal resistance in a circuit. This additional resistance actually decreases or stops the flow of current.

FIG. 5-34. **Example of voltage drop test on dim headlight. Voltmeter shows 1.6-volt drop between ground connector and chassis ground. After cleaning headlight ground, voltage drop returns to normal and headlight regains brightness.**

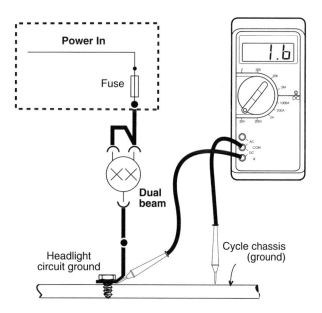

A voltage drop produces symptoms and problems ranging from dim headlights to a weak horn. Some common sources of voltage drop are faulty wires or switches, dirty or corroded connections or contacts, and loose or corroded ground wires and ground connections.

Voltage drop can only be checked when current is running through the circuit, such as by operating the starter motor or turning on the headlights. Making a voltage drop test requires measuring the voltage in the circuit and comparing that reading to what the voltage should be. Since these measurements are usually small, a digital voltmeter must be used to ensure accurate readings. If you suspect a voltage drop, turn the circuit on and measure the voltage when the circuit is under load.

A voltage drop test is generally more accurate than a simple resistance check because resistance levels involved are often too small to measure with most ohmmeters. For example, a resistance as small as 0.02 ohms results in a 3 volt drop in a 150 amp starter circuit. (150 amps x 0.02 ohms = 3 volts).

Keep in mind that voltage with the key on and voltage with the engine running are not the same. With the ignition on and the engine off, full charge battery voltage should be approximately 12.6 volts. With the engine running (charging voltage), voltage should be approximately 14.5 volts. For exact measurements, first measure battery voltage with the ignition on, then with the engine running. Remember not to create a spark near a hot or possibly defective battery! An explosion could result. If necessary, take your battery voltage reading at the primary battery terminal block (typically at the starter solenoid), well away from the battery.

The maximum voltage drop, as recommended by the Society of Automotive Engineers (SAE), is: 0 volt for small wire connections; 0.1 volt for high-current connections; 0.2 volt for high-current cables; and 0.3 volt for switch or solenoid contacts. (On longer wires or cables, the drop may be slightly higher.) A voltage drop of more than 1.0 volt usually indicates a problem.

FIG. 5-35. *Warning*: Solenoid junction block and other points that lie well away from the battery provide alternate battery testing sources. Avoid direct voltage checks at the battery, especially after heavy charging from the alternator or a battery charger. Explosive hydrogen gas can surround the battery and ignite violently from the slightest spark.

Testing Battery and Charging System

When checking the battery and charging circuits, be careful and considerate of battery hazards. High amperage applied to a defective battery is, literally, a potential bombshell. When you know your cycle's charging system is functional yet the battery acts dead, proceed with extreme caution. A minute spark near an overcharged or defective battery is a safety hazard. Avoid the risk of igniting explosive hydrogen gas. Always unplug your battery charger before connecting or disconnecting the clamp leads. If in doubt, make volt/ohmmeter tests well away from the battery, at the alternator, a factory wire junction or the fuse/relay.

Find a good ground, and attach the correct meter probe (based on your system's polarity). Attach the other probe to the hot wire source and read battery voltage. If you get a reading of 12.30 or less volts on a 12-volt system, with all known current drains (including lights, ignition and accessories) shut off, the battery's state of charge is at 50% capacity or lower. This indicates poor electrical connections, weak alternator output, excessive current drain from accessories or a defective battery.

You can check each of these possible problems with the volt-ohmmeter. Start the engine and begin at the alternator. The battery signal to the voltage regulator should say, "I'm low on voltage, flow some current my way!"

In response, the normal charge circuit will call for a heavy amperage flow. Use the voltmeter mode of the tester, and probe the charge wire at the alternator with the positive lead. On a negative ground system like your Harley-Davidson, attach the negative lead to ground.

Charging properly, the alternator should now read well over 12.6 volts on a 12-volt system. (See factory service manual to determine voltage settings and acceptable readings.) With current flowing toward the battery, voltage could read 14.8 volts or higher, depending upon the parameters of the voltage regulator and output capacity of your cycle's 12-volt alternator.

FIG. 5-36. If you cannot get a normal voltage reading from the charge circuit, a wiring or fusible link problem may exist. Trace the route of the alternator and regulator wiring leads, then test these circuits with an ohmmeter.

If you see no increase in voltage over your static battery test reading, the alternator or regulator is not performing properly or there is a short circuit or open in the charge circuit wiring. If the wiring is okay, refer to your factory service manual for further troubleshooting details and how to repair or replace the alternator and/or voltage regulator.

For determining a wiring fault, begin your ohmmeter test at the first junction between the alternator and battery. Zero the meter and set for DC-Ohms and K-Ohms. Check the wire for continuity and conductivity by holding a probe at each end of the wire and reading the scale. If no opens or shorts exist, the meter will rest at the zero line. If there is too much resistance, as with a slight open in the lead or a poor connection, the needle will read upward on the scale. An actual open in the wire prevents the needle from registering at all.

Repeat this procedure along the wire path toward the battery. Eventually, you will locate the short or open. Resistance readings help locate corrosion within wire leads, too. Battery cables, starter motor leads, or battery terminal connections often develop such problems. Unseen in a visual inspection, a current blockage cannot fool your ohmmeter! The force necessary to keep current flowing is measurable.

The meter can also test headlight and dimmer switches, the starter solenoid switch, relays, breakers, fuses, ignition circuits and the turn signal switch. Tracing poor ground wires, troubleshooting faulty gauges, finding nuisance shorts, isolating worn spark plug cables and most other electrical tests are well within the volt-ohmmeter's ability.

Quick Check of Starter Motor

If the battery charge is full and wires are intact, your starter motor should perform well. When the starter turns slowly but wiring tests okay, either the engine has too much internal friction/resistance or the starter solenoid and/or starter motor have troubles.

Before condemning the starter, make sure the engine turns over freely. Remove the spark plugs. You can then carefully move the primary chain or belt assembly to rotate the crankshaft, or you can push the cycle by hand, then re-

FIG. 5-37. Check your ignition cables periodically with an ohmmeter. Electronic ignitions with higher firing voltages and wider spark gaps place more stress on high tension carbon cables.

lease the clutch lever with the transmission in a higher gear. Once you know that the engine rotates freely, you can look to the starter motor.

I make a quick test of the starter draw by using an induction meter to check current (amperage) flow through the starter cable while cranking the engine. If this reading exceeds maximum draw for my motorcycle's starter, the next move is to test the solenoid switch on the starter.

Another method of testing the starter is a voltage reading while you crank the engine. Hook voltmeter (–) probe to a good ground source. Hold voltmeter (+) probe at the starter's solenoid terminal or battery cable junction—safely away from the battery. Compare cranking voltage with specifications found in your factory service manual.

If the solenoid meets continuity and resistance specifications found in the factory service manual, remove the starter and solenoid for bench testing. Isolate starter from solenoid problems on the bench, and consider the repairs described in the factory service manual for your model. Once you are certain the starter motor or its drive mechanism is defective, you can decide whether to repair or replace the assembly.

FIG. 5-38. Starter defects often give warning. A clicking solenoid or erratic, dragging motor indicates trouble. An amperage draw or voltage draw test helps determine condition of the starter. Here is a simple induction meter test for quick troubleshooting. With tester laid across high amperage cable to starter, crank engine over. Meter reads approximate amperage flow/draw through cable.

0021714

6

ENGINE TROUBLESHOOTING AND SERVICE

My approach to motorcycle mechanics has always been academic. I am grateful that most of us have the ability to read, as quality service literature provides the vital details and step-by-step directions for performing successful repair work. After three decades of turning wrenches professionally and fifteen years of writing magazine technical features, reader Q&A columns, and numerous books on subjects dealing with a variety of motor vehicles and applied mechanics, I value one skill above all others: *How to accurately move from a general observation to in-depth troubleshooting and appropriate repairs.*

My primary technical aim with this book is to *help you think and respond more like a professional Harley-Davidson mechanic.* This requires insight into the nature of your motorcycle, plus the ability to move from the realm of simple, more general observations to the level of complex deductions and the necessary actions that follow. You do not have to subscribe to a particular philosophy to become proficient or better skilled at motorcycle mechanics. *The key here is acquiring experience, a sensory "feel" and knowledge of the machine.*

As awareness of your Evolution motorcycle increases, you will find that troubleshooting and repair work become increasingly less difficult and far

FIG. 6-1. One benefit of HOG membership is towing insurance. You may find that troubleshooting is impossible under certain field conditions. Rather than risk damaging a cycle, many owners now have access to a closed trailer. *Always make sure the tow company has suitable equipment for towing or, preferably, trailering your Harley-Davidson.*

more rewarding. From this chapter forward, we will move up the learning curve, beyond basic service, lubrication and minor tune-up, to the realm of in-depth mechanical troubles and their remedy.

The first part of this chapter serves as an orientation to your engine's service needs and provide a foundation for practical troubleshooting. If your troubleshooting leads to the conclusion that you need to rebuild your engine, the second part of the chapter deals with the rebuilding process.

Routine Engine Service

Harley-Davidson has reduced engine service demands dramatically. An inductive discharge (breakerless) ignition system, a carburetor with pre-set jets and mixture modes, and zero-maintenance charging and starting systems minimize the concerns of owners.

FIG. 6-2. While earlier Harley-Davidson OHV hydraulic tappet engines offered adjustable pushrods, today's Evo valvetrain has non-adjustable pushrods and is fully maintenance free. During an engine rebuild, you must carefully match valve stem heights and pushrod lengths to specifications found in your Harley-Davidson factory service manual. When assembly is correct, non-adjustable pushrods should provide proper valve clearance.

Evolution V^2 engines offer an advanced design that follows engineering principles evolving from the earliest V-twins. Your Evo's engine has the lowest maintenance requirements of any Harley-Davidson engine to date, complemented by the highest reliability record!

Unless there is a defect or malfunction of a component, you will content yourself with lighter chores like lubrication, oil filter changes, air filter cleaning, a minor tune-up (Chapters 4 and 5), and listening to the rhythms of your engine as it motors down the road. If you maintain your cycle regularly, there is less likelihood of a mechanical breakdown or an episode of embarrassingly poor performance. For the core engine assembly of both F-series and XL V-twin Evos, including valvetrain components, there are no periodic service demands: Harley-Davidson offered maintenance-free hydraulic valve tappets as early as the 1948 Panhead engines.

While the primary chain, clutch and other areas of the powertrain require periodic inspection and adjustment, your Evo engine unit should run efficiently between overhauls. When parts wear out prematurely, however, troubleshooting can pinpoint the cause and extent of damage.

TROUBLESHOOTING ENGINE WOES

Despite regular maintenance, care and sensible riding habits, your Harley-Davidson motorcycle engine may develop troubles. Properly diagnosing these problems will help you determine the extent of wear or damage, whether you have the skills and needed tools to perform the repair, and how much the repair or, in the worst instance, complete engine rebuild will cost.

Unless there is an obvious knock or rattle deep within the engine, troubleshooting or locating a loss in performance usually involves a methodical process of elimination. You begin by checking engine tune: proper ignition and fuel system functions. Then you advance to a compression check and, if necessary, a cylinder leakdown test. This will help pinpoint whether the engine is capable of producing adequate and reliable performance. (See Chapter 2 for details on leakdown and compression tests.)

Low Compression; Internal Friction

LOW COMPRESSION can result from a pressure leak at either cylinder. There are several causes for compression loss: Leaking or improperly clearanced intake or exhaust valves, worn or defective piston rings, a leaking ("blown") head gasket, or casting cracks can each lower compression. So does a severely worn camshaft, defective tappets, pushrods or valve rocker arms.

Diagnosing low compression requires a compression gauge or cylinder leakdown tester. (See Chapter 2 for details on these test procedures.) One roadside field testing method involves shorting cylinder spark leads, one at a time, and comparing the engine rpm drop per cylinder. A high rpm drop indicates a strong cylinder, while a low rpm drop reveals a cylinder that has either low compression or an ignition, fuel or vacuum related problem. This simple procedure is much like the "dynamic compression test" found on many oscilloscope engine analyzers.

FIG. 6-3. To perform a "dynamic compression" test, make sure ignition spark function is normal. With transmission in neutral, start engine and set throttle at high enough rpm for engine to run on one cylinder. Safely unplug first spark lead. (Grip spark wire boot with insulated pliers.) Observe rpm drop. Re-install spark lead and bring idle to where you set it for start of test. Now you can remove other cylinder's spark lead and measure rpm drop. Compare rpm drop between cylinders. Weaker cylinder will show less rpm drop.

FIG. 6-4. A compression test reveals cylinder pressure with engine cranking. A cylinder leakdown test (shown) is made with piston stopped at T.D.C. of compression stroke. Pressurized air is fed through spark plug hole; percentage of air "leakdown" from cylinder gives condition of rings, valves, and head gasket. 8–10% leakdown reflects an engine in top shape. If leakdown is okay and the engine still runs poorly, suspect a flat camshaft lobe(s), fuel or ignition troubles, vacuum leak, timing, or internal friction.

FIG. 6-5. An unlikely but possible cause of cylinder leakage is that a cylinder head or barrel has warped, resulting in a head gasket failure. Rarely will re-torquing head bolts remedy this trouble. Removal of heads for repair or replacement, plus installation of new head gaskets, would be necessary.

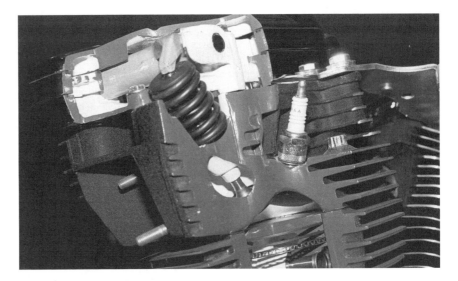

INTERNAL FRICTION indicates major engine trouble. If the engine will not crank easily, first rule out the obvious battery or starter/electrical problems. Place the transmission in neutral. Remove both spark plugs and rotate the crankshaft either by pushing the cycle in a higher gear and releasing the clutch, or by rotating the primary drive at the clutch hub. The engine should turn freely, with only moderate (normal) resistance from the valvetrain.

OVERHEAT/SEIZURE can prevent the engine from cranking or rotating after a severe overheat or running without oil. Pistons can distort from heat, gall the cylinder walls and destroy crankshaft bearings and other parts.

FUEL STARVATION results from low fuel supply. (This can include low fuel supply pressure or volume on an Evo with SFI/EFI.) Common fuel starvation causes are a plugged fuel petcock, fuel filter or stuck carburetor needle. (SFI systems require special testing procedures. As of this book's printing, SFI/EFI induction systems have limited model application. Currently, troubleshooting is a dealership service. For SFI troubleshooting techniques, you should check the Harley-Davidson service manual for your model.)

FIG. 6-6. To check for internal friction, remove spark plugs and rotate crankshaft with transmission in neutral. High resistance indicates internal engine damage, primary binding or a transmission bearing and/or gearset seizure. Have a helper disengage clutch at lever, and rotate crankshaft. If engine will not turn freely with clutch disengaged, suspect bearing, piston, connecting rod or valvetrain damage.

FIG. 6-7. Lubrication generally fails during a severe overheat, resulting in glazed and scored cylinders, warped pistons, failed rings and piston galling of cylinder walls. Valve stems can seize in their guides; a spinning engine can drive pistons into the open valves. Head casting cracks from severe overheat are common, especially near exhaust valves and valve seats. Camshaft and crankshaft bearings can also fail and seize.

FIG. 6-8. SFI-equipped engines (shown) can suffer from restrictions in fuel supply or return lines, pressure regulator troubles or fouled/defective injectors. On carbureted engines, rule out a sticking carburetor float needle and also make certain that ignition V.O.E.S. system functions properly.

FIG. 6-9. Before suspecting fuel pressure or carburetor/injector troubles, consider the fuel filter(s) or fuel filter in the gas tank. A single fuel fill-up with watery gasoline is enough to impede fuel flow and engine performance. A fuel pressure gauge (far photo) can quickly determine fuel pump pressure output on SFI/EFI systems that operate under precise pressure and require these kinds of tests.

WEAK IGNITION creates hard-starting problems and lack of power. Check the ignition output and spark timing. (See Chapters 5 and 6 for details.) A common mistake is to condemn the coil or ignition module. As for troubleshooting these two items, I would test the module before the coil.

Electronic ignitions are vulnerable to wiring failures and poor connections, the major causes of poor ignition performance. Check carefully for insulation breakdown and shorts to ground. Evolution engines dissipate a great deal of heat, and road vibration also takes its toll. Embrittled wire insulation, wiring failures and shorts can be a prime source of trouble.

Test wires between junctions. You will find engine and chassis wiring diagrams in the factory service manual. Factory manuals devote sections to electrical and wiring needs. If an electrical or ignition problem is not readily apparent, test circuits with your volt-ohmmeter or sublet the task to a local Harley-Davidson dealership that has special testing equipment.

FIG. 6-10. Wiring shorts, fraying and bad grounds cause the majority of field failures. Look closely at routed wires and connections. (For details on troubleshooting your cycle's wiring and electrical components, see Chapter 5.)

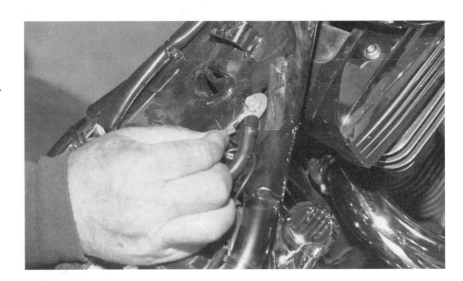

VACUUM LEAKS, if severe, will prevent the engine from running. A sufficient leak creates low manifold pressure, stalling, lean air/fuel mixtures and backfire. Even small vacuum leaks can lean the air/fuel mixture, cause idle speed to drop and prevent smooth performance.

The engine's sudden inability to idle indicates a vacuum leak or plugged fuel circuits. Check the V.O.E.S. and emissions vacuum hoses and circuits. Intake manifold and carburetor flange hardware can loosen over time, resulting in poor gasket sealing and possible vacuum loss. Periodically check torque at manifold junctions and carburetor attachment hardware.

WARNING —
Always keep volatile solvents away from hot engine parts. When checking for vacuum leaks, use a spray substance that will not ignite if it contacts a hot surface or spark.

FIG. 6-11. A non-volatile spray solvent or penetrating oil helps detect engine vacuum leaks. With engine idling, spray toward intake manifold sealing edges and carburetor base. If a leak exists, rpm will change.

Engine Will Not Run Properly

Three essentials for optimal engine performance are 1) normal compression, 2) correct valve lift and 3) proper valve timing. When troubleshooting reaches beyond spark timing adjustment, vacuum leaks and changing fuel filters, make certain your engine meets these essential requirements.

If compression registers normal for each cylinder, verify valve lift by first removing the valve cover(s). Consult the Harley-Davidson service manual or your dealership for valve lift data. Measure either the height of each valve from its closed position to fully open (actual valve lift) or the amount of tappet lift at the pushrod end of rocker arm. (Pushrod measurement indicates the camshaft's actual lobe lift.) Note whether valves open to specification.

In addition to valve lift, make note of valve timing variance that can result from a worn timing gearset. Timing gear troubles are rare, as gear-drive camshafts have been a mainstay on Harley-Davidson engines. Gearsets provide a positive, durable method for rotating a camshaft.

If a camshaft/valve timing gearset were worn or damaged enough to allow valve timing to jump one or more gear teeth, one sign would be radically re-

FIG. 6-12. A worn camshaft lobe or improper valve clearance will affect valve lift. Check valve clearance before testing valve lift. On rebuilding an Evo V-twin engine, note use of color coded pushrods; each must be removed and stored in proper order. Colors signify length and location for each pushrod. (See rebuilding tips in this chapter for assembly details.)

FIG. 6-13. If ignition timing has suddenly become retarded, yet the ignition sensor plate remains securely bolted to engine case, suspect excess slack in timing geartrain. This is a rare occurrence with Harley-Davidson engines. Although somewhat noisier, a gear-driven camshaft and ignition timing drive prove superior to all other designs.

tarded ignition timing. (A fully stripped set of timing gears causes catastrophic damage to a running engine. Moving pistons slam into open and immovable valves.) Typically, even high mileage timing gearsets show minimal wear, perhaps exhibiting milder symptoms like gear noise.

TUNE-UP CAUSES include faulty ignition, inadequate fuel supply, flooding or vacuum leaks. Even your cycle's electronic ignition requires spark timing adjustment. Fuel system troubles involve a dirty filter, plugged carburetor passages, a sticky needle/seat assembly in the carburetor, a defective float or a defective fuel pressure system (SFI engines).

Isolate problems. Verify the strength of the ignition spark, check spark timing and ensure that the engine has an adequate fuel supply. Check vacuum circuits. Make certain that the emission control system is functional, along with the crankcase breathing system. If indicated, remove, strip and clean the carburetor thoroughly and install a rebuild kit, available at your local Harley-

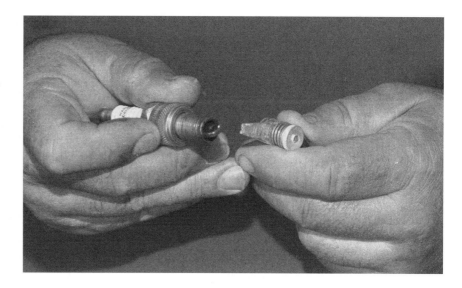

FIG. 6-14. Tune troubles include improper spark timing, restricted fuel supply and malfunctioning emission control components. V.O.E.S. switch uses vacuum for its signal. Check vacuum and fuel lines for leaks. Periodically test V.O.E.S. function to avoid spark timing malfunctions and fouled spark plugs.

Davidson dealership. You will find carburetor overhaul instructions within the kit and also in your factory service manual.

EXHAUST SYSTEM RESTRICTION has vexed plenty of troubleshooters. Check the exhaust system! Restricted exhaust can prevent the engine from starting or developing full power. A muffler or catalytic converter may show no external damage yet have broken baffles or internal restrictions. Include the exhaust system on your engine inspection and performance checklist.

FIG. 6-15. Exhaust system restriction can cause power loss. Tap muffler and catalytic converter gently with a rubber head or sand filled plastic hammer. Listen for loose baffles. *Tap lightly! These expensive chromed components do not need hammer dent marks.*

Engine Will Not Crank

WEAK BATTERY OR CHARGE CIRCUIT TROUBLES remain primary sources of starting problems. The simplest cause is dirty or corroded battery posts. Periodically testing the battery, adding distilled water to cells as needed, and cleaning the posts and case can help prevent hard starts and a stranded motorcycle. (See Chapter 4.) Make certain cables are clean and connections snug.

FIG. 6-16. Battery maintenance is best preventive care
for starting circuit. Don't buy
a new starter, voltage regulator or alternator components
before thoroughly cleaning
the battery and its cables,
then testing specific gravity
with a hydrometer. Here is a
terminal and cable end in
need of thorough cleaning.

FIG. 6-17. A wise precau-
tion, even for a battery that
shows no sign of weakness, is
the hydrometer test. Specific
gravity of a fully charged battery should read uniformly at
each cell. Perform this test before cold weather begins.

Alternator troubles are quick to identify. A charge current induction meter
or a simple volt-ohmmeter can provide useful test results. (See electrical section in Chapter 5 for details on testing your charge system.) Begin with the
voltmeter "OFF." Take care not to generate a spark near the battery. Securely
attach the negative (black) probe to a good chassis or engine ground point.
Attach the positive (red) probe to a battery current source some distance from
the battery, such as the solenoid switch. Switch the voltmeter to "D.C."

Measure the voltage level before cranking, during cranking and after starting the engine. Make certain that the maximum charge voltage reads within
the regulator's normal charging range as outlined in the Harley-Davidson service manual for your model.

DEAD BATTERY CELL(S) present a difficult diagnostic problem. A quality
battery can limp along with a dying cell for months. It often takes a deep
overnight freeze to bring out the worst in a battery. To avoid being stranded
after parking overnight in a cold climate, test each of your battery's cells reg-

ularly with a hydrometer. Specific gravity should be normal and uniform at each cell.

STARTER MOTOR PROBLEMS generally give warning. A solenoid switch or starter drive unit often shows signs of weakness before it fails. Run-on, clicking and erratic cranking are signs of starter and solenoid troubles. (See Chapter 5 for details on your starter's function, requirements, and testing.)

Poor cranking when hot is often due to worn brushes or extreme armature bushing wear that allows the armature to drag on the field coils. Aftermarket exhaust pipes passing too close to the starter motor may also cause hard starting when hot. (Poorly clearanced pipes can overheat and expand the starter motor's armature.)

GEARTRAIN FRICTION OR DRAG can prevent cranking. Among geartrain causes are seizures of a transmission bearing or gearset. With a seized transmission gearset, you can still turn the engine over with the clutch disengaged. When clutch plates have bound up but the transmission is okay, the engine should still crank over with the gear selector in the neutral position.

FIG. 6-18. Even with seized transmission parts or internal shifting components (shown), engine should crank with clutch disengaged. Engine will likely stall as you engage the clutch. (Before suspecting a damaged transmission, check clutch adjustment and operation. See Chapter 7 for further details.) A seized transmission can result from poor lubrication, severe parts stress or excessive wear.

MOTORCYCLE WILL NOT MOVE means several possibilities. A failed clutch is the first consideration. A clutch that is permanently disengaged (clutch cable binding, disc plates worn completely or clutch springs broken) might still allow shifting of gears.

The opposite situation is a damaged clutch cable, linkage or defective clutch components that prevent the clutch from disengaging. Raise the motorcycle on a cycle lift or suitable and secure hoist, with the rear tire able to spin freely. Leave the ignition switch "OFF" and disconnect the spark plug cables at the plugs. Remove the spark plugs. Place the transmission in low gear. Using a remote starter switch to crank the engine, click or crank the starter. This should rotate the cycle's rear tire. Perform this procedure in each of the other gears.

WARNING —

Perform remote starter switch test only with ignition "OFF" and spark plugs removed to prevent engine from starting. Make sure nothing contacts the rear tire. Make sure cycle is securely balanced. If necessary, you can set a slight load on the engine/powertrain by applying the rear brake lightly as you crank the engine.

Abnormal Noises, Knocks and Rattles

Your Harley-Davidson service manual details troubleshooting techniques for every kind of problem associated with your motorcycle. You can easily trace troubles through charts and outlined information found in that book. Here, I will quickly review the common causes of knocks and unusual engine noises that might occur.

FIG. 6-19. Harley-Davidson V² Evolution engine is a precise and sophisticated piece of machinery. Although Harley-Davidson critics have bashed the traditional appearance and fundamental engineering that has characterized models since the Knucklehead Era, Evolution engines offer a high degree of refinement and reliability inherent to a product with nearly a century of development.

The use of roller bearings on the crankshaft and a highly protective lubrication system makes the Evolution engine a survivor. Unless your engine loses oil pressure, there is a high likelihood that the crankshaft assembly, or "lower end," will run trouble-free for over a hundred thousand miles.

When you hear what sounds like a lower end bearing noise or knock, the first concern is oil pressure. Even if the oil pressure light functions properly, consider checking pressure directly with a test pressure gauge attached to the engine's oiling system. (See factory service manual for test gauge and adapter part numbers, plus directions for hook-up on your Evo engine.) Verify oil pressure, and compare these figures to specifications found in your Harley-Davidson factory service manual.

Be certain that this suspected lower end noise is not the transmission or primary chain drive. With the engine running, pass the stethoscope or sounding device along the primary chain area, and see if the sound emanates from this assembly. If the noise is clearly from the area of the crankshaft, you could have big troubles. Do not run the engine any further. Get used to the stethoscope before listening for troubles. Noise becomes exaggerated, and even

FIG. 6-20. A main bearing knock or rattle is usually a deep throated grating sound within the engine. You can use a stethoscope or sounding tube to isolate the area of bearing whir or knock. Note location of your main bearings and listen carefully here for noise.

normal machinery may sound like severe troubles. Know the difference between normal sound levels and a defect.

A loose piston, wrist pin or upper connecting rod bushing will produce an audible signal at the cylinder barrel. Wrist pin noise is often a "double knock." Piston "slap" or excess clearance is generally more pronounced when the engine is cold and you tip-in the throttle gently from a slow curb idle to a brisker idle.

Double-rap noises under this kind of throttle movement, or when accelerating the cycle under load or while lugging the engine, suggests a loose piston pin and/or loose upper rod bushing. A cracked or distorted piston, or a warped and worn cylinder wall, will produce a sound similar to a loose piston pin, but more like a pronounced "pinging" sound. Possibility of broken rings exists with this kind of damage.

A loose set of tappets or worn tappet guide bores might confuse your search for lower end or cylinder noises. The stethoscope can pinpoint tappet, guide, upper valvetrain and timing gear noises. Work your way around these components before condemning the crankshaft assembly, pistons or cylinder bores. Hydraulic tappets bleed down when your cycle is parked. It is not abnormal, when starting the engine cold, to hear slight tappet noise until the tappets pick up oil. This noise should disappear quickly. When listening for tappet or tappet guide bore troubles, first warm engine completely.

When I suspect a connecting rod knock, the first step is isolating the cylinder. With the engine running at a brisk idle, enough to produce the noise, I disconnect one spark plug wire carefully with an insulated pliers. (Grab plug boot only, and do not pull on ignition wire.) Keeping the engine running, I listen for the rattle or knock.

If the knock disappears or diminishes substantially, suspect the piston, rod or crankshaft bearings of this sparkless cylinder. If the noise becomes more pronounced, suspect the other cylinder. Re-connect the loose spark plug wire and disconnect the other cylinder's spark lead. Run the engine at a brisk idle, and listen for noise. If the noise has disappeared or diminished greatly, you've found the culprit cylinder.

Valvetrain noise telegraphs up and down the pushrod tubes. A stethoscope will pick up this noise readily, and you can then focus on the rocker arm/valve mechanism or the tappets and tappet guides. Worn valve guides or broken valve springs will sometimes echo near the intake or exhaust valve ports. More likely, this noise will resonate at the rocker box cover(s). Exhaust valve guides and valve stems typically wear faster than intakes.

A bent or worn pushrod, worn rocker arm or defective hydraulic tappet will cause valve clearance to increase. This noise sounds like excessive valve clearance in a mechanical tappet engine. Failure of this kind is both rare and usually symptomatic of other troubles—like poor or restricted oil flow to the tappets.

Beyond these problems and oil leaks, there is always the issue of normal wear. The main wear areas in your engine will be at piston rings, upper cylinder walls (tapering toward top of piston ring runs at the upper cylinder), valves and valve guides, valve guide seals, the upper connecting rod bushing, piston skirts and, less frequently, the timing gears. The crankshaft, per se, is a highly rugged item, and other than bearing replacement, or the rare need to replace a crankpin, the crankshaft assembly is the least likely area to fail.

Oil Burning: The Blue Smoke Blues

If your engine is visibly using oil, with blue smoke coming from the tailpipe and a consistent loss of oil, analyze the cause. Blue smoke on start-up after the engine has set for awhile usually means valve, valve guide and guide seal wear. When the engine puts out a steady stream of blue smoke under hard acceleration, suspect piston ring and/or cylinder wall troubles. Oil is pumping past the rings. (This type of oil consumption is commonly referred to as "blowby.")

Riding down a long grade under compression, observe your tailpipe emissions as you begin to once again accelerate. Blue smoke here means piston ring or valve guide and guide seal wear. This is the result of high manifold vacuum. High vacuum will suck oil past worn valve stems and guides, and also draw oil past the piston rings and into the upper cylinders.

Dark brown or black smoke may simply be accumulation of a rich air/fuel charge in the cylinders under a long period of deceleration. This would be considered normal, especially at higher altitudes, where your air/fuel mixture may already be rich from rarified air.

Oil Pressure Loss, Seal Leaks, and Crankcase Pressure

In your factory service manual, you will find a detailed description and "map" of your engine's oiling system. Few problems occur with Harley-Davidson Evo oiling systems, however, if a problem does arise, be alert. A loss of oil pressure could ruin your engine quickly—especially if you are motoring at cruise speed when pressure fails.

NOTE —

Watch the light as you would an oil pressure gauge. Some owners prefer to install a quality aftermarket oil pressure gauge to monitor true oil pressure at all times. I prefer this approach, too.

The oil pump drive gears fit firmly on their shafts, fitted with shear-type keys. In the unusual event that metal fragments should run through the pump, gear jamming may cause key failure and immediate loss of oil pressure.

Oil pressure loss can also occur from restrictions in the oil tank feed lines. One kind of restriction is slush or ice formation. This can occur when condensation and water content in the oil tank build to the point that ice can form. Regular oil changes and periodically flushing the tank (generally with kerosene) can offset this risk. See your factory service manual for recommended flushing procedures.

You can quickly check oil flow by observing the return of oil to the tank. There should be a steady flow of oil through the tank inlet. Remove oil fill cap with engine running, and observe oil flow.

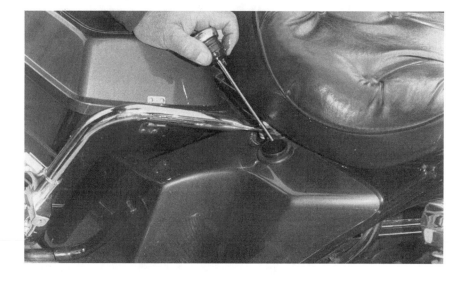

FIG. 6-21. Observe oil return flow at tank now, while oiling system is in top shape. This way you will know what to look for later, when you suspect that oil pressure has dropped or if oil switch malfunctions. On the road, you can stop and verify oil flow, then check actual pressure (PSI) at your earliest opportunity.

There is a connection between sudden oil seal leaks and crankcase pressure. Your Evo engine's "dry sump" lubrication system requires a sophisticated crankcase breathing system. If the breather system becomes restricted or does not allow crankcase pressure to vent properly, there is risk to seals and a likelihood of oil leaks.

When your engine develops a sudden, "mysterious" engine oil leak(s), inspect and thoroughly service the crankcase breather system. You may find that seal leaks will stop at this point. If not, repair the crankcase breather system, then replace damaged seals as necessary.

The different lubricants in the engine, primary and transmission units will help you distinguish engine oil leaks from those in other areas of the powertrain. Know the smell, coloration and texture of each oil. This way, if a leak develops, you can pinpoint which area of the powertrain to troubleshoot.

ENGINE REBUILDING FOOTNOTES

My sourcebooks for information on rebuilding or repairing Harley-Davidson engines have always been the factory service manuals. My current factory service manual library for Harley-Davidsons includes information spanning 1917–present. Earlier coverage is from factory re-prints of original shop manuals. Evolution Era manuals are always on the shelf at better stocked dealerships. I am confident that if you understand the language, reference terms, tools and hands-on steps described in a Harley-Davidson factory service manual, you can rebuild your motorcycle.

FIG. 6-22. Terms like "engine overhaul" have become widely abused. A valve regrind, even with a piston ring set replacement, is not a major overhaul or rebuild. A major engine overhaul or complete rebuild should restore all tolerances and parts fitups within the engine. Labor flat-rate guides clearly define steps of repair jobs versus complete rebuilding. If you sublet engine work, know whether your engine is undergoing a component repair, a valve-and-ring job, or a complete rebuild.

Before starting an engine rebuild project, read the factory service manual sections devoted to this task. Decide whether this is the kind of project that fits your allotment of spare time, your tool assortment, your skills and your temperament. If you suspect that this task is beyond any one of these factors, *do not begin the work*. Bringing a thorough "basket case" (or even a partially disassembled bike) to your local dealership will surely cost more than toting your fully intact motorcycle to the service department for repairs. Basket cases are often hard to sort out and incur hours of extra labor charges to wade through scattered, lost or misplaced pieces.

If your tools, skill or understanding fall short of these requirements, you will at least be a better informed consumer. This knowledge will help you work with your dealer around the maintenance and repair of your motorcycle.

When you have determined what is wrong with the engine, view your repair prospects as one of three group tasks: 1) in-frame cylinder head work (including valve grind job), 2) cylinder head and piston/ring assembly (involves removal of cylinder barrels while engine is still in-frame), or 3) a full rebuild. A full rebuild entails removal of the engine assembly from the frame and complete disassembly, cleaning, inspection and measuring of parts before re-fitting new pieces.

Many home mechanics can handle valve grind and cylinder head in-frame repairs. Even piston and ring replacement is within the scope of the more accomplished home mechanic. Head and valve work, cylinder re-boring and honing of cylinders will be sublet tasks. Home mechanics should stick to disassembly, clean-up and careful re-fitting of new or freshly machined parts.

Rather than paraphrase the step-by-step rebuilding techniques described thoroughly in your factory service manual, let's focus here on those issues I call "footnotes." These are the unwritten comments that only years of work as a professional mechanic can cultivate, the insight gleaned from repeated hands-on experience and research.

Building A Quality Engine

FIG. 6-23. Whether a cylinder head overhaul or complete engine rebuild, the focus is renewal or replacement of key parts. Wear items to consider are piston rings, valves, valve guides and guide seals, the oil pump, tappet guides and tappets, pushrods, rocker arms and shafts, the camshaft(s), bushings and bearings, timing gears, crankshaft and rod bearings, sprockets, all gaskets and seals.

FIG. 6-24. Oil pump renewal is a must during a rebuild. (Near photo of 1340cc engine; XLH oil pump shown in far photo.) A disassembly, inspection and replacement of worn pieces will assure adequate oil flow to your expensive "new" engine. Follow oil pump guidelines and specifications found in your factory service manual. Make sure all oil lines and hoses are thoroughly clean and in top condition before assembly.

FIG. 6-25. Valvetrain wear points include camshaft lobes and bearings, timing gears, tappet guides, hydraulic tappets, pushrods (check tips and shaft trueness), rocker arms and shafts, valves, valve guides and seals, valve springs, retainers and locks, and valve seats. These parts each require close inspection for fatigue and wear. Take measurements and compare with factory tolerances (as described in service manual). Thoroughly clean any reusable pieces and store in a dust-free, dry area.

FIG. 6-26. Valve grinding, generally a sublet task, requires disassembly and thorough clean-up of cylinder head components, valves and all related parts. Inspection of valve stems and faces will determine whether valves can be re-faced and put back into service. I prefer replacement of valves, valve guides and valve springs on a higher mileage engine to assure reliable performance. Exhaust valves and guides, in particular, take a beating over time.

FIG. 6-27. Three-angle valve seat cutting is a norm today. This assures a properly located, correct width valve seat for the new valve. Harley-Davidson recommends initial 31- and 60-degree cuts to narrow and locate valve seat. Final cut is 45-degrees when using a grinding process or 46-degrees with cutting tool. This will help prevent carbon buildup during normal valve seat-in.

FIG. 6-28. Commonly, automotive machine shops will cut valve stem ends to restore valve height after machining. On Harley-Davidson Evo engines, valves have hardened tips and *cannot be shortened by grinding at their tip end.* Your dealer can, if required, supply special short stem (0.030-inch shorter) valves to attain proper fitup after head and valve seat machining. These special valves also assure proper valve spring fitted height and pressure.

WARNING —

Do not remove material from valve stem tip ends. Valve is hardened here, and removal of material will expose softer metal that would wear rapidly in service. If you must sublet your valve job to a local automotive machine shop, advise them of this fact.

FIG. 6-29. Among tools needed to perform a thorough engine rebuild are micrometers, both inside and outside types. Cylinder barrels and bearing or bushing bores require an inside "mike" for roundness and taper. Shafts, valve stems, camshaft lobes and the crankshaft require outside measurements. Precise motorcycle engine timing kit (upper right), including a dial indicator, has served me well for decades. Magnetic stand helps hold dial indicator for a variety of inspections.

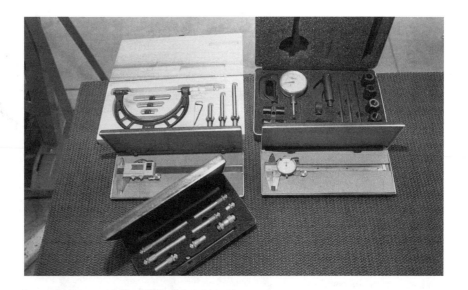

FIG. 6-30. Any blue discolored parts should be replaced. Galled or scored parts need re-machining or replacement. Why take a chance on marginal or fatigued parts? Pay for your rebuild once, not twice. Discard or machine those parts that show wear or signs of stress.

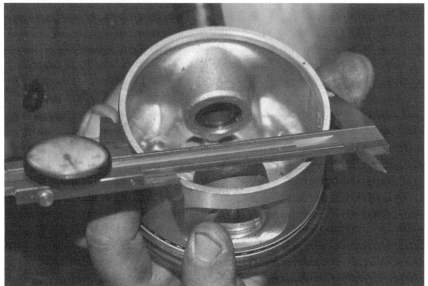

F*IG.* 6-31. Inspect cylinder barrels and pistons for signs of overheat, scoring and distortion. Blue discoloration is a clear sign of overheating. Use an outside micrometer or precision caliper to measure piston and piston pin diameters. Use an inside micrometer or dial indicator (shown) to measure cylinder bore for taper, wear and distortion. (See factory service manual for tolerances.)

F*IG.* 6-32. Unless pistons, pins and cylinder walls check well within tolerance, re-bore and power hone both cylinders, and install new pistons and wrist pins. Inspect bushing-to-pin fitup and make sure upper end rod bushings (shown in cutaway view) are in top shape. If not, replace rod bushing(s).

FIG. 6-33. Shafts, timing gears, bearings and bushings need inspection and micrometer measurement. Gears and shafts require specific backlash or shaft end play. Use a dial indicator or feeler gauge (shown here at crankshaft), and compare readings with specifications found in your factory service manual. These measurements and tolerances are critical and indicate wear. Parts fitup must be within specification for long service life.

FIG. 6-34. When you disassemble the engine, it is essential that you lay out parts in their proper order for reassembly. Items like timing or oil pump gears, or even pushrods, may look alike. *They are not.* Note color coding on cam and timing gears, pushrods and other parts. Your factory service manual describes color markings of fitted parts.

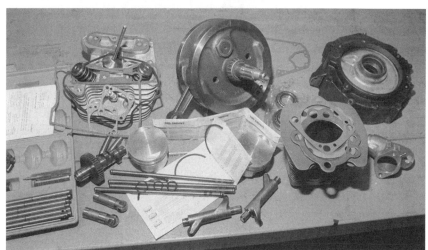

FIG. 6-35. Since complete engine rebuilding exposes primary chain or belt and sprockets, this is a wise time to closely inspect these pieces and replace them if necessary. Primary chain adjuster slipper has usually worn enough for replacement. Replace any worn parts in primary system.

FIG. 6-36. Use Genuine Harley-Davidson parts when performing an engine repair or rebuild. By doing so, you have assurance of latest update parts for your engine. Cylinder base gaskets have gone through several parts supercedures to reach stage where they will not leak oil. You want the latest Genuine Harley-Davidson parts or well known aftermarket products designed to remedy problems.

FIG. 6-37. Even racing or high performance components are available through your dealership. Genuine Harley-Davidson parts meet a high standard of quality, backed by a factory parts warranty. Some non-factory aftermarket racing and high performance parts, described in the performance chapter of this book, do serve well in special use applications.

FIG. 6-38. Importance of cleanliness cannot be overstated. During disassembly, use clean coffee cans, or sealed plastic jars, to hold labeled and separated hardware. Clean these parts and keep them clean for re-assembly. Cover exposed crankcase, oil tank, oil lines and other assemblies to prevent contamination by abrasive dust or grime. Your work area must be free of dust during engine assembly.

7 PRIMARY CHAIN, CLUTCH, AND TRANSMISSION

Your Evolution engine delivers power from its crankshaft through an enclosed primary chain system. At the rear of the primary chain is a wet-plate clutch assembly. When the clutch and transmission function properly, power flows smoothly from the clutch unit into the gearsets.

Within the transmission, a shifter mechanism directs power flow through the gearsets. Lower gear ratios provide the increased torque needed to get your cycle rolling from a standstill. Powerful intermediate gear ratios can accelerate the cycle readily and also meet the challenge of grades. Higher gears bring the cycle to highway cruise speed, where the engine rpm becomes steady, and fuel economy rises.

Power flows from the transmission to the rear wheel via a final (secondary) drive sprocket. An Aramid belt or traditional roller chain, depending upon which model, delivers power to the rear wheel's drive sprocket.

In Chapter 4, I shared information on routine service and adjustment of the secondary drive belt or chain. This chapter focuses on the primary chain, clutch assembly and transmission systems of your Evolution motorcycle. The F-series 1340cc engine uses the classic "divorced" (separately mounted) trans-

FIG. 7-1. On primary case of F- and XL-series engines, there is an inspection plate for checking primary chain adjustment. Look closely at the condition of links throughout chain's length. Measure hot or cold chain play as described in your factory service manual. Compare play at various points along the chain.

mission assembly. The XL models retain their unit construction layout, familiar from the original '57 Sportster forward.

While a few of the early F-series Evolution cycles feature a four-speed transmission, most models have offered the five-speed. (Evolution XL models began with four-speed transmissions, then evolved to the current five-speed design.) Despite internal gearbox changes to accommodate the additional fifth gear, service procedures remain fundamentally the same for four- and five-speed gearboxes.

PRIMARY CHAIN SERVICE

The primary chain drive requires periodic checks for proper chain tension and wear. Like any other chain drive mechanism, the primary chain can stretch. When it stretches to the point that safe adjustment is no longer possible, the primary chain must be replaced.

FIG. 7-2. Primary chain temperatures run high. Change primary or primary/transmission lubricant regularly. (See lubrication details in Chapter 4.) When cycle has seen a hard, long run, consider changing this fluid, regardless of mileage since the last service. Oil is cheaper than a chain, a new adjusting shoe and sprockets.

FIG. 7-3. If primary chain needs minor adjustment, find tightest spot on chain. In factory service manual you will find procedures for raising or lowering the adjusting shoe. Shoe has nylon rubbing surface and can wear to excess over time.

WARNING —
Rotating chains and sprockets can cause injury. Disconnect the battery negative cable before exposing the primary system.

FIG. 7-4. When chain adjustment cannot bring chain tension into tolerance, either primary chain and/or adjusting shoe have reached their service limits. You need to remove primary cover and test primary chain for stretch and abnormal wear. Inspect adjuster shoe and replace if necessary. Adjust new chain and/or shoe assembly to proper specification. Recheck tension after 500 miles of operation.

CLUTCH TROUBLESHOOTING AND SERVICE

Wet plate clutches are a popular motorcycle design, although Harley-Davidson has used dry type clutch assemblies as recently as the primary belt-drive era just prior to the introduction of Evolution motorcycles. I like wet clutches and a "bathed" primary chain, as oil has a cooling effect. On air-cooled engines, a wet clutch and primary chain help alleviate fatigue and also lower the risk of parts damage from excessive heat.

Clutch styles vary between models. Before working on your clutch assembly, review the Harley-Davidson service manual for your motorcycle. Become familiar with parts layout and function. If you have the right tools, consider clutch service within the realm of home mechanics.

When the clutch shows symptoms of trouble, run through the list of possible fixes. Simple cures include a clutch adjustment and cable/lever adjustment. You may need to replace a worn clutch cable. Worn clutch plates and other

FIG. 7-5. A Harley-Davidson wet-plate clutch is not a complicated mechanism. You can easily understand its function and even consider rebuilding such a unit. A wet clutch consists of a series of plates. Friction plates are driven by the clutch shell, which receives power from the rear primary sprocket.

FIG. 7-6. Steel plates sandwiched between friction plates have inner teeth that drive the clutch hub. This clutch hub powers the transmission input shaft or mainshaft. In middle of a later model clutch plate stack is a spring plate, and at the outer face of all wet-plate clutches you will find a pressure plate and diaphragm spring. This diaphragm spring applies necessary clamping force to press together friction (drive) and steel (driven) plates.

parts require an overhaul of the clutch. Always attempt an easier fix before condemning the expensive clutch assembly.

Troubleshooting the Clutch

Clutch troubles fall into three categories: 1) The clutch slips under load or on take-off and changing gears; 2) the clutch causes the engine or whole cycle to shake when you release the lever (roughness called "chatter"); and 3) you cannot completely disengage the clutch.

If the *clutch slips*, there is either insufficient free-play upon releasing the lever, or the clutch unit diaphragm spring has weakened severely. Always maintain correct free-play at clutch lever, and if slip still occurs, adjust the clutch. (See below.)

When the clutch *will not disengage completely*, there is gear clash on shifting. In the worst case, you may not be able to stop the cycle without the engine stalling. Sometimes the cause is as simple as too much slack in the clutch cable and/or the need to perform a clutch adjustment.

Causes of *clutch drag* can be as simple as too much free-play at cable/lever. This means you cannot move the cable far enough for the clutch to disengage completely. Always adjust the clutch before adjusting cable/lever free-play.

More severe causes of drag include the need for a major clutch adjustment or damage at clutch plates and elsewhere within the clutch assembly. Such damage will not permit clutch plates to separate completely when you apply the clutch lever. This creates drag.

Clutch Adjustment

Clutch adjustment is not difficult. It should always begin at the clutch unit. Although procedures change with different model years, the overall approach is similar. The proper clutch adjustment will establish free-play at the clutch release mechanism. Once you have set the adjuster correctly, you can adjust cable/lever free-play.

If you have performed this adjustment correctly, with the clutch adjuster and cable/lever free-play set properly, your clutch should be smooth and operate without roughness or chatter. Full disengagement should be easy to achieve. If not, it's likely time to rebuild your clutch.

FIG. 7-7. When adjusting the clutch, you must first relieve all tension at clutch cable. This will enable an accurate adjustment at clutch unit.

FIG. 7-8. This particular clutch design calls for a diaphragm spring plate adjustment. A series of bolt hole combinations allows spring plate to apply different degree of pressure to clutch stack. (This alters spring diaphragm shape and, as a result, the clutch apply pressure.) You can adjust this kind of clutch spring plate with common tools and a feeler gauge set. See factory service manual for exact details on your model.

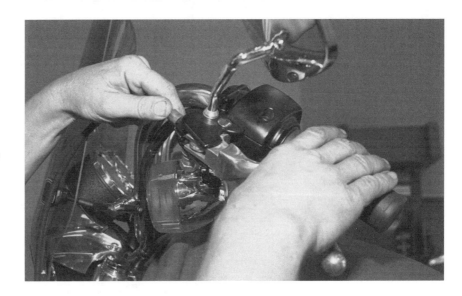

FIG. 7-9. When adjusted properly, your clutch lever will have enough travel to completely disengage the clutch. Once you release the lever completely, the cable and adjuster free-play will permit clutch spring diaphragm to apply full pressure at the clutch plate stack.

NOTE —

Do not attempt a clutch adjustment at the clutch cable only. You could get a false reading. For the clutch to work properly, there must be adequate free-play at the release rod or spring diaphragm in the clutch unit. Always adjust the clutch in the manner described in your factory service manual.

**Clutch Cable
Replacement**

Your cycle's clutch cable is a wear item. Periodic inspection, required lubrication and adjustments will extend cable life. When the cable shows wear or has stretched to the point that adjustment is no longer possible, you must replace the cable. This is one task that you can readily perform at your home shop— or even on the road if necessary.

You will find step-by-step clutch cable installation instructions in your factory service manual. Rather than describe installation methods for the wide range of Evolution motorcycle models, I will share general concerns. Each model has specific cable routings. Do your clutch and throttle cable replacements "by the book"—use your factory service manual.

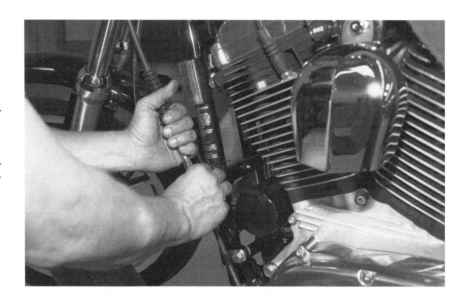

FIG. 7-10. Before replacing your cycle's clutch cable, look carefully at its routing. Make certain that you follow OEM path on re-installation. If you suspect that cable routing may not be original, review illustrations found in your factory service manual. If still unclear, look at a similar model motorcycle or consult your dealer's service or parts department.

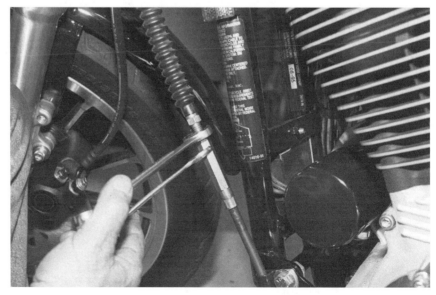

FIG. 7-11. Clutch cable replacement involves loosening adjuster completely to allow disconnecting cable from hand lever and at clutch linkage end. (Models differ, so consult your factory service manual.) Note method of attachment to pivot pin at lever. Some earlier models use a pivot pin with a flat side that must face toward lever.

FIG. 7-12. Before making adjustments on your new cable always adjust clutch at clutch unit. This will assure proper free-play at clutch release mechanism. Now you can adjust new cable to achieve correct lever free-play. Work lever several times to seat parts. Check adjustment again.

FIG. 7-13. Cables stretch. After riding your motorcycle for 500 or so miles, re-check cable free-play adjustment at lever. Normal stretch and seating-in may require a re-adjustment at this point. You can extend cable life by periodic inspection, lubrication (shown) and adjustment. When excessive stretch or fraying occur, replace cable.

Clutch Overhaul Tips

The factory service manual describes the removal, disassembly, inspection and re-assembly procedures for your clutch. Clutch design and specifications vary between models; however, all F- and XL-series Evolution clutches can be overhauled without removing the transmission.

Clutch overhaul, with the right tools, is within the capacity of many home mechanics. In general, you will need to remove the primary cover. (Disconnect the battery negative cable first, to prevent the engine from cranking during the procedure.) Then follow the steps in your service manual.

> *CAUTION —*
> *The transmission shaft nut and shaft thread is of left hand type. Turn the nut clockwise to loosen. Turn the nut counter-clockwise to tighten.*

You can determine clutch wear by looking closely at the clutch components on the bench. Visible defects include wear, nicks or pits in friction lining, a rough surface on the steel plates, warpage of plates and blue discoloration, which indicates heat fatigue.

FIG. 7-14. On this application, one way to prevent clutch unit's sprocket shaft from turning while you loosen this nut is to place transmission in high gear and have a helper apply the rear brake firmly. You should now be able to loosen mainshaft nut. If necessary, use this technique when setting nut's torque on re-assembly of clutch unit.

FIG. 7-15. Check steel plates for flatness. An inexpensive surface that works well here is a flat piece of safety glass with edges sanded smooth. In your service manual, you will find clutch specifications and limits for maximum plate warpage. Using a feeler gauge, hold plate flat on glass and measure beneath gaps around plate/disc. Replace any warped or defective plates to assure proper clutch operation.

FIG. 7-16. Measure thickness of plates with an outside 0-to-1-inch micrometer or precision caliper. Compare plate thicknesses to specifications in your service manual. (Make sure data is for your type of clutch, as manuals often cover several years and models.) Friction disc material determines thickness of each disc. Make sure there is ample material on each disc. Replace any marginally worn discs.

FIG. 7-17. Soak new clutch plates in appropriate Harley-Davidson primary case oil for your motorcycle. (F- and XL-series cycles use different primary and transmission oil.) This readies your clutch parts for re-assembly and start-up. Clean primary case housing and cover thoroughly before you install fresh clutch assembly.

FIG. 7-18. Pilot bearing must not show signs of wear. Watch for discoloration (bluish) from excessive heat. Unless this bearing feels absolutely free and smooth when rotated, replace it with a new one. Call this "insurance," the assurance of trouble-free service and no need to do the job twice.

FIG. 7-19. Inspect crankshaft/sprocket nut, sliding cam and compensating sprocket, when your engine features this equipment. Replace any of these parts if worn or damaged. Check splines on shaft extension for wear, galling or fatigue. While you have these parts off, replace any marginal pieces.

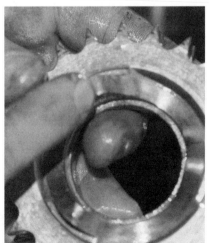

Fig. 7-20. Consider the adjuster shoe a wear item. Unless like new, replace this nylon slipper. A new or serviceable chain can be adjusted periodically as long as the adjuster shoe has enough material. New adjuster shoe can serve as a reliable guide for chain wear.

Fig. 7-21. Clutch or clutch adjustment problems can create hard shifting and "clunks" on shifting. If clutch does not disengage completely, you cannot get transmission to shift properly. Damage will occur if you persist in riding your motorcycle in this condition. (See earlier section of this chapter for clutch adjustment details.)

Transmission Trouble and Diagnosis

In this section, I'll share highlights of transmission repair and overhaul. Here, you may prefer subletting the cycle to the dealership. For F-series models with a divorced transmission unit, you may want to remove the transmission assembly yourself and take the unit to the local dealership for disassembly, repair or overhaul.

Before delving into a major transmission job, rule out other possible troubles. In cold climate start-ups, let your cycle warm completely before riding. Place the gear selector in neutral and keep the clutch engaged during warm up. Allow engine heat and primary chain movement to thoroughly warm up the lubricant. If hard shifting prevails, suspect troubles beyond oil type.

Look first at the need for a clutch adjustment (or replacement if worn badly). You can cause rapid wear of the transmission shifter mechanism and transmission internal parts by shifting gears without completely disengaging the clutch. Also look for a problem with the shift linkage.

FIG. 7-22. The only "simple fix" for a hard shifting transmission is changing gear lube. In winter, a heavier gear lubricant in a colder climate can cause hard shifting. This usually goes away, however, as engine and transmission assembly warm up.

FIG. 7-23. Some models have more elaborate shift linkage than others. Make sure, especially on F-series cycles, that linkage is not binding or obstructed. Although this sounds simple, symptoms of transmission trouble can result from problems as basic as a binding lever or cable, or linkage that needs lubrication. If your cycle's transmission jumps out of gear, make sure there are no linkage obstructions that could prevent shifter from engaging gears completely.

FIG. 7-24. Shifter pawl adjustment (XL models) and shifter rod adjustment (F-models) are the only transmission related shifting problems that do not require opening the transmission. (F-series shift control cover and drum are accessible without removal of transmission.) If your cycle has a shifting problem, try a pawl or shifter rod adjustment before considering a transmission assembly overhaul.

FIG. 7-25. Transmission shifter mechanisms fit externally and internally on Harley-Davidson cycles. XL models have most shifter parts within transmission assembly. This means that in-depth repairs (shifter forks and drum) involve extensive disassembly work. Consider this major service, tasks requiring greater experience and a higher skill level.

Transmission Repair Overview

Specifications for transmission tolerances and clearances are detailed in your factory service manual. You will also find steps for removing the transmission unit from an F-series motorcycle chassis. On XL models, transmission work can take place with the engine/transmission assembly still in-frame.

FIG. 7-26. Do not attempt a transmission overhaul without first consulting your factory service manual. Gear, shaft and bearing parts are expensive, and a trip to your dealer's parts counter may tell you whether to proceed with this repair or not. At these costs, you want to be certain that this is the source of trouble.

There are both four- and five-speed transmissions in Evolution Era motorcycles. From a repair standpoint, the skill required to overhaul any of these transmissions would be similar. You need a variety of specialty tools and pullers, the factory service manual, and an appreciation for detail when overhauling a Harley-Davidson motorcycle transmission. You cannot improvise here, as the result could be severe damage to alloy cases and bearing bores.

FIG. 7-27. Removal of the transmission drive sprocket is a part of transmission work. *Sprocket nuts use a left hand thread, so be sure to turn nut clockwise when removing it.* Replace sprocket if there are signs of wear. Look at rear wheel sprocket, and if wear exists here, replace rear sprocket as well. You will find details on sprocket removal and installation within factory service manual for your model.

FIG. 7-28. Rear sprocket removal is just a few steps beyond a wheel and tire removal for a tire change. In Chapter 8 you will find information on wheel and tire removal. Factory service manual offers wear limits for secondary (final) drive chain, belt and sprockets. The general rule for parts replacement is wear that creates a chain or belt stretch equal to 3/4ths of a sprocket tooth.

FIG. 7-29. When wear is present, you will notice a rust-red gap on secondary chain sprockets. On belt drive sprockets, look closely for damaged or chipping chrome. This can ruin an Aramid belt. Belt, sprockets and drive chain play vital roles in your cycle's powertrain. Although these pieces are expensive, be glad you don't have a driveshaft with ring-and-pinion gear assembly to maintain or rebuild.

FIG. 7-30. If you decide to rebuild your transmission, your first aim on F-series cycles is getting the unit onto a work bench. Shifter control unit troubles do not require transmission removal. In most instances, you can repair an F-series shifter control unit by removing primary case and/or accessing shifter at top of transmission assembly while gearbox is still in-frame.

FIG. 7-31. Among tools needed to overhaul a transmission are special pullers and a hydraulic press. Use of special fixtures and extreme care will prevent damage to expensive cases, bearing bores and transmission parts. If you do not have these tools, and if motorcycle repair work is not an ongoing function in your life, plan on subletting these steps to a Harley-Davidson dealership or similarly qualified shop.

8 WHEELS, HUBS, TIRES, AND BRAKES

Much of your motorcycling safety depends upon routine service items. Of special concern are tires, wheel assemblies and brakes. Failure of a tire, seizure of wheel bearings or a malfunctioning brake component can place you and your motorcycle at high risk. Periodic inspection and service can help prevent these kinds of problems.

Tire and wheel rim inspection, adjusting spokes (if required), repacking and adjusting wheel bearings, thorough brake system inspection and full brake service are within the scope of home mechanics. Although sometimes awkward work to perform, maintaining your Harley-Davidson's wheels, tires and brakes can help assure your safety and riding pleasure. Performing your own wheel, tire and brake service also provides the skill and knowledge of how to make repairs on the road.

While much of the tire, wheel and brake work performed within this chapter reflect a dealership environment, you can do similar work with more modest tools. With practice, changing a tire with only hand spoons and rub-

FIG. 8-1. Wheels rated for tubeless tires will be marked as such. Never attempt to put a tubeless type tire on a wheel rim designed and rated for tube-type tires and vice versa. Use front and rear tires recommended by Harley-Davidson for your model. Mount tires in manner prescribed by Harley-Davidson.

FIG. 8-2. Tubeless tire rims are easy to maintain. Check valve stem for leaks, dabbing soapy water at stem seat and valve core. Note condition of tire, looking for irregular belt shape, oxidation, deteriorating rubber and worn tread. I advise tread replacement at a minimum tread depth of 1/8-inch. "Lincoln's head on a U.S. penny" is too thin for high speed runs on hot asphalt or riding a rain slick stretch of foggy, mountainous road.

ber lubricant is possible. Likewise, you can do most brake work with basic handtools. The objective is care and concern for those components involved.

> **WARNING —**
> *Never let your tires' tread wear to 1/16th inch. Your safety is largely dependent upon tire condition. I would replace tires at 1/8th inch tread, although some sources accept maximum wear to 3/32nds of an inch.*

WHEEL AND RIM SERVICE

There are three types of wheel/rims used on Harley-Davidson Evolution motorcycles: traditional laced-spoke types, modern one- or two-piece cast alloy assemblies, and two-piece "disc" wheels. Laced spoke wheels remain popular for their aesthetic appeal and classic look. Maintenance-free cast and disc wheels provide an added safety margin and installation simplicity by allowing use of tubeless tires.

Laced spoked wheels require periodic inspection for loose, broken or fatigued spokes and damaged nipples (adjustor/nuts). Special care is necessary when changing a tire on laced spoke wheels. Since the tire must be a tube type, a protective rubber rim-band separates and protects the tube from the rim center, nipples and spoke ends. Whenever you replace a tire or tube, inspect the condition of the rim band and make certain that it covers spoke nipples completely. Replace rim bands at the slightest sign of fatigue.

The steel outer rim on laced spoke wheels is durable and somewhat flexible. With the exception of damage from collision, slamming into a curb or extreme jarring from a pot-hole in the road, the rim stays true. "Tuning" the spokes (tapping on them gently with a metal tool) and adjusting them as required will help keep these wheels in alignment and running true.

Cast alloy wheels, a 1970s breakthrough, were a major advance in motorcycle tire and rim technology. The traditional laced spoke wheel, rim band and tube were no longer necessary. Tubeless tires, proven in automobile use, provided wider resistance to blowouts caused by heat buildup and friction. They also are far easier to mount. Cast alloy wheels require no routine maintenance. Inspection is simply for signs of casting fatigue, damage, stress and valve stem problems, and noting the condition of tire tread and sidewalls.

Most Harley-Davidson dealerships and better equipped independent shops now have electronic wheel balancing equipment. Using a spin balancer, there is a quick check for wheel rim trueness. With the tire dismounted from the rim during a tire change, have the shop spin your wheels on the balancer and check rim "runout." Start with a visual check. Then, if you or the technician suspect damage, use a dial indicator and magnetic stand to precisely measure wheel rim runout.

The traditional way to assess runout, and also a means for assembling and truing a laced spoke wheel, is on a truing stand. If you were to lace and true wheels regularly, it would make sense to invest in a quality wheel truing stand. For the home mechanic, however, there are ways that you can determine rim runout without using a stand.

After reviewing the factory service manual procedure for lacing your wheels, decide whether you have the equipment and desire to perform this work yourself. If not, your Harley-Davidson dealership or an independent motorcycle shop with proper truing equipment can assist. Whichever shop you approach, make certain that their guide for wheel lacing is a Harley-Davidson service manual.

FIG. 8-3. Lacing a spoke rim is an art form. Assembly of a wheel requires painstaking care and patience. If you want to perform this kind of work, review wheel lacing section in your factory service manual. You will find details on assembly techniques, the sequence in which you install sets of spokes, how to center a rim, true the rim and tighten spokes in sequence.

Wheel Lacing Tips

If you decide to lace or true your wheels, there are several precautions to observe. To remove a wheel and hub assembly, follow instructions in your factory service manual. You will find this is an opportune time to repack your wheel bearings and install new grease seals. (See later section in this chapter.)

Once you have your wheel(s) removed, you can set the assembly in a truing stand. Use a stand like Harley-Davidson Part #HD-95500-80 or an equivalent aftermarket truing stand. I like the Harley-Davidson stand for its sturdy legs and hefty arbor shaft diameter. When setting up a Harley-Davidson laced wheel, be certain to consider radial runout, axial or lateral runout, proper rim offset on hub and uniform tightness of spokes.

FIG. 8-4. Lacing a wheel involves factory procedures. You must select the right spokes (long- and short-style) and follow an exact pattern for placing spokes onto hub. Then you "lace" and attach spokes to rim in a specific pattern ("cross-four" shown here). Unless you follow this sequence closely and with patience, lacing a wheel can be a frustrating task.

FIG. 8-5. You can improvise, at least for preliminary on-cycle testing of wheel trueness. Using fork or swing arm legs for a "stand," set up dial indicator at a leg or arm. With motorcycle raised enough for tire to clear floor safely, rotate rim slowly and read wheel rim lateral runout much like on a truing stand. (Weight of wheel will set bearings against their cups as you rotate assembly.) This is a simple, roughly accurate test for runout.

FIG. 8-6. NEAR: Radial runout is the relationship of the rim to the hub. If you were to measure from the hub centerline to the tire mounting surface on the rim, this distance should be equal around the entire rim.
FAR: Measure axial or lateral runout at *inside* edge of rim, where tire bead seats against rim edge. This will assure tire alignment and straightness when cycle runs down the road.

FIG. 8-7. Many Evolution cycles have factory rim offset. This offset measurement varies between models and wheel designs, so check the factory service manual for details on your cycle's requirements. Any aftermarket wheel should come with detailed instructions that address assembly methods and proper offset.

FIG. 8-8. To true a wheel, always loosen spokes in pairs, counting turns carefully. Once a pair of spokes is loose, tighten opposite spoke pair same number of turns. True rims to within factory specification for runout, using initial set of spokes as described in factory service manual. Once rim is true, remainder of spokes can be tightened, beginning at valve stem hole. Harley-Davidson recommends tightening these remaining nipples one turn at a time as you rotate rim.

FIG. 8-9. Seat spoke/nipple heads in rim with a mallet and flat punch. (I suggest using a brass punch to prevent nipple damage.) Once again check trueness of rim and tightness of spokes. Next, you can file or carefully grind off excess spoke lengths. Threads should not extend above nipple heads. This will prevent a spoke end from wearing through rim band and puncturing tire tube. After filing or grinding, remove all metal debris before installing rim band, tube and tire.

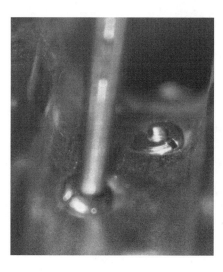
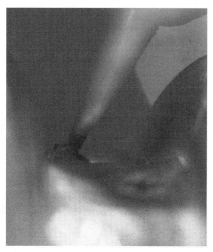

FIG. 8-10. Overtightened nipples will distort rim seats or worse. "Snug" is tight enough. You can determine uniform tightness by tapping middle of each spoke gently with a steel tool. Listen to pitch of ring. You can hear difference between tighter and looser spokes. Adjust spokes until sound is reasonably uniform. If you do not know correct pitch, test a wheel that is correctly laced, preferably on a newer motorcycle. Try to match this pitch.

CAUTION —
If you tighten spokes first, then loosen opposite pair, you can warp or damage wheel rim. Never create an overtight situation. Always loosen, then tighten spokes to true the rim.

NOTE —
Spoke types, shapes and lengths differ. Make sure you identify spokes and place them at proper locations.

WHEEL HUB AND BEARING SERVICE

Routinely, your Harley-Davidson Evolution motorcycle will require wheel bearing service. Whether you true a wheel, change a tire or follow the periodic maintenance schedule for your motorcycle, wheel bearing repacking should be on your safety checklist. When you have properly cleaned, repacked and adjusted your cycle's wheel bearings, this service is good for 10,000 miles on most models. (See lubrication schedule in your factory service manual.)

WARNING —
Refer to your factory service manual for specific details on disassembling, reassembly and proper torque settings for axle nuts and other wheel hardware. These procedures vary between the many Evolution models, and a generic approach will not do. Make certain you follow wheel bearing service guidelines for your specific motorcycle.

There are general requirements for any wheel bearing repack or service. Although your factory service manual offers vital details for safely adjusting and assembling wheel bearings and hubs, several details apply to all bearing service. Once properly adjusted with a dial indicator, wheel bearing end play can be felt by hand. With wheel and tire safely suspended off the ground, hold tire at six and twelve o'clock. Rock wheel on axle shaft and bearings. Know this amount of play *by feel*. Once you know feel of proper bearing play, a quick check on the road is possible. Here is one more way to become familiar with the inner workings of your Evolution motorcycle.

FIG. 8-11. Follow factory service manual when removing your wheels. Procedures differ between models and wheel types. Safely support your cycle while performing wheel service.

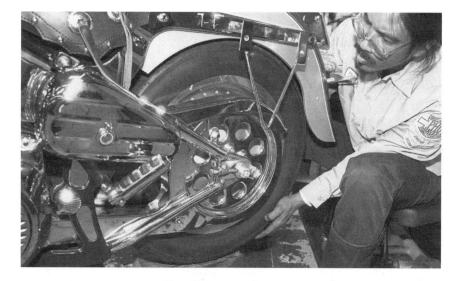

FIG. 8-12. Disassemble axle and wheel bearing components as described in your factory service manual. Lay parts out carefully and in order. Never mix bearings or swap from side to side. After thorough cleaning, inspect all pieces for damage or fatigue. Replace any marginal parts. Always replace bearings in sets, including cups (outer race) and cones (caged roller bearing assembly).

FIG. 8-13. Use a suitable solvent to clean all old grease from bearings. Once bearing is thoroughly clear of grease, you can air dry completely or blow parts dry with pressurized air. *Never spin a bearing assembly with compressed air.*

WARNING —
Never spin or rotate a roller bearing with air pressure. A spinning bearing could score or fly apart, causing serious bodily injury. Always blow air from sides, and prevent bearing from spinning.

FIG. 8-14. Bearing must be completely dry and free of grease and debris before re-packing. I use the hand method, pressing grease through the wide side edge until it comes up through the rollers. Make certain that grease fills each roller and cage. Go around bearing several times to eliminate gaps.

FIG. 8-15. Whether you use this grease packer or hand method, smear a good film of grease around outside of cage and rollers as your last step. Coat new seal's outer edges and sealing lips with a film of grease. Install clean bearing spacer in hub. Next, install bearings, one at a time, driving their grease seals into place. (See factory service manual for seal depth.) Pack grease into cavity between each seal and wheel bearing before installing axle shaft.

FIG. 8-16. Install wheel, axle shaft and related pieces as described and illustrated within your factory service manual. When you have fitted all parts properly and set torque on axle nut, you can verify wheel bearing end-play. This is a critical measurement, listed in your service manual. End play confirms bearing adjustment, and this adjustment affects handling, wheel stability and safety.

FIG. 8-17. Wheel bearing end play is lateral or axial movement of hub on axle shaft. Set up a dial indicator as shown here. With wheel elevated off ground, push wheel/tire firmly toward a fork leg with hands held at either 6 and 12 o'clock or 3 and 9 o'clock. Note reading on dial. Now pull wheel away from fork leg, with hands held at same clock positions as before. Again, note dial reading. Difference between these two dial indicator measurements is bearing end-play.

FIG. 8-18. If endplay reads out of tolerance, look for problems like a new bearing cup that does not fit squarely, improperly installed pieces, or parts out of order. (Bearing spacer width is set at factory.) Even a bearing set change should not cause wheel bearing end-play to go out of range. Fitup between original and new OEM bearings should be nearly identical.

FIG. 8-19. When wheel bearing endplay is incorrect, yet all parts and assembly procedures check okay, adjust wheel bearings by installing a new selective fit bearing spacer or proper thickness shims. These are available from your Harley-Davidson parts department. Know how much end-play correction you need before purchasing new spacers or shims.

FIG. 8-20. Parts assembly order must be correct, including which direction you install axle shaft. On some Evolution cycles, installing axle shaft in wrong direction can damage muffler or other parts. Some axle shafts require a coating of anti-seize compound during assembly. Check your factory service manual for specific details.

TIRE SERVICE

You can perform several aspects of tire service on your Evolution motorcycle. Details like tire balancing, however, will require subletting the wheel and tire assembly to a dealership or independent shop that has appropriate tire balancing equipment.

On the road, even the best maintained motorcycle may some time get a flat tire. I once had a rear tire go flat during the era of laced spoke wheels and tube-type tires. At 70 mph, I had ample time to reflect on what it would be like as the cycle slowed to a stop. Fortunately, I was able to stop the motorcycle completely before all the air had left the tire. That ride was still unique.

I trust that you will have few, if any, flat tires on the road. (If you do have a flat, keep in mind the safe operating tips I shared in Chapter 3 of the book.)

FIG. 8-21. Your saddlebag tool kit should include a tire patch kit. A tubeless tire with an obvious nail hole in the tread can be repaired with a plug (left). If tire bead still seats on rim, you may be able to plug hole without removing wheel assembly. Harley-Davidson's string/plug with liquid cement (right) can be fitted from outside of tire. However, a puncture at sidewall presents a hazard that only a new tire will fix. (See "Warning" on next page.)

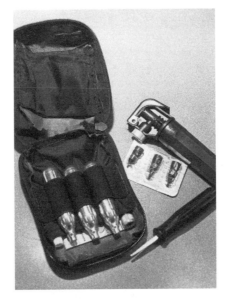

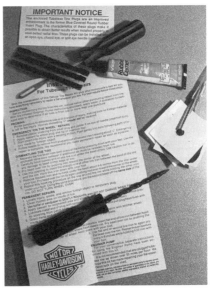

Should you have to repair a tire in the field, as I did late that night over twenty years ago, you can do so with a minimal amount of tools. On an Evolution motorcycle, the most challenging aspect of emergency road service will be getting the wheel and tire off if necessary. You need to support the motorcycle carefully, then remove the wheel assembly in the most practical manner.

On full-dressed FL-models, field tire service is not a graceful task. You may need to call HOG Road Service (if you're a member in good standing—and you surely should be!). It is far easier to perform emergency tire work or road repairs on a Sportster or FX model. Don't take a chance and accidently drop or damage your motorcycle. Call the tow truck or trailer.

For the sake of emergency road service, I will share the step-by-step fundamentals of repairing a tire in the field. These measures are intended to get you back on the highway and motoring toward a town with a Harley-Davidson dealership, a dependable independent motorcycle repair facility or a tire store equipped to service motorcycles.

I have patched tubes with small nail holes without removing the wheel and tire assembly from the cycle. In this case, the bead had broken loose as the cycle came to a stop. With the wheel raised off the ground, the tire and wheel could be rotated as spoons worked one side of the tire off the rim. I pulled the tube out just enough to access and safely patch the nail hole, then reassembled the tube and tire as if the wheel was on a work bench. Assess the situation thoroughly before attempting this kind of "creative" emergency fix. Make a proper repair, if necessary, as soon as possible.

WARNING —

Automotive string type plug repair is strictly a temporary, emergency effort. Harley-Davidson recommends that repairs be made from inside of tire with a patch and plug combination, chemical or hot vulcanizing patches or a head-type plug. Do not cause additional damage to tire's cords when inserting a string plug. Maximum hole size of 1/4-inch is Harley-Davidson's limit for a safe, repairable tire. Repairs can only be made in tread area of tire. If tread wear is at 1/16th of an inch or less, do not repair a tire under any circumstance. Some of these steps are not considered permanent fixes nor safe for long or high speed travel. Once back on the road, do not stress your emergency tire and/or tube repair. Ride with extreme caution, and repair tire properly at earliest opportunity.

FIG. 8-22. Before disassembling tire, always note tire's direction of rotation and position on rim. You will find rotation arrows at sides of tires. (Harley-Davidson has determined best direction and sizing.) Typically, balance mark on a tire is placed at valve stem. Always mark tire location on rim before attempting to disassemble tire. Reassemble tire at same location to preserve balance.

FIG. 8-23. For tube-type tires, you will likely need to remove wheel assembly and at least break down one-half of tire to access tube. If hole is minor and nail is removed, you may be able to leave tire on rim and remove tube with both beads broken and just one side of tire dismounted. Use caution when dismounting a tire. Use special tire spoons and Harley-Davidson Rim Protectors (part #HD-01289) or equivalent. These tools can fit in your saddlebag.

FIG. 8-24. Tire machine is often the only safe method for breaking a tire bead. In an emergency, weight on the tire sidewall near rim edge may break the bead. Support back side of rim with a block of wood. Avoid placing weight on the rim edge, which could damage the wheel. Bead broken loose on both sides of rim will allow removal of one or both tire beads. "Drop-center" (right) design of rims means that if you press opposite section of tire bead into center of rim, you can gain useful clearance that will ease tire work.

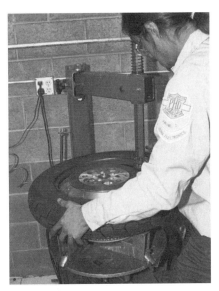

FIG. 8-25. If you need to apply brute force, something is wrong. Either tire has climbed out of drop center, or a bind exists. Tire mounting takes strength but not ripping force. Take small bites with tire spoons, and use at least three spoons to ease task.

FIG. 8-26. Main objective during mounting of tire is to avoid pinching tube with tire spoons. Work spoon carefully over rim edge. Begin at valve stem area. Stretch tire just enough to go over rim. Keep tire bead in drop center to increase radius at area you are working with spoons. Soapy water or a dish detergent like Ivory Liquid can act as a mounting lubricant for an emergency tire fix. Shops use a specially formulated rubber lube (right) for tire work.

FIG. 8-27. On tube type tires, make sure tube is well within tire cavity before attempting to air assembly. Do not pinch or fold tire tube during inflation. Air tire only to normal recommended pressure. Effort here is to fill out and seat tire bead on rim. Deflate tube to take out any folds, then inflate again to recommended pressure for your model. (See Harley-Davidson service manual or operator's handbook for correct cold inflation pressures.)

FIG. 8-28. Evolution tubeless tire rims have used a variety of valve stem types. These stem designs are not interchangeable. *Do not attempt to replace a stem with a type not recommended for your cycle.* Use only OEM design valve stems. Advise tire technicians to do same.

FIG. 8-29. When mounting new tires, check tire radial and lateral (axial) runout. Tires are not often defective, but when they are, you have a serious safety problem. Factory service manual discusses runout tolerances for tires. If not within specification, check rim runout. If rim runout tests okay, you have a defective tire. Replace it.

ALIGNMENT

We don't often think of motorcycles requiring a wheel "alignment," a term that commonly applies to four-wheeled automobiles and trucks. Alignment, however, can be a problem on your motorcycle. Some cures for misalignment are as simple as setting axle adjustors properly. Other problems can be as serious as a bent or "tweaked" frame or fork set.

FIG. 8-30. Simple alignment gauge made from welding rod serves well. This gauge can quickly check rear wheel/axle misalignment. Your goal is to equalize measurement between swing arm pivot shaft's centerline and rear axle shaft centerline. A pattern for shaping this rod is in your service manual.

Take secondary belt or chain tension into account when adjusting rear wheel alignment. When adjusted properly, axle centerline to swing arm pivot centerline will measure same length at each side. Belt or chain tension must also be correct. Achieving this may take awhile.

FIG. 8-31. Some models have offset tread mid-lines between front and rear tires (top). When traveling in a straight line, front tire's centerline tracks on a slight lateral offset from track of rear tire. See offset specifications, if applicable, in your factory service manual. Verify measurement on your motorcycle. Using two long straight edges on floor, follow factory procedure for verifying horizontal wheel offset. (Straight edges must press tightly against each side of rear tire.) Front wheel (top) must be turned straight (equal space at front and rear of rim on each side). Offset is difference between left and right side spacing. Compare with service manual chart. If not correct, check rear wheel alignment (bottom).

FIG. 8-32. You can measure vertical alignment by placing a "clinometer" against one brake rotor face. Stand cycle to its vertical centerline. Hold or strap cycle steadily in this position *with fork pointed straight ahead*. (Do not compress fork legs.) Measure vertical angle of each wheel's disc brake rotor. Reading between front and rear rotors should be within 1/2-degree variance. More than this suggests bent front fork legs, a bent or tweaked frame or a sprung swing arm.

FIG. 8-33. An accurate alternative to a clinometer is a simple plumb bob on a string. Level cycle vertically at rear brake rotor, using plumb bob. (Measure carefully from string to uppermost and lowest points on rotor's face, as shown here.) Secure cycle steadily in this position, without compressing front fork. Repeat measurement at front brake rotor, making sure front tire/rim remains parallel to a pair of wheel alignment straight edges on floor. Measurement at uppermost and lowest points on front brake rotor's face should also be equal.

BRAKE SERVICE

Your motorcycle has the benefit of disc brakes front and rear. Hydraulic brakes of this kind provide maximum stopping power. They also lessen risk of fade or overheating. Water from rain, puddles, snow or slush has far less effect on disc brakes than on earlier drum type brakes.

Another advantage of disc brakes is their ability to self-adjust. The distance between lining and rotor remains constant throughout the normal service life of brake pads. For this reason, brake fluid level and rear pedal adjustment (if applicable) are the only routine service concerns between brake pad changes.

Two master cylinders, one for front brakes, the other for the rear, provide pressure to calipers through brake pipe and hoses. By splitting the system into separate front and rear braking, there is an added safety margin. Failure of a front system part will not impact rear braking, and vice versa.

Harley-Davidson cautions that only a qualified technician should work on your cycle's brakes. I would agree that brake work requires special consideration. Before attempting a master cylinder or brake caliper rebuild, consult your service manual. You can find instructions in your factory service manual on rebuilding these components, but they are footnoted by a number of "cautions." You may decide to sublet this job to your local dealership.

There are some service adjustments, like rear brake pedal height, that you can readily perform. You can also replace the master cylinders. Several service precautions will prevent troubles with your brakes. I will highlight some of these concerns here.

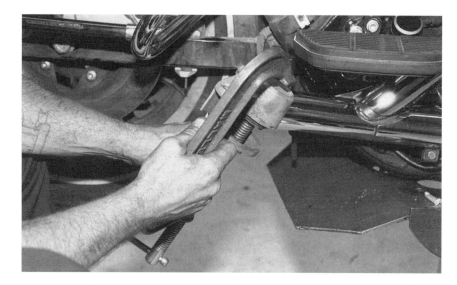

FIG. 8-34. Make certain you have proper brake work tools and know how to use them. Routine pad replacement generally calls for common tools. Shown here is tool for retracting caliper piston. Most home mechanics can perform safe and successful brake pad replacement.

FIG. 8-35. Brake fluid checks are part of your routine service. Especially after a pad replacement, you will need to verify fluid levels. Typically, rear master cylinder requires fluid to within 1/8th inch of reservoir top. (See your factory service manual for exact specifications and recommended brake fluid, typically D.O.T. 5 silicone type.)

FIG. 8-36. Front brake master cylinder reservoir usually requires fluid to base of cover gasket (some models to 1/8th inch below rim of reservoir). Check fluid with handlebars in straight ahead position.

FIG. 8-37. Position of master cylinder piston upon release of brake lever or pedal is a crucial concern. Improper pedal rod adjustment or poor master cylinder assembly technique could prevent a master cylinder piston from retracting far enough. If relief (compensating) port is blocked or not uncovered, fluid could become trapped within brake system when you apply brakes. Wheel lock-up or brake drag can result, each a highly hazardous condition.

FIG. 8-38. Harley-Davidson has used two types of hydraulic line banjo washers. Early types and later types differ, one being a zinc coated copper washer, the other using steel with a rubber O-ring. These types cannot be mixed or fluid leaks will occur. Note original type for your cycle. Replace with similar kind of OEM washers or washer/O-rings (if so equipped).

FIG. 8-39. Some Harley-Davidson Evolution cycles do not use an adjustable brake pedal for the rear master cylinder. Do not attempt to alter such a master cylinder's pedal settings. Know which type of master cylinder and pedal type your cycle uses. Consult factory service manual for details.

**Disc Brake Pad
Replacement**

Working on your braking system takes care and attention to detail. You may have the requisite skills to safely perform particular brake work or work your way through an emergency repair. Brake pad wear, fade or glazing could occur on a long trip, and you might find yourself in a very deserted place, with only a Greyhound bus to bring a new set of pads. Equipped with your factory service manual and this book, you just might be the best motorcycle brake mechanic in that crossroad town!

In this pictorial step-by-step, I share a pad replacement job on a late Evolution motorcycle. While your cycle may differ from this model, the general requirements will likely be similar. Use this information in an emergency or field service situation, supplemented by detailed information found within your Harley-Davidson factory service manual.

FIG. 8-40. Wear limit for most Harley-Davidson brake pads is 1/16-inch. I prefer changing pads well before this point, especially with a long trip ahead. Compared to fresh, thick lining, brakes with worn lining heat up faster and cannot resist fade as well.

FIG. 8-41. Removing this front brake caliper involves removal of upper mounting bolt and lower mounting pin. Caliper will slide upward at this point and free of rotor. Make sure you do not stress brake line as caliper clears the rotor.

FIG. 8-42. On some cycles, you may find it easier to disconnect brake line from fork leg. Sometimes it may be practical to loosen banjo fitting and disconnect brake line at caliper. (Cover line and caliper to prevent fluid contamination.) This requires new banjo washers upon reassembly. You must also use fresh and clean D.O.T. 5 silicone brake fluid and air bleed the brake line. Consult factory service manual for procedures.

FIG. 8-43. Pads are now accessible. On this application, there is a screw that holds pad retainer. Loosen screw and retainer, then remove inboard brake pad.

FIG. 8-44. This caliper type uses a pad holder. Remove pad holder and spring clip. Inboard pad will now come loose from pad holder. On a simple pad replacement, disassembly can stop here.

FIG. 8-45. Most mechanics scour brake rotor, just enough to remove glaze and give lining chance to seat-in. This will help prevent brake squeal. A special grease (typically Dow-Corning 44 Grease or equivalent) is used on caliper mounting pin to allow caliper to center freely. If you disassemble caliper further, you also apply this lube to inside bore of caliper threaded bushing, outside threaded bushing, and inside lower caliper mounting pin bore.

FIG. 8-46. Install pad into pad holder. Spring clip holds pad against holder. Note position of parts in this assembly. Pad holder upper mounting screw hole is at upper right side. When assembled properly, pad lies flat within bore, and both spring clip loop and pad's friction side face away from caliper's piston. Now inboard pad can be placed in its seat. Pad retainer screw torque is snug. (Follow factory service manual recommendations for proper torque settings.)

FIG. 8-47. Make certain that pad holder aligns with caliper's fork leg mounting bolt as you install caliper. Otherwise, caliper will not center properly and pads could lock up brakes. When mounting caliper, make certain threaded bushing is in place, if so equipped. Coat lower mounting pin's machined shoulder with Dow Corning 44 Grease or equivalent. This application calls for 25–30 ft-lbs torque at lower and upper pins. Verify torque specifications for your application.

FIG. 8-48. Installing new pads causes caliper piston to retract, which will force fluid to master cylinder. You may not need to add fluid. (If bleeder valve has been opened to relieve excess fluid, make certain bleeder valve is secure after mounting caliper.) Bleed brake system to remove air. Top off with clean D.O.T. 5 brake fluid.

FIG. 8-49. On this brake application, rear brake pad replacement begins with removal of pin bolts. Push on caliper to relieve piston tension. You can now lift caliper free of rotor. Slide caliper upward and tie safely aside with mechanic's wire. Leave pads in mounting bracket.

FIG. 8-50. Remove spring retainer clip. Once clip is loose, you can remove outside brake pad (pull outward and off mounting bracket). Next, push inner pad inward and away from mounting bracket. This is extent of disassembly needed to change this style pad set. Unless you find fluid leaks, caliper can be left assembled with brake line attached.

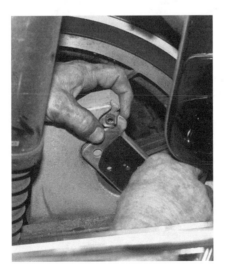

FIG. 8-51. Install pad set with friction lining facing inward (toward each side of rotor surface). At this stage, pads stand within caliper mounting bracket. Carefully install retainer spring. Verify proper location of pads, shims and retainer spring.

FIG. 8-52. Now caliper can slide over pads, shims and spring retainer clip. Caliper should slide on without much effort. (You may need to retract piston further to gain clearance.) Once holes align for caliper locating pin/bolts, you can coat bolts with Dow Corning 44 Grease or equivalent, then install bolts.

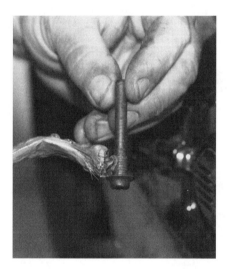

With caliper and new brake pads in place, apply brakes several times to seat parts. Check rear brake pedal height. Some models call for adjustment of pedal height, others do not. Verify brake fluid level and top off with D.O.T. 5 silicone hydraulic brake fluid. Although air is not likely to enter hydraulic brake system during this kind of service, for safety sake, *always take time to bleed brakes.* Harley-Davidson advises a 100 mile "wear-in" of new brake pads. This is simply a period where you avoid hard braking if possible. Allow brakes to wear-in before riding down long grades.

Brake Bleeding

There are times when bleeding your cycle's hydraulic brake system may be necessary. Atmospheric pressure differential, extreme heat and other climate variables may cause spongy brakes. Always inspect for leaks at master cylinders, calipers, hoses, lines and banjo junctions before bleeding air from brakes. If no leaks are present and fluid appears at normal height in reservoirs, try bleeding brakes to eliminate spongy feel. When you rebuild cylinders, replace a defective line, or have a sufficient leak, air gets into brake lines. This also requires "bleeding."

Although some shops use pressurized bleeding equipment, a one-person brake bleed is possible, using a simple method that has stood the test of time. Note the steps in Figs. 8-53 to 8-56. If you find yourself on the road with a brake problem, you can duplicate this procedure.

Silicone D.O.T. 5 hydraulic brake fluid has been the only recommended brake fluid for Evolution motorcycles. Although expensive, this product is vital to your safety. For this reason, you must always use clean and fresh D.O.T. 5 brake fluid. Minimize waste and spillage.

WARNING —
Brake fluid is toxic. If available, wear light industrial gloves when handling brake fluid.

FIG. 8-53. Carefully clean brake bleeder valve. Take a length of clean plastic hose (clear helps), and attach it to bleeder valve. Place end of hose in a clean container (preferably clear plastic).

FIG. 8-54. For front brakes, turn fork assembly straight ahead. Fill master cylinder with clean, fresh brake fluid, and install cover. Depress brake pedal or pull brake lever to develop some kind of pressure in line. Hold front brake hand lever or rear brake pedal under pressure. Open the respective bleeder valve with plastic tube attached, approximately 1/2-turn or enough to feel pressure drop. (Allow a drop of 1/2- to 3/4-stroke of lever or pedal.) Close bleeder valve, and release pedal/lever *slowly*.

FIG. 8-55. Repeat these pump-up, hold and bleed steps. Watch for air and fluid coming from plastic hose. If much fluid comes out, stop and verify fluid level in master cylinder. Top off cylinder, as necessary, with clean and fresh D.O.T. 5 silicone brake fluid. Install cover.

FIG. 8-56. When you have evacuated all air, snug bleeder valve to no more than 100 in/lbs (8 ft/lbs) torque. Top off master cylinder once more with clean, fresh D.O.T. 5 silicone brake fluid. Carefully install brake reservoir gasket, cover and screws. Apply brakes and test for a sure, immediate response before operating the motorcycle.

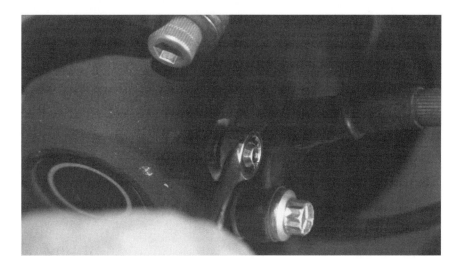

9

CHASSIS, FORK, AND SUSPENSION

The pleasures of safe motorcycling have no parallel. Unlike any other kind of motorized transportation, it affords the greatest sense of freedom and oneness with the environment, and the ultimate feel for "the road."

Motorcycle operators and passengers develop an intimate relationship with the machine. At best, a good chassis' ride quality can provide one of the best days of your life. At worst, a poor suspension system and rough ride quality could mean kidney trauma, pale-knuckle handling on corners, and a bad case of saddle soreness.

The anticipation that precedes the purchase of an Evolution cycle barely approaches the thrill of riding such a machine. When an Evo's suspension and handling work properly, cruisin' doesn't get any better!

Handling and suspension rely on a well engineered chassis, front fork assembly and rear suspension. Harley-Davidson goes far toward meeting the wide variety of owner needs. Each bike comes ready to perform and handle within a given range of rider demands, and some Evolution models have even more refined agility or ride quality than others.

No one cycle design can suit every kind of riding environment. Selecting the right model chassis is certainly the first consideration when you want a motorcycle that will handle well on your favorite roads and highways.

FIG. 9-1. Ride quality is largely dependent upon the suspension tuning of your motorcycle. Harley-Davidson has gone far toward satisfying the needs of long distance road riders. Some models, like FLH/FLT-series touring cycles, can turn a sunrise-to-sunset day of riding into a silky stream of serene memories.

You will likely experiment to determine what kind of suspension tuning works best. There is some latitude for tuning the suspension of any Evolution motorcycle, but the process becomes a lot easier when you begin with the right chassis design. (See later section in this chapter. Also see Chapter 10 for high performance handling tips.)

CHASSIS "TUNING"

Most of us choose a motorcycle for its aesthetic appeal as much as its engineering. In Chapter 2 of this book, I emphasized the various chassis available in the Evolution model lineup. At the heart of your motorcycle is its frame. All features of your motorcycle's suspension depend upon this durable member. The frame acts as the foundation for the entire chassis.

The term "chassis tuning" applies to the various factors that make a motorcycle handle better under particular riding conditions. To serve owners'

FIG. 9-2. Front fork assembly plays a large role in your cycle's handling and steering response. Two basic fork types serve Evolution cycle owners. Most common is telescoping tube and spring type (top). Patented Springer front end (bottom) carries look of pre-1949 Harley-Davidson fork design into Evolution Era. Current Springer models include FXSTSB Bad Boy, FXSTS Springer Softail and FLSTS Heritage Springer. FXSTS and FXSTSB blend "chopper" look with contemporary styling. Heritage Springer brings back the classic profile of pre-Hydra-Glide F-model hardtails. Springer models stand out at the hamburger joint.

needs and riding habits, each Evolution model offers some degree of suspension adjustment. There are also provisions for altering the handlebar angle and the seat position to achieve a comfortable riding posture with the stock cycle. All of this, the rider and the machine, make up the handling dynamics of your Evolution motorcycle.

Before attempting to adjust the suspension on your particular model, review the factory service manual section dealing with adjustments. Know the proper technique and goals of each change. Consult your dealer's service department if your cycle has a handling quirk or problem. If the cycle is still under warranty, your dealer may be able to assist. Your dealer can provide helpful suggestions on suspension, handlebar and seat adjustments.

Knowing how and when to adjust the cycle's suspension, handlebars and seat position will go far toward improving your riding experience. Let's look first at the various suspension tuning measures that Harley-Davidson has provided for your motorcycle.

FIG. 9-3. Telescoping fork sets use long internal springs (one in each leg/tube) for handling movement and countering dive. Fork oil, routed through oil flow orifices, helps dampen spring rebound. This oil and valving serve much like hydraulic shock absorbers on an automotive chassis.

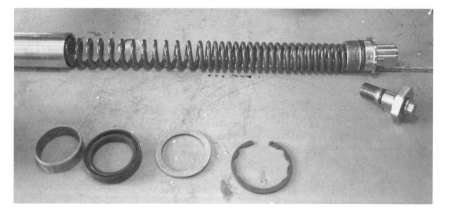

FIG. 9-4. Coil springs on both telescoping and Springer front ends come with a select wire size, diameter and length. Harley-Davidson has engineered these springs to match chassis demands, ride height requirements and handling needs of each motorcycle model. Spring rates are factory pre-set for necessary flexibility.

WARNING —
Do not overfill forks with oil under any circumstance. Overfilling does not improve the cycle's handling and will likely cause failure of seals. Always drain forks completely when servicing. Refill with exact amount specified in your factory service manual.

FIG. 9-5. Personalized tuning of hydraulic fork begins with controlling fork damping rates. This can be as easy as changing fork oil viscosity. Harley-Davidson's Type E 5-Wt. oil is best for most Evolution cycles. Screamin' Eagle 10-Wt. fork oil will increase damping and stiffen handling slightly for those who corner hard or like to push the margins when braking and cornering.

FIG. 9-6. A hydraulic (airplane/automotive type) shock absorber dampens Springer front fork. This is a simple device that cannot be adjusted. If damping suffers, suspect trouble here.

FIG. 9-7. FLT touring models use an air-adjustable suspension for both fork and rear shock absorbers. On this FLT model, the handlebar acts as an additional air reservoir for fork legs. Adding pressure at valve (left end of handlebar) increases load capacity and helps resist excessive fork dive when you brake. Soft pressure and damping will allow front fork legs to compress too far and too rapidly.

WARNING —
Never exceed top air pressure recommended in your factory service manual or owner's manual. Damage to expensive components and a safety risk will result.

FIG. 9-8. Typical maximum rear pressure setting is 35 PSI. Front anti-dive settings vary from firm (20 PSI), to normal (15 PSI), to soft (10 PSI). Considering passenger and cargo demands on these cycles, air adjustable suspension provides the simplest, quickest way to improve handling and safety. Consult factory service manual for settings and pressure limits on your cycle.

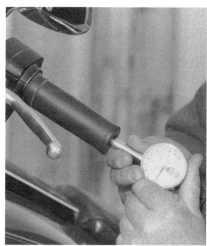

FIG. 9-9. Air adjustable suspensions still rely on fork oil. Change fork oil at regular intervals to assure safe handling and long service life of seals, damping components and fork tubes.

FIG. 9-10. Some earlier Harley-Davidson models equipped specifically for sidecars use an adjustable steering stem damper. Evolution motorcycles have a fixed steering stem bearing load. Bearing load is set carefully during assembly or service, and fork stem requires no further input between service intervals.

FIG. 9-11. Steering head bearing adjustment is crucial to safety and good handling. Harley-Davidson emphasizes proper service and adjustment of steering head bearings. If you set these bearings too tightly, your cycle will suffer from high speed "weave" and "hunting." Set too loose, violent shimmy of front fork assembly will reach "tank slapper" stage. (See later section in this chapter for service tips and adjustment.)

FIG. 9-12. NEAR: Rear shock absorbers on non-Softail models have provision for adjustment for heavier loads. Most spring/shock sets have five settings. Here is a special spanner wrench to set spring adjustments. FAR: On 1989 and newer models with Softail suspension, this tool adjusts rear springs. 1988 and earlier Softail suspension has no provision for adjustment and relies strictly on variable rate springs and 15 PSI nitrogen gas charged shock damping system.

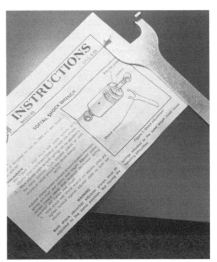

FIG. 9-13. On 1989 and later Softail rear suspension, compressing springs will produce a stiffer ride, while loosening springs offers a softer ride. First loosen lock nuts, then loosen or tighten adjuster plates the same amount at each spring. Tighten lock nuts, then experiment with each setting until you achieve correct ride quality and load capacity. Always perform your motorcycle testing away from traffic.

FIG. 9-14. When earlier Softail nitrogen gas over oil damping system fails, owners often opt for an aftermarket torsion bar suspension kit (shown). Nitrogen gas and oil system is expensive to repair and may offer less satisfaction than other options.

CAUTION —
Never loosen pressure lines on early Softail rear shock system. These units are pre-oiled and gas charged at the factory, and are not serviceable. Loosening a line will cause loss of pressurized nitrogen gas, rendering system useless.

Proper Seat and Handlebar Location

Although many owners believe they must learn to accept their motorcycle just as it comes, this is simply not true. All human bodies are not the same, and special consideration for height, arm length and leg requirements play a vital part in assuring owner satisfaction. Fitting yourself to the chassis should take place before you ever attempt to ride an unfamiliar motorcycle. Getting your body correctly postured on a new machine can make the difference between "being at one" with your Evo motorcycle and fighting a losing battle.

No Evolution cycle is weak in the performance arena. One more reason why you need to make sure your riding position is right is to aid safe riding and control of your motorcycle. Your dealer can help determine the correct seat height, or retrofit seat, for you and your favorite passenger. Change seat height before altering handlebar location. Once you establish the correct seat height, adjust the handlebar to allow a comfortable, accessible feel.

Many Evolution owners tailor their cycle's ride height with a lowering kit. Harley-Davidson "Profile Low Suspension" and other aftermarket suspension kits can lower the chassis and seat height to meet rider needs. In combination with correct handlebar set, a suspension lowering kit can be part of an overall fitment approach. Kits can change fork height, rear shock height, and position of swing arm and frame. I will share some of the adjustments that can make your motorcycle more accessible and easier to handle.

WARNING —
Any lowering kit must be installed to manufacturer's specifications. Harley-Davidson's kits often require front and rear lowering as a package. In such cases, always install a matched front and rear suspension lowering kit at the same time. Beware of reduced cornering clearance/angles and location of kickstand ("jiffystand"). Some kits include a new jiffystand to accommodate lower chassis height.

FIG. 9-15. Seat height and handlebar position affect visibility, your relationship to controls and vehicle's center-of-gravity. For some touring models, seat height adjustment is possible. On other cycles, lower profile seats are available from Harley-Davidson and reputable aftermarket sources.

FIG. 9-16. In some instances, OEM handlebars do not have correct shape and contours for your body type. A variety of handlebars are available through your Harley-Davidson dealership and aftermarket sources. Genuine Harley-Davidson Motoring Accessories is a ready source for handlebars, pegs and suspension lowering kits.

FIG. 9-17. On touring models with running boards, you can adjust boards for both operator and passenger. Tilt angle and proper height help riders achieve comfortable foot location for balance, control and easier riding.

Frame and Mount Damage

When your cycle has been through an accident, or if you have purchased a pre-owned model that handles strangely, your primary concern is frame damage. It takes a great deal of force to damage a Harley-Davidson Evolution motorcycle frame, but such accidents can happen.

If you suspect frame damage, the first place to check is frame alignment. In Chapter 8, I shared two techniques for verifying frame alignment. Frame, fork and swing arm or Softail damage will readily show up in these kinds of wheel alignment and frame checks.

Broken frame joints and engine mounting tabs, loose motor mounts or fatigued suspension attachment points are serious trouble. In addition to symptoms like excessive vibration and shudder, handling and safety can suffer drastically. Since personal injury is likely with these kinds of flaws, consider frame and mount inspection a regular part of your cycle's service.

FIG. 9-18. Note condition of frame tubes, welds, motor mounts, mount tabs and suspension attachment points. Loose hardware, broken mounts and misaligned parts can cause engine/transmission vibration, wander and other handling quirks.

FIG. 9-19. Evolution Sportster models have used a traditional rigid engine mounting system. This puts torque loads directly to frame tabs. Inspect these tabs and Heim joint braces regularly.

FIG. 9-20. FL and FX motor mount cushions also require inspection. Look for tears, deterioration and any softening or damage from oil. When excess cushion wear exists, see factory service manual for replacement procedure on your motorcycle.

FIG. 9-21. Closely check steering stem/head bearing set for looseness. A loose or misadjusted set of head bearings can cause serious handling defects, including wander, wobble, tank-slapper fork shimmy and other quirks.

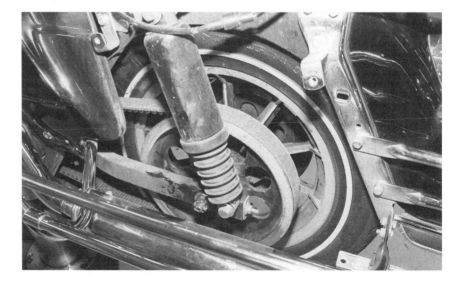

FIG. 9-22. Rear tire wobble, wander and a mushy, non-compliant ride will result from worn or defective swing arm or Softail pivots. Using a stand to raise your cycle's rear tire free of floor, you can check rear swing arm bearing or "Clevbloc" bushing movement. Follow factory service manual details for servicing bearings or re-bushing your swing arm.

Steering Head Bearings

Steering head bearings play a vital role in the handling and safety of your motorcycle. When these bearings become worn or loose, steering shimmy and loss of steering control follow. Consider steering head bearing inspection and required service of special importance. Inspect for bearing play regularly.

Steering stem/head bearing service and removal procedures vary among Harley-Davidson models. Always consult factory service manual before attempting steering head bearing service. Considering safety and handling factors, plus the expense of your motorcycle's frame, you would be wise to sublet this kind of work to your local dealer. If you decide to perform steering head/bearing work yourself, proceed with extreme caution. Follow factory service manual procedures for disassembly, repair, service and reassembly.

WARNING —
Improperly adjusted steering head/stem bearings pose a serious safety hazard and could cause loss of steering control. Adjusting steering head/stem bearings requires experience and sensitivity to bearing settings. If you are not certain how to adjust bearings, do not attempt this procedure. Have your Harley-Davidson dealership perform this service.

FIG. 9-23. Adjustment of steering head bearings is achieved by setting adjustor nut or bolt until you remove play. Steering stem must turn freely from side to side without any looseness or roughness in bearing set.

FIG. 9-24. Some Evolution cycles have bearing races that can be removed with a special Steering Head Bearing Race Removal Tool, Part #HD-39301, used with driver handle part #HD-33416. Other models may have a variation on this removal tool number. This kind of tool, if applicable to your model, allows removal of steering head bearing races without risk of damage to frame head.

FIG. 9-25. You may not feel qualified to rebuild steering stem/head bearing assembly. You can, however, check bearing play without disassembling any components. Lift the cycle's front wheel free of floor, and gently swing forks left and right. Feel for roughness in bearings, binding or any kind of looseness. With handlebar straight ahead, push forward and pull bar back evenly as you watch closely for any movement between steering triple clamps and head. Play here is an indication of bearing wear or misadjustment that requires immediate attention.

FIG. 9-26. On later Evolution cycles, the steering head section has a grease fitting to enable lubrication of steering head bearings without any disassembly. Grease with Harley-Davidson Wheel Bearing Grease #99885-89, or as specified in your service manual. Apply grease with greasegun until grease flows from each end of steering head. Flush out old grease, then stop. With a clean rag, wipe off all excess grease to avoid attracting abrasive dirt. With front wheel off floor, check bearing movement and for any signs of bearing looseness after greasing.

Routine Fork Service

Although steering head bearing service may require more time, tools and skill training than you care to invest, you can perform routine fork oil changes and inspection of the fork assembly. Fork oil changes are a part of regular maintenance on all Evolution cycles except the Springer front end. You will find details and fork oil change procedures outlined in your factory service manual. Here, I will share a general overview of how to change fork oil.

> **WARNING —**
> *Use extreme caution when removing fork tube caps. Fork springs are still under some compression, even with fork legs fully extended. Harley-Davidson recommends use of goggles to lower risk of eye injury during cap removal.*

FIG. 9-27. Place a drain pan beneath leg, remove drain plug, apply front brake, and push forward and downward in a hard manner to compress forks and force fluid from fork leg. Replace drain plug and repeat procedure at other leg. Check drain oil for any signs of moisture (emulsified oil). This would indicate leaking seals. Once you have drained fluid, raise your cycle's front wheel free of ground to allow fork legs to extend fully. By doing so, dangerously high spring pressure can be reduced.

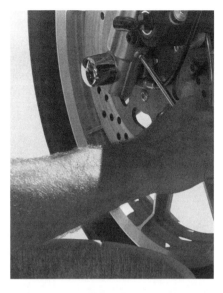

FIG. 9-28. Clean any debris from around fork tube caps, and very carefully remove caps. Springs are still under some pressure, so stay back from tube as you remove tube cap. (Wear safety goggles.) Keep debris out of tubes. Unless you have rebuilt the fork and thoroughly washed out all oil, you will follow capacity data for a "wet" fork tube refill. Fill each leg with specified amount and type of oil for your cycle. Install a new O-ring(s) (shown at right) if any wear exists. Carefully install fork tube caps. Torque each cap to specification.

FIG. 9-29. On FL models with air suspension, there are two methods for changing oil. Method shown here involves use of special tools described in your factory service manual. Use compressed air for pressure and also vacuum. This is an easier, quicker service method, common to shops.

FIG. 9-30. To change fork oil regularly on models with anti-dive suspension, invest in HD-34633 air suspension pump or equivalent, a valve core removal tool, an air operated vacuum tool (shown), Harley-Davidson's #65995-88A battery vent tube (detach vent ends) or equivalent, and a clean measuring cup. You can empty and refill forks without removing any components other than fork leg drain and fill plugs. Alternate conventional method involves removal of fairing and much more, a time consuming and excessive approach.

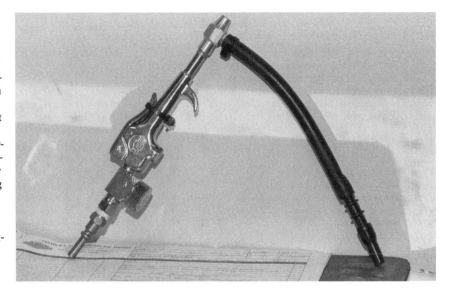

Alternative method for changing fork oil on an FL model with air suspension involves removing instrument panel, handlebar, front light bar and outer fairing. Harley-Davidson advises that instrument panel cannot be rotated upside down, or fuel gauge damping fluid may leak out and damage the gauge face. I would invest in tools described at Fig. 9-30 before removing all of these components to perform a fork oil change. Another alternative, of course, is subletting air suspension fork oil changes to your local dealership.

Suspension System Inspection and Repairs

Beyond fork oil changes, your front fork may need service at some point. Wear areas are the telescoping tubes, seals and O-rings on hydraulically damped telescoping fork systems. Rocker bushing, spring and hydraulic damper shock wear on Springer fork assemblies are also areas of concern.

These kinds of wear could be obvious, either from changes in ride quality or stability, or visible leakage of fluid at fork seals. Any of these symptoms require a thorough check of your fork assembly and suspension.

FIG. 9-31. Fork wear and damage includes seal leaks, fatigued springs, worn tubes or slider bushings, and air suspension troubles. Factory service manuals cover repairs on these components. You can check for bent frame, fork or swing arm components by verifying alignment and closely inspecting fork legs. (See Chapter 8.)

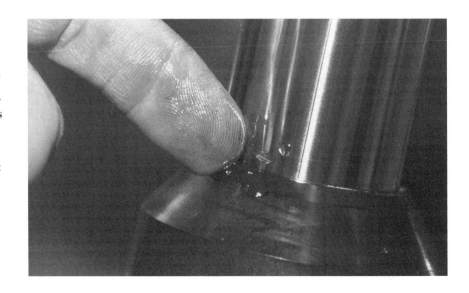

Periodically check your cycle's rear shocks and swing arm. Look shocks over carefully for leaks and signs of fatigue. With cycle on the ground and held upright, press on rear end heavily, and note rebound damping of shocks. On air systems, verify that shocks and lines hold pressure without leaking down. The rear swing arm bushings can be readily tested for play and bushing/bearing wear.

While suspension inspection and repair work are possible with the right tools, this kind of service requires care and proper technique. Your safety and the safety of passengers depend upon the condition of your cycle's fork assembly, steering head bearings, swing arm bushings or bearings and rear shock absorbers. If you have any doubt about your skill at diagnosing or repairing suspension troubles, see your Harley-Davidson dealership or a competent independent shop.

FIG. 9-32. To check for fork wear, raise front wheel and tire above ground. Make sure cycle is secure. With fork legs fully extended to relieve some spring pressure, grab lower fork legs and rock legs fore and aft. Observe any play at slider/tube bushings, and also check for play at seals. In this position, also check for steering head bearing play.

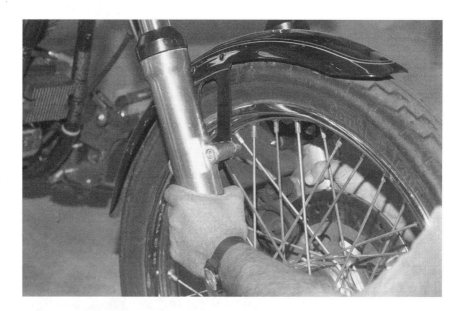

FIG. 9-33. Check rear air shock system for leaks. If you suspect a line or shock leak, pressurize system and note drop in pressure. Leaks are easy to detect with system pressurized. Apply soapy water solution (with a clean paint brush) at connections, shock rod and any other sealing areas. Bubbles indicate a leak, much like checking for a tire or tube leak.

FIG. 9-34. Lift your cycle's frame and rear tire safely above floor. Make sure swing arm is free of any pressure. Hold cycle steady with tie-downs or similar means, and carefully move swing arm laterally (sideways). Note any movement at pivot bushings or bearings.

FIG. 9-35. If you detect swing arm pivot bushing or bearing wear, consult factory service manual for your model. Review procedure for removing swing arm or Softail cradle. (Note section devoted to replacing worn pivot bushings or bearings and reassembling these components.) If you have necessary skill and tools for such repair work, follow steps outlined in the Harley-Davidson service manual for your model.

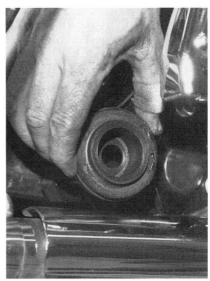

10

PERFORMANCE UPGRADES

Harley-Davidson motorcycles have always symbolized performance. Early on, the company recognized racing as both an engineering testbed and showcase for the reliability of various models. Today's AMA-sanctioned XR750 and liquid-cooled VR1000 racing machines carry forth a long tradition of Harley-Davidsons that have dominated the winner's circle.

Performance and Emission Concerns

For the Evolution era owner and rider, federal and state emission control restrictions have eroded interest in all-out engine modifications for highway use. Along with the Clean Air Act amendments of the 1990s, states have made strides to further legislate and enforce motor vehicle pollution laws. Motorcycles have survived with the least restrictive emissions regulations. That phenomena has begun to change, however. The overwhelming popularity of Harley-Davidson's Evolution motorcycles and a growing interest in road motorcycling have attracted the attention of clean air agencies.

Positioned for the new millennia, Harley-Davidson engines feature a closed crankcase emission system, an evaporative emission system for capturing gasoline fumes, an emission sensitive CV carburetor or precisely tuned

FIG. 10-1. The Sportster, Buell and some FX models have earned the classification "superbike." It is important to recognize that your V-twin Evo engine, in totally stock form, is a formidable powerplant that can propel your motorcycle with ease. Even the weighty FLH-series touring cycles, fully dressed and two-up with luggage, can climb grades or effortlessly pass a slow moving vehicle. Factory EFI/SFI makes these chores even easier, regardless of altitude.

electronic (sequential) fuel injection, plus a tamper proof electronic ignition with staged timing advance. Each of these measures complies with steadily rising air pollution control standards.

For the current owner of an Evolution motorcycle, emissions laws also place limitations on the kinds of modifications and alterations you can make to your cycle's engine. By the strictest legal standard, which is clearly enforceable in states like California, your motorcycle cannot operate on public roads with any retrofit device that does not comply with emissions regulations.

In California, an approved retrofit device will bear an Executive Order (E.O.) exemption number. An E.O. number indicates that the retrofit part does not in any way defeat the emission controls, nor does it lower the pollution standards that the vehicle met when originally certified by the manufacturer. Defeating an emission control device is also a federal offense under the Clean Air Act, although until recently, these regulations were seldom enforced within the motorcycle community.

In the wake of such changes, the Evolution motorcycle owner interested in increasing performance faces several concerns: 1) Do you want performance at the risk of violating enforceable emissions laws? 2) If you make changes not affected by laws in place today, will you need to reverse these changes later, as many automobile enthusiasts have been forced to do? 3) Is it sensible to modify a street use Evolution engine, and if so, which modifications work? 4) If you modify the Evolution engine or chassis, how can you preserve the reliability, value and integrity of your substantial investment?

As for violating the law, many dealerships and shops are now unwilling to make certain modifications for fear of fines, court charges and doing a disservice to their customers. As for what to expect in years ahead, the issue of emission enforcement is real, especially in non-attainment areas (those regions identified for tougher emission enforcement). Annual or biennial emission inspection for motorcycles is likely.

Regarding the practicality of modifying your Evolution engine or chassis, there are some changes that can enhance performance without violating current emissions laws or reducing the reliability of your motorcycle. In this chapter, I will share information on engine modifications that fall within these parameters.

NOTE —
Making decisions about the legality of your motorcycle remains your choice, not mine. In this book, I have consistently emphasized quality engineering and safety. As we explore options that can improve the overall performance of your motorcycle, I will continue to follow that standard.

What Is "Better Performance?"

Considering the stakes, safety must be the foremost aim when making changes to your motorcycle. Before deciding how much more horsepower your motorcycle needs, let's focus on the safest ways to wield that horsepower on the open road. My first concern with any large motorcycle is the *chassis*. You can only apply horsepower if the cycle has balance and handles predictably.

CHASSIS TUNING

Unless you intend to use your cycle strictly for drag racing or boulevard light-to-light forays, sooner or later you will meet a corner at a fast and questionable speed. The time to assess your cycle's chassis and the kind of suspension tuning that you take into this challenging corner is long before you reach it.

As I emphasized in earlier chapters, there is an Evolution motorcycle best suited for each riding environment. If the open highway or a curvy mountain pass is your calling, then the handling, steering, braking and balance of your motorcycle is of paramount concern. If, by chance, you have selected a chassis that does not suit your customary riding habits and road venues, *don't spend money and energy trying to make this cycle work right.*

FIG. 10-2. Harley-Davidson devotes considerable effort to the design of Evolution niche market models. Each model has its attributes and limitations. *When it comes to basic chassis design and handling, you cannot turn a Springer FX Softail model into a Buell—or even a Fat Boy.* Don't try.

FIG. 10-3. On the track, a minor change in fork damping or spring rate can mean the difference between setting up neatly for a sweeping corner, holding a straight line while drag racing, or crashing unceremoniously into hay bales with an out of control motorcycle.

Fortunately, the overwhelming popularity of Evolution motorcycles makes them easy to sell and re-sell at a premium price. There is no loss in admitting that you simply made the wrong choice. You cannot make an informed judgement without first trying a particular cycle and developing a set of expectations for your next bike. This is all part of motorcycling.

Once you select the right model, tuning a road cycle's chassis is a matter of refinement. You can focus on adjustments, and even some modifications, that will enhance chassis performance. In racing parlance, "tuning" a chassis aims at improving the steering, braking and handling. Racers in the V-Twin Harley-Davidson Superbike class face a far greater challenge than road riders. Ultra high speed cornering taxes handling to its limit.

Tuning your street motorcycle's suspension begins with riding the cycle and carefully noting its performance under a wide range of conditions. Since every rider has a slightly different body profile and riding style, the standard for your cycle's chassis tuning must be your own.

Fork Tuning

When trying to determine the correct fork or swing arm spring rates and damping, a good test is hard braking. Always perform these tests in a straight-line environment, on clean pavement and away from any traffic. Bring the cycle to a rapid stop, just short of skidding. Make this a balanced effort between front and rear brakes, applied as they should be in a hard panic stop.

If your cycle's front end "dives" (rapid and complete compression of fork legs) under a hard pull on the front brake lever, the chassis will pitch forward and downward violently, as if unchecked. Typically, this indicates that fork damping and/or spring rates are too soft. On models equipped with air suspension, you can experiment with higher anti-dive air pressure settings in the front fork assembly.

FIG. 10-4. If possible, use a hand air pump and "no-loss" gauge when changing air suspension rates. Using an unfamiliar service station or garage compressed air system could accidently blow out your fork's air suspension seals. Always stay within Harley-Davidson's recommended PSI settings to avoid damaging this expensive system.

For models with long springs in telescoping fork legs, try increasing the fork oil viscosity to create a better damping effect. This will usually eliminate the yo-yo feel that lighter oil and weak damping create. In the worst case, if dive is persistent, talk to your dealer's parts personnel about optional or retrofit fork leg (long) springs that will increase the spring rate and resist dive.

NOTE —
If, when attempting to compress the front forks under severe braking, you discover a shuddering and shaking of the handlebar, check closely for loose fitup of steering stem/head bearings. (See earlier suspension and fork service chapter for details on stem bearings.)

The result is right for street and highway riding when *you* can stop the motorcycle in the harshest manner and still maintain control with a responsive front fork assembly. This may take considerable experimentation, and the variables could change when you add a passenger or luggage, or even when the climate and ambient temperature change.

FIG. 10-5. On a lighter motorcycle and a bumpy road, stiff rear suspension spring rates can lead to sensations like wheel hop and bounce. Sometimes, a stiffer ride quality is exactly what you do not need. Overly stiff rear suspension can cause a harsh ride and erratic wheel movement. Buell rear spring and damping rates are easily adjustable for quick changes on the road (lower left). When tuning your cycle's suspension, avoid an overly soft ride that allows mushiness or wobble on cornering. Buell offers special tuning feature: an accessible adjustor for changing front fork damping (lower right).

Rear Suspension

Rear suspension tuning reflects the kind of movement you expect beneath your seat. Beyond "ride quality," there are other expectations that your rear suspension can meet. Signs of an overly soft rear swing arm or Softail spring rate include the wobbling sensation that occurs on cornering. This feels like the motorcycle is moving laterally over moguls, a very unstable, unsettling movement.

This kind of mushiness is often mistaken for wobbling fork legs (loose sleeve bushings) or worn suspension/swing arm bushings. Once you are certain this is not the cause of your mushy wobble on curves, look to soft spring rates and/or weak hydraulic damping.

The other extreme is setting your spring rates or air suspension so stiff that the swing arm actually tramps on curves. At worst, this can include wheel hopping and loss of control, or a rear end that wants to bounce and slide outward rather than stick to the road. If you tension or air up the suspension for a passenger and luggage, remember to reset the system when you return to solo riding. Otherwise, when riding alone without extra weight over the rear wheel, you could find the back end wanting to hop outward across the pavement on a curve. This becomes even more likely and pronounced if the pavement is rough or irregular.

If you cannot find the right spring or damper settings within the parameters established for your showroom stock Evolution motorcycle, talk to your dealer about solutions. Different shock absorber assemblies or front fork leg springs from another model may provide the right setup.

For Softail models, an aftermarket improvement is KT Components "Sofspension." A complete retrofit torsion bar system, Sofspension replaces the short travel OEM shock absorbers that mount horizontally beneath the frame's engine cradle.

FIG. 10-6. "Sofspension" by KT Components eliminates OEM shock damping of Evolution Softail rear suspension. This easy to install torsion bar suspension retrofit kit also provides a simple ride height adjustment. A torsion bar, with its variable rate of resistance, offers compliant yet predictable suspension for meeting road challenges and harsh handling conditions.

A torsion bar can steadily increase resistance as the suspension compresses. This also helps control unwanted movement, serving much like a shock absorber. (The damper included in the Sofspension package is simply to counter swing arm oscillations. Beyond this, no rebound damping is necessary.) Sofspension satisfies Harley-Davidson Softail owners who want the look of a hardtail but appreciate a more predictable ride and better handling.

Fork Rake Angle and Effect on Handling

As a rule, less degrees of fork rake will afford better low speed stability and easier turning. Extended forks, like the FX or Springer FX assemblies, have a higher degree of rake angle. This, generally, means straight line stability at road speeds—at the expense of low speed stability.

The Hugger 883, lowered to accommodate shorter legged riders and those wanting a lower saddle height, has a 30.1-degree rake with 4.7-inches of trail on a 59-inch wheelbase. All other current Sportster models offer a 29.6-degree rake and 4.6-inch trail measurement on a 60.2-inch wheelbase. The latter formula most closely serves as a performance benchmark for stock Harley-Davidson road handling. Reflecting the boulevard cruiser end of the scale is the popular 32-degree and higher rake angles of FX factory custom bikes. The FXSTC Softail Custom currently tops the list at a 34-degree rake angle with 5-inches of trail.

If you are reasonably satisfied with the handling of a given cycle design in its stock form, you may be able to fine tune the fork rake angle. There are lowering kits for some of the cycles, available through Harley-Davidson. (See Accessories chapter.) Although the frame shape and steering head position remain the same, a kit might alter the rake angle and trail enough to make a difference. If this does not meet your expectations, consider another Harley-Davidson model that will better serve your riding needs. It's a lot easier to find another machine than re-invent the one you now own.

NOTE —
If you install front and rear lowering kits simultaneously, as generally recommended by Harley-Davidson, the change in handling might be minimal. Share your objectives with the local dealer, and work out an approach that will provide the kind of ride and handling you want.

FIG. 10-7. Touring and police cycles of the FLH-series lineup offer 26-degrees of front fork rake with 6.16-inches of trail and 16-inch wheels. This kind of cycle will bend well to the road but still behaves satisfactorily at low speed U-turns in a parking lot.

MORE STOPPING POWER

Some of us take full advantage of the potent power-to-weight ratios in models like the Evolution Sportster 1200. I rode predecessors of these modern superbikes during the era of drum brakes and Nevada's "basic speed law." On a bright, dry day with no traffic on Highway 395, I could leave the speed zone at the north end of Minden and enter the speed zone at the south end of Carson City, 13 miles away, just nine minutes later—while never violating the law! (One such occasion, I was casually passed by a blue and silver Nevada Highway Patrol car that cruised well above its speedometer's century mark.) All this speed, and our motorcycles had mechanically actuated drum brakes. Ignorance was bliss.

FIG. 10-8. Even in the Muscle Car Era, with unbridled horsepower and high octane on tap, a cammy Sportster (shown) or warm Knucklehead, Panhead or Shovelhead needed to *stop*. We rode on tube type tires with wire laced spoke wheels, our lives depending upon mechanically actuated drum brakes. Brakes on Evolution models, disc-type front and rear, offer far better performance than older drum designs (right).

FIG. 10-9. Carefully follow instructions when installing a dual disc brake conversion kit. For safety's sake, note which brake pads work correctly with dual rotors and/or a ventilated rotor retrofit kit. Use the correct brake pads. By converting to a double-flange hub or complete wheel assembly, you can install dual disc front rotors and calipers on 19-inch laced spoke wheels. Although cast wheels require less maintenance and fuss, dual disc front brakes are a significant upgrade.

Today's Harley-Davidson boasts safer hydraulic caliper and disc rotor brakes at each wheel, designed for the recommended gross weight of the cycle under normal use. If you feel the need to upgrade due to a performance increase or for carrying more weight, you can make brake upgrades on the XL, FXR and FXD series models with OEM accessory parts.

Through Harley-Davidson's Genuine Motor Accessories program, you can readily upgrade the front brakes of '88-up models with 19-inch cast wheels. On a 19-inch laced spoke wheel this Dual Disc Brake Kit conversion will work if you first install a double-flange hub. (You can also buy a complete laced spoke wheel with the double flange hub.)

I strongly recommend an investment of this kind. The use of two rotors, each with its own caliper, provides a level of safety unparalleled by any single disc brake system. Doubling the swept area (the surface contact area of the rotor faces) on the front braking system, this conversion lessens the braking effort at the lever and brings the cycle to a faster, more positive stop.

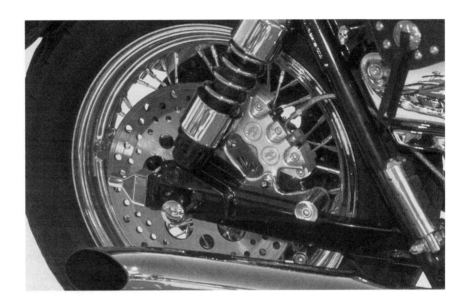

FIG. 10-10. Ventilated rotors help resist brake fade and work well at the front and rear of cycle. These rotors serve single or dual front disc braking systems. Upgrade calipers and ventilated rotors offer sure response during panic stops, on long downgrades and under heavy load conditions. See your Harley-Davidson dealer or a quality aftermarket source for details about available upgrades for your cycle's braking system.

TIRES, FINAL DRIVE, AND GEARING

Evolution motorcycles use either a chain or belt secondary drive system. Both types have proven their worth, and neither has a considerable edge for street use. While some owners change over to a belt drive for ease of maintenance, you will find that both belt type and chain drive systems are reliable.

FIG. 10-11. Gearing is the product of the primary sprocket tooth counts, transmission gear ratios and final drive primary and secondary sprocket tooth counts. Tire diameter can also effectively alter gearing. An oversized tire makes for higher (numerically lower) gearing. Undersized tires effectively lower gearing. Harley-Davidson chooses tires carefully for the various Evolution models and does not recommend deviating from these sizes.

One area where performance can improve, however, is final drive gearing. Factory gearing depends upon a given cycle's image and the perceived usage by buyers. The lowest geared current models are sport cycles and the touring cycles intended to carry a massive load. Here, acceleration is improved, although fuel economy can suffer slightly from the engine running higher rpm at highway cruise speeds.

If your cycle needs better acceleration, consider a secondary drive system sprocket change. By decreasing the number of teeth on the front sprocket, you can effectively lower the gearing. (Increasing the rear sprocket tooth count has the same effect.) See the local dealership about options. The parts department can determine your cycle's current tooth count and gearing, and you can compare this with available sprockets.

NOTE —
While changing to a larger diameter tire is much like gearing your cycle taller, neither I nor Harley-Davidson recommends altering tire size to achieve different gearing. When you compare gearing between two models, always consider any difference in tire diameter.

FIG. 10-12. Officially, there is only one set of tire types recommended for your Evolution cycle. When you replace tires, according to manufacturer's warranty and safety standards, you need to select an identical tire size, tread design and make of tire. Most owners willingly comply with this reasoning, as experimenting with exotic tires can be a risky game.

FIG. 10-13. Cast wheels and tubeless tires are generally regarded as safer at high speeds. They tend to run truer and cooler, thus resisting blowout. Cast alloy wheels were a major safety breakthrough, although many owners prefer the aesthetics of classic laced spoke wheels.

FIG. 10-14. Every tire has a speed rating. Consult with your Harley-Davidson dealer or a tire dealer if you have questions about the speed range and safety ratings of your tires. Always use recommended air pressures described in your owner's handbook.

FIG. 10-15. If you change the final drive gearing or tire size, expect speedometer error. See your dealer's parts department for help with speedometer calibration.

FIG. 10-16. Tread types suit different chassis and riding dynamics. Buell relies upon high speed tires and a grasping, wraparound tread for fast cornering. This is typical of superbikes set up for traction and a safety edge when cornering at high speeds. FLH-series touring model (shown) uses a proven highway tread that will carry a cargo, track well under a variety of road and weather conditions plus deliver high mileage.

Tire pressure affects load capacity, safety and handling. If tires are low on pressure, the load capacity drops. This is even more crucial when you have a passenger on board, full saddlebags and the air temperature hovers above 90° F in July. Use an accurate "no loss" gauge to assure correct pressure. Check tire pressure after your cycle has parked for at least a few hours in a totally shaded environment.

STREETABLE ENGINE UPGRADES

The goal of this book is to help assure your satisfaction with a roadworthy Evolution motorcycle. Owners intent on racing a Harley-Davidson in Sportster/Superbike competition or all-out drag racing should consult with their local dealer about factory parts and dealer support for competitive events.

There are many aftermarket manufacturers and specialists who build Harley-Davidson competition motorcycles and racing components. All-out racing engines, however, fall beyond the scope of this book. If you need sources for racing modifications, I have listed manufacturers, vendors and machine shops under "Racing Parts" and "Machine Shops" in the Appendix section.

If you have ambitions of racing a Harley-Davidson, the AMA and other motorcycle racing associations lend encouragement to entry level cyclists who want to build competitive racing machines and begin racing. Enthusiast magazines provide references, ads and insights into notable fabricators, custom machine shops and parts manufacturers that specialize in Harley-Davidson racing motorcycle components.

> **NOTE —**
> *If you have developed an interest in racing your motorcycle, whether in drag strip or road course competition, consult with professional builders and racers before spending energy and financial resources. Also see the Appendix for "Racing Schools."*

Although I share some details in this chapter that apply to both highway use and racing, my main aim is the kind of modifications that are street legal and deliver reliable service over time. I want your motorcycle to provide years of top performance and retain its exceptional value right to the point that you trade for your next Harley-Davidson.

> **NOTE —**
> *Even though emission legality is on the line, some owners modify and replace their cycle's OEM carburetor with an exotic mixer. This defeats the simplicity and careful factory tuning of an OEM Evolution carburetor. The two carburetor designs used as OEM equipment on Evolution era cycles each offer flexible performance and utility. They meet emission standards, provide reasonably good performance and offer good fuel economy. The later CV-type carburetor features a degree of flexibility not found in previous Harley-Davidson designs.*

Air Induction and Carburetion Improvements

In any row of parked Evolution motorcycles, you will find cycles with aftermarket induction systems. Some changes are as mild as a custom air filter assembly or K&N's proven filter replacement for the Harley-Davidson OEM air cleaner. Other cycles may boast a different carburetor or a performance intake manifold.

If you live in states with mandatory emission control inspection, it is very easy to violate regulations. Even a Genuine Harley-Davidson aftermarket air cleaner may not be designed for a California evaporative emissions system.

NOTE —
Over time, aftermarket products will likely come into emissions compliance. At the present, however, many aftermarket air cleaner assemblies for Evolution engines would fail California's stringent visual inspection.

While some states allow for a thoroughly sensible tailpipe emissions inspection only, other states, like California, demand a full visual inspection to make certain the crankcase breather, carburetor, air cleaner and evaporative emissions systems appear as certified when the vehicle sold new.

In states requiring visual emissions inspection, an air filter change that exposes the EVAP or closed crankcase breather system to atmosphere will be ruled "illegal" and result in complete failure of the test—regardless of whether the tailpipe pollutants come within the allowable levels or not.

CAUTION —
States like California have tightened emission requirements. As wider enforcement of regulations and an increase in motorcycle sales continue, expect that your Evolution motorcycle may have to comply with annual or biennial inspection.

Expect that Harley-Davidson and other aftermarket sources will soon supply E.O.-exempted air filter assemblies that have earned California/"50-State legal" status. A low restriction, emission legal air filter kit may include a new main jet along with the air cleaner, emissions fittings and instructions for a legal installation. If your motorcycle must comply with periodic visual emissions inspection, make sure aftermarket components meet 50-State legal status.

There are numerous high performance carburetors and improved intake manifolds available for Harley-Davidson motorcycles. The Edelbrock Quik-

FIG. 10-17. An aftermarket easy-flow filter may lean out the air/fuel mixture and require that you increase the main jet size. Lean mix can cause detonation, or in the worst case scenario, engine damage as severe as a holed piston. Despite the necessity to either resize (drill out) or replace the main jet in order to restore a normal air/fuel ratio, jetting changes violate current emissions law.

Silver II series carburetors have become popular among Evolution owners, notably for their American-made identity and bolt-on ready nature.

NOTE —

Harley-Davidson has offered Screamin' Eagle performance replacement carburetors. As emission requirements for manufacturers become more stringent, however, an OEM will be less likely to offer any kind of performance replacement carburetor for its emission certified engines.

Another quality, street legal performance carburetor is Mikuni's race-bred HSR42-series. Select models of this unit now bear California E.O. exemption numbers. In "50-State legal" form, an HSR42 42mm carburetor will meet emissions regulations on designated Harley-Davidson models. An E.O.-exempted Mikuni carburetor and installation kit, while replacing your Evo's original carburetor, can easily pass a visual or tailpipe emissions inspection.

Edelbrock, a noted name in automotive performance for over half a century, has now expanded its focus to include Harley-Davidson's popular Evolution motorcycles. Due to automotive aftermarket experience and the

FIG. 10-18. Main jet sizing drills were once viewed as engine tuning tools. Some clean air agencies would like to fine or punish a mechanic for simply possessing a set of these main jet sized drills!

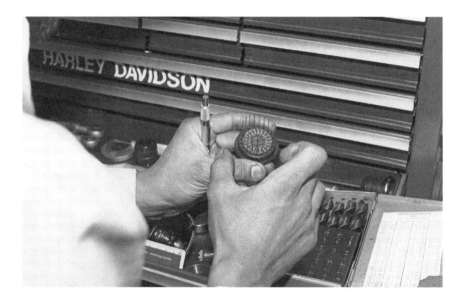

FIG. 10-19. Any mechanic tuning a cycle properly would not resize a main jet unless exhaust content or spark plug readings indicate an excessively lean mixture. In shops outside California, a low restriction air cleaner typically includes carburetor re-jetting to restore original air/fuel ratios and prevent engine damage. Vendors need to pursue California E.O. numbers and offer legal air cleaner kits that include a new main jet matched for a specific Evo application.

corporation's headquarters within California, Edelbrock is fully familiar with Air Resources Board requirements.

Many of Edelbrock's automotive parts have earned E.O.-exemptions and street legal emissions status. Several replacement items for Harley-Davidsons have also earned E.O. numbers, including the Performer aluminum cylinder heads, which are 50-State legal under California's E.O. #D-215-15.

In addition to improved cylinder heads (covered later in this chapter), Edelbrock offers aluminum intake manifolds for Evolution Big Twin (1340cc) engines. These manifold kits will work on stock as well as modified engines.

Performer manifolds are available for buildups that include longer stroker cylinders, milled OEM cylinder heads or Edelbrock's machined and unma-

---

Bolt-on Mikuni Carburetion Upgrade

Sometimes, a replacement carburetor may have entirely wrong jetting and tuning for a particular Evo engine. The engine may run lean or rich mixtures, or there may be "flat spots" and hesitation at various points in the engine's rpm range or under load. Each of these symptoms are signs of improper calibration or staging.

Mikuni's HSR42 and HSR45 series carburetors, by contrast, have Smoothbore Venturi designs for improved air flow. A flat slide helps atomize fuel, while eight roller bearings on the slide allow for easier throttle pull. A large fuel bowl and a high performance needle valve assure adequate fuel supply under extended heavy throttle operation.

These Mikuni carburetors have an adjustable accelerator pump system for crisp low-end response and instant passing punch. To start the engine cold, the HSR carburetors offer an enrichment system. Carburetors for Harley-Davidson applications have the correct jets and are available in emission legal calibration.

Depending upon the motorcycle model, HSR Mikuni carburetor kits include items like an intake manifold, K&N filter, a chrome air filter cover, fitted cables, mounting and installation hardware (even a throttle grip assembly in some cases) plus instructions. For Evo California emission legal carburetor kits, all HSR calibrations are set for an otherwise stock engine.

Mikuni's long and impressive list of motorcycle racing successes make the HSR emission legal carburetors right for owners seeking more horsepower and crisper throttle response across the entire power band, plus more power at the top rpm range than any other carburetor of this type. Whether you make other modifications or not, Mikuni carburetion is a proven choice.

Dependable and easy to field service, Mikuni's latest HSR42-series flatslide throttle valve carburetors offer a perfect blend of simplicity with a wide range of tuning possibilities. California emission legal for a variety of Evo 1340cc applications, these 42mm carburetors offer superior overall quality. Precision ball-bearing slide mechanism and tunable accelerator pump system are a few of the features that distinguish this carburetor. (Photo: Mikuni)

FIG. 10-20. An Edelbrock QuikSilver II 50-State legal carburetor (coupled to a Performer intake manifold) offers several improvements over Harley-Davidson's OEM carburetors. QuikSilver carburetor compensates well for altitude. With its flat slide design and no accelerator pump, this is an easily tuned mixer, available in emission legal form. (Photo: Edelbrock)

FIG. 10-21. K&N filtration is always a safe bet from both a performance standpoint and for meeting street legal emission requirements. I have used K&N filters in each of my motorcycles and on automotive projects for magazines. These are top quality parts that make a difference. K&N Filter Kits are available through Harley-Davidson's Motor Accessories program and other motorcycle parts suppliers.

chined custom cylinder heads. There is a smoother flowing manifold available for engines ranging from showroom stock to fully modified.

Refinements like a low restriction air filter, an Edelbrock Performer aluminum intake manifold and a properly calibrated and jetted carburetor can make your Evo engine move out. Add precise ignition tuning, and most owners would be perfectly satisfied with this kind of bolt-on performance.

Ignition System

Evolution V^2 engines benefit from an advanced fully electronic OEM ignition. The module determines spark timing advance, and the "spark timing curve" is factory programmed into the module. Unlike older motorcycles, there is no need for replaceable breaker points or a centrifugal advance mechanism.

For street performance with a reasonably mild camshaft grind and a near stock compression ratio, you will find that the Harley-Davidson ignition's spark output is sufficient. I would not invest in exotic aftermarket ignition enhancements unless an engine build includes a radical increase in compression, a camshaft with considerable valve overlap and high spark plug firing loads.

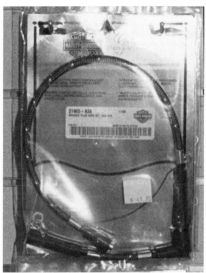

FIG. 10-22. Harley-David-son's own Screamin' Eagle high performance ignition module, performance spark plugs, braided spark plug wires or High Temp 8mm wire sets can enhance performance and your cycle's appearance. Braided wires feature integrated ground leads. This means your electronic ignition or CB and other radio equipment will not suffer from interference.

For an all-out racing buildup, with a modified induction system, boosted compression ratio and radical camshaft profile, the spark timing curve will also need attention. Harley-Davidson's own Screamin' Eagle line and other aftermarket sources can provide high performance electronic ignition modules with more suitable spark timing curves for maximum power.

MSD, Jacobs Electronics, Mallory and others offer electronic ignition enhancements for high performance and racing use.

For the Evolution owner looking for good highway performance from a stock ignition, the local Harley-Davidson dealership can offer enhancements. I would consider Harley-Davidson Gold or Screamin' Eagle performance spark plugs as a basic step. Always check plug gaps before installation.

FIG. 10-23. A subtle and often overlooked consideration is use of Harley-Davidson's electrical contact grease. Multi-pin connectors are often disconnected for service and troubleshooting. Apply H-D Electrical Contact Grease #99861-90 at bulb sockets, multi-pin connectors and other wiring junctions to provide a moisture barrier, resist corrosion and help prevent faulty ignition and electrical system performance.

Camshaft Upgrades

Whenever performance talk takes place, camshaft changes are a hot topic. The original camshaft in your Evolution motorcycle's engine is a grind that will deliver smooth performance, offer a stable idle, meet most highway performance requirements and maintain good fuel economy.

FIG. 10-24. A camshaft change can result in an immediate and noticeable increase in power. By installing a 1995-up California emission grind in your 49-State Evo engine, you can increase performance. This is unusual. Typically, more stringent emission parts will de-tune an engine. Designed as a grind for California models with catalytic converters, this camshaft offers a hotter, more desirable lobe profile.

So why change a good thing? Well, there are some camshaft changes of a milder nature that can actually increase your Evo engine's performance without sacrificing desirable qualities.

One of the most sensible camshaft changes for the street, and one that makes excellent sense to dealers outside of California, is the use of the later (1995–up) California grind camshaft in your 49-State cycle. If your Evolution model was sold outside of California, it likely has the 49-State camshaft grind and can benefit from the California model camshaft. This is a common dealership modification these days, as it complies with emission laws and satisfies customers who want friskier performance. You can verify by your serial and identification numbers whether the cycle was built for California sale.

For those looking for even more street performance, Crane, Competition Cams, Andrews Products, Leineweber Enterprises, S & S Cycle, Carl's Speed Shop, Red Shift, Rev-Tech and other reputable aftermarket vendors can supply high performance street use or all-out racing camshafts plus valvetrain pieces and other high performance engine products. (See Appendix of this book for High Performance/Racing Parts sources.) A few words of caution here: Radical camshaft profiles require valvetrain improvements and other modifications.

Do not expect exceptional performance from an otherwise stock engine by simply installing a radical camshaft(s). In fact, you may very well find that the only thing impressive about the finished product is the lopey exhaust note. Consult with manufacturers about the systematic changes that should accompany a given camshaft grind. (Cylinder head machining, increased valve and port size, new valve springs and retainers, pushrods, new lifters, modified lifter guides and other upgrades may be required.) Outfits like Crane, CompCams, S & S Cycle, Edelbrock, Mikuni/American and others have technical hot lines to answer these questions.

A safe approach is to consult with more than one vendor to confirm the correct strategy for building up your high performance Evo engine. Remember, any significant engine changes will likely violate federal, state and local

FIG. 10-25. A hot, racy camshaft grind will provide a lopey idle and distinct exhaust note. Some owners strive for this sound. Power is the game, but keep in mind that a lopey idle means greater valve overlap and longer valve opening durations. This translates as a higher carbon monoxide and hydrocarbon count from an idle through mid-range speeds, the check points for emission tailpipe tests. If your cycle is subject to a tailpipe emissions inspection, a lopey idle camshaft(s) will likely fail the test.

emission laws. Even a "warm" camshaft(s) can increase the hydrocarbon and carbon monoxide content of your cycle's exhaust system. Many high performance and racing modifications, as vendors and manufacturers must quickly assert, are "not for use on public streets and highways."

The market is rife with custom camshafts. Popularity of Harley-Davidson Evolution motorcycles has created a high demand, lucrative market for performance parts. With so many camshafts and aftermarket valvetrain assemblies available, keep in mind your cycle's performance needs. A high-revving grind that offers increased mid-range to high speed power is just what your FLH touring bike or a heavier Evo cycle *does not need* for highway use.

In such an application, camshafts like the Rev-Tech EV05, CompCam's EVL-2000 and Crane's Fireball series work best. These manufacturers and others also make more radical grinds that can enhance performance on Sportsters, the Buell, boulevard cruisers, drag strip bikes and all-out track or stroker motor applications.

Cylinder Head Upgrade

The popularity of the Evolution V-twins has encouraged a growth in aftermarket Harley-Davidson performance products. Currently, Edelbrock's emission legal street cylinder heads and intake manifold make the best possible upgrades short of an exotic, and expensive, racing buildup.

Singling out three areas for improvement over the stock head design, Edelbrock set out to make an Evolution V-twin engine perform far better—without any change other than the cylinder head assemblies.

The switch to a rectangular-shaped, raised intake port was the first step, resulting in an increase in air flow and velocity. Next, a unique dual-quench combustion chamber design causes air/fuel mixtures to tumble and mix more thoroughly as they enter the cylinder. The 72cc volume of this combustion chamber effectively raises compression from 8.5:1 to 9.5:1, while the head design is fully legal for 50-State emissions requirements.

FIG. 10-26. NEAR: Edelbrock's raised rectangular intake port increases surface area of intake floor. This translates as much easier air flow and a higher velocity for air moving toward the cylinder. FAR: D-shape to Edelbrock's exhaust port helps thwart reversion, the nemesis of exhaust flow. Intentionally mismatching shape of exhaust port and pipe opening results in less risk of reversion. Pipes more easily scavenge exhaust. Performance increases.

Lastly, the unique D-shaped exhaust port, due to intentional mismatching of port-to-pipe shape, serves an unusual and beneficial purpose. By lowering the risk of "reversion" (the tendency toward backflow of exhaust into a cylinder), the Edelbrock head's exhaust port offers far better flow. Even when used with stock exhaust pipes, a pair of these Edelbrock Performer cylinder heads provide a dramatic difference in performance.

In tests performed independently, results have been impressive. Starting with a totally stock California Big-Twin (1340cc) model, with nothing added beyond a pair of Edelbrock's Performer heads and a Performer aluminum intake manifold, peak torque and horsepower increased by 10%. While the OEM cylinder heads (stock) peaked torque on the dynamometer around 2500 rpm, the stock engine steadily lost torque above this speed. By comparison, Edelbrock's heads maintained a higher, more useful torque output well beyond 2500 rpm.

When Edelbrock added items like Crane's #316-2B camshaft, a set of aftermarket exhaust pipes and an aftermarket carburetor, the performance leaped. Using the same California model cycle as a baseline, these items and

FIG. 10-27. Edelbrock's assembled Performer alloy heads feature stainless steel valves with 1.850-inch intake and 1.610-inch exhaust diameters. Seats are ductile iron, as are valve guides, with 1.460-inch O.D. valve springs, Teflon valve stem seals, new retainers and valve locks. Edelbrock casts these heads of 356 aluminum, heat treated to level T-6. These parts are all-American in design and manufacture.

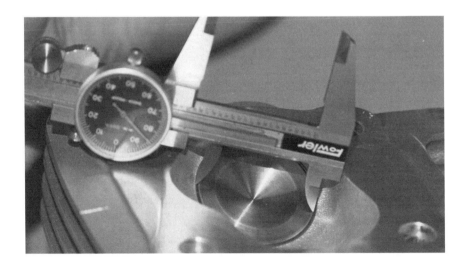

the Edelbrock Performer heads bumped dynamometer horsepower to 75 @4900 rpm. Torque jumped to 89 ft/lbs at 4000 rpm.

This test claimed a 92% increase in peak horsepower over the stock cycle's dyno readings! The modified engine also showed a tendency to hold torque longer. Peak torque hung above 80 ft/lbs from 2600 rpm all the way to 4900 rpm. For road riders, this translates as a substantially wider power band for acceleration and passing power.

The independent test did not specify which kind of aftermarket carburetor or exhaust was used in these dyno runs. Emission legal street use would require a carburetor and tuned exhaust that each have E.O. exemption numbers. (Mikuni and Edelbrock each offer such carburetors.) The potential of Edelbrock Performer cylinder heads is obvious. For street and highway use, a sensible buildup would be the Edelbrock cylinder heads and intake manifold, an emission legal performance carburetor and a proven aftermarket exhaust system. A warmer camshaft would be optional.

A Glimpse Of The Wild Side

Edelbrock's success with the Performer line of cylinder heads has its parallel in the Performer RPM racing head designs. These heads promise a fast ride for the quick and ready.

Performer RPM heads come without valve pieces and with uncut valve seats. The valves in this case are of 2.100-inch intake O.D. and 1.812-inch exhaust O.D. These heads are readied for ductile iron valve guides with shoulders. Valve spring pads feature extra material to allow for custom machining.

The Performer RPM heads have no provision for a crankcase breather and use the later ('92-up) short head bolt design. (Casting allows for 3/8-inch diameter bolts and larger.) To accommodate the huge valve diameters, Edelbrock has relocated the spark plug holes and changed their thread diameter to 12mm.

These bare all-out performance heads aim at the owner building a racing cycle. Most users have plans for a stroker kit (longer stroke crankshaft and rod configuration for more torque and cubic inch displacement) or a big-bore kit.

Stroker and big-bore formulas have been a key part of Harley-Davidson drag racing engines for years. The Edelbrock Performer RPM series cylinder heads, however, provide a noticeable improvement over buildups using radically modified stock head castings.

Racing engine buildups involve blueprinting and precise fitup of machined parts. Without substantial reinforcement of the engine's lower end, a set of radical cylinder heads, higher compression, a radical camshaft(s) and high output ignition would quickly waste even the rugged Harley-Davidson Evolution engine's crankshaft assembly. Edelbrock's Performer RPM cylinder heads are for racing use only and not legal for use in a pollution controlled motorcycle.

Exhaust Tuning

For the stock Evolution motorcycle, factory exhaust tuning works well under most circumstances. When you begin to modify your engine, however, exhaust tuning becomes a consideration.

For later Evolution cycles with catalytic converters or a model with EFI/SFI, the factory exhaust system calibration is vital. Modifying any Evolution cycle's exhaust system must also take into account the induction tuning, carburetor jetting and ignition calibration.

Although many aftermarket exhaust systems will produce dramatic increases in peak performance, there is always a price for top end performance. Exhaust tuning is a precise science that addresses low-end torque, mid-range power and top-end performance as three distinct goals. Unfortunately, it is virtually impossible to maximize performance at all three of these levels with only one exhaust system.

For this reason, most aftermarket exhaust systems for motorcycles concentrate on mid-range to top-end power. The kind of low restriction exhaust system that achieves gains in this rpm range might even help the engine breathe better in general. But torque seldom improves much at an idle, tip-in or low-speed lugging mode with this kind of exhaust system. For top-end performance, the goal for high rpm engines is a maximum exhaust flow that simultaneously produces a "scavenging" effect.

Unless you have made radical changes to the compression ratio, camshaft profile and cylinder head flow to achieve all-out performance gains, Evo 1340cc engines basically develop "stump pulling" low-end torque. The stock Sportster 883cc and 1200cc engines skew more toward mid-range and top-end performance. Peak torque for 1340cc 49-State engines is at 3500–3600 rpm, and California engines peak out around 2400 rpm. (This quick torque rise on California catalytic converter engines is the prime reason for popularity of the California camshaft.) The Sportster 883 develops peak torque at 4600 rpm, while the 1200cc model reaches its peak at 4000 rpm.

Engines that produce this kind of torque and operate at relatively low rpm do not benefit from high rpm exhaust designs. Most street riders, whether they are aware or not, typically do not run their engines much above 3000 rpm in traffic. When a rider wants an engine that leaps briskly to 6000 rpm, only the Sportsters and Buell can meet the demand.

The very nature of FL, FX and FLH models is such that a radical aftermarket exhaust system might actually defeat the power dynamics of a motorcycle that depends upon a quick torque rise. For the Sportster bent on maximum acceleration or drag racing success, an aftermarket tuned exhaust would make more sense. With such an exhaust system, plan on re-jetting the carburetor to assure engine survival.

Unless you intend to modify your Evo engine with a camshaft(s) that delivers more mid-range and higher rpm power, consider Harley-Davidson OEM exhaust systems for their aesthetic appeal and function. If you do plan a switch to a hotter camshaft(s) profile, either lower your cycle's secondary drive gearing or strip weight from the bike. You will need this kind of leverage to get rolling and prevent a performance lag at take-off and lower speeds.

Upper and Lower Engine Footnotes

If you need to rebuild your Evolution V^2 engine for the street, consult your dealer's parts department about upgrade and superceded factory parts. There is nothing lacking in the latest Evo's pistons, connecting rods, lubrication system, valvetrain pieces, crankshaft assembly, camshaft(s) and bearing sets.

You will find, however, that the Evolution engine designs have evolved since their inception. Gaskets and even hard parts have undergone changes and factory improvements. Most of these later and better pieces will retrofit to earlier Evo engines. This is one more reason to source your parts directly from a Harley-Davidson dealer.

If your engine unit is completely apart, this is an opportunity for blueprinting and precision balancing of parts. Although Harley-Davidson does a good job in original assembly and balancing, you can, with access to the right machine shop, exceed these production standards.

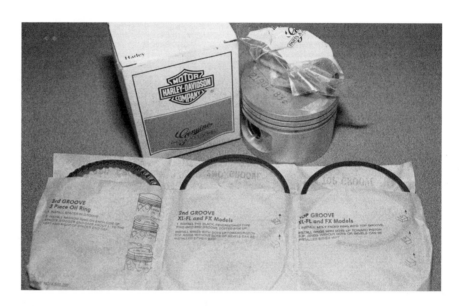

FIG. 10-28. Always use Genuine Harley-Davidson replacement parts. You will find that precise tolerances and fitup will restore your engine to like new performance. Accept no substitutes, other than those high performance upgrade components recognized for their superior design and purpose. (See this book's Appendix for suppliers of quality high performance replacement parts.)

FIG. 10-29. Harley-Davidson's multi-piece crankshaft design makes bearing and crankpin changes complex. Assembly of these parts requires a special fixture to true and align flywheels and shafts. You cannot improvise this kind of tooling. If tool cost is out of range, sublet crankshaft bearing installation and crankpin work. When servicing the crankshaft, consider custom balancing of the assembly.

FIG. 10-30. The factory service manual for your model provides engine rebuilding steps and a listing of all tools necessary for engine disassembly and reassembly. Read the entire section before attempting to perform an engine teardown. Instructions will indicate whether this job is within your tool and skill range. It's less costly to sublet work in one piece than to have a professional reassemble your "basket case" engine or transmission.

FIG. 10-31. United Engine & Machine builds Keith Black (KB-series) hypereutectic T6 alloy pistons for Evolution engines. KB design makes a top upgrade for highway performance. Closer tolerances, reduced risk of detonation and improved piston ring location are some of the manufacturer's claims. I have used KB type automotive pistons for years and find them superior for performance, oil control, quiet operation, fuel economy and longevity.

CLUTCH AND DRIVE ASSEMBLY UPGRADES

No chain is stronger than its weakest link, and this surely applies to Harley-Davidson primary and secondary drives. The late model wet-plate clutch designs offer tremendous reliability when adjusted periodically and not abused.

For the user whose engine produces more than stock horsepower, however, upgrade clutch components may be necessary.

Only use a high apply pressure clutch if your cycle requires it. Heavier spring pressure can cause heavier shock loads to gears, drive chains or belts. Do not install a racing clutch unless your buildup has enough horsepower to demand this kind of stamina and force. Avoid power shifting whenever possible. Your cycle's geartrain and drive system will suffer drastically if you hammer shifts with a high force clutch.

FIG. 10-32. Aftermarket belt drive primaries grew in popularity when Harley-Davidson offered a dry clutch and a belt primary drive at the tail end of the Shovelhead era. For the street, however, a wet clutch, proven by every kind of superbike, offers a long service life and relatively low maintenance.

FIG. 10-33. High horsepower gains warrant use of a heavy duty clutch assembly. Racers and high performance users rely on aftermarket components. (See Appendix, and contact vendors for details.) If you bump up the horsepower on your Evo engine, consider using stronger clutch pieces. Note installation of DFI Vibration Damper in this application.

Balance and a smooth running engine are appealing thoughts, especially for owners who have grown tired of engine vibration (sometimes great enough to cause finger numbness). For getting rid of the continual buzzsaw sensation, one item that works is the Doug Fisher International (DFI) Vibration Damper assembly.

The DFI damper unit fits in place of the compensator on an Evolution engine's primary system. If you can change a primary chain, you are qualified to replace your engine's compensator assembly with this DFI device.

Vibration dampers have been a proven part of automotive engine design for a very long time. The DFI unit uses two inertial rings, springs and friction discs to capture the crankshaft's vibration, using friction to eliminate unwanted energy.

Available for all Evolution V-twin engines, the proven design claims a 60% reduction in engine vibration. Anecdotal testimonials by owners assert this and more. Some even claim noticeable improvements in acceleration, plus smooth engine operation from an idle to redline.

DFI also offers a full-service facility for precisely balancing an Evolution crankshaft, connecting rods, pistons and other reciprocally moving parts. (See Appendix.) Although the DFI Vibration Damper will eliminate a good deal of vibration, DFI recommends a full balancing job during engine rebuilding.

FIG. 10-34. DFI's Vibration Damper helps alleviate a time-honored motorcycle nemesis. Harley-Davidson V-twins with compensating sprocket drive (left) create a nice exhaust note and thunderous torque but have even more shake than most motorcycles. DFI device (right) claims a 60% reduction in crankshaft/engine vibration. If you can change a primary chain, installation of this damper unit should take just a morning.

Whether you decide to wax, polish and service your cycle, leaving everything stock, or gradually personalize the appearance and increase the performance capability of your Evolution motorcycle, I trust that you will "Ride to Live" and "Live to Ride" again!

11

ACCESSORIES

Walk into any Harley-Davidson dealership, and you will find a storehouse of quality accessories for Evolution motorcycles. Owners continue a long-standing tradition of personalizing their motorcycles, supported by Harley-Davidson's willingness to offer scores of useful aftermarket components.

Evolution cycles come from the factory with an array of appealing features. Accessorization of most Evolution motorcycles consists of subtle improvements in function and lighter aesthetic enhancements. For some machines, this may require nothing more than a few add-on items.

Aftermarket accessories fall into three categories: 1) enhancements to appearance (a subjective choice in most cases!), 2) increasing the motorcycle's function and riding comfort, and 3) improvements in performance.

I cover the latter category, those changes that will enhance the cycle's power output, cornering and overall handling ability, in the previous chapter. Now we'll concentrate on safe and practical accessories that can make your cycle look better and offer more versatility.

FIG. 11-1. Ot230
FIG. 11-2. n tour, you can find dealerships in distant places with a completely different line of accessories. Here, at Harley-Davidson of Reno, Nevada's seasonal climate and higher elevation encourage full fairings, warm leathers, hefty gloves and other quality riding apparel.

0021201

Where To Shop

My first outlet for accessories is the local Harley-Davidson dealership. Why? Because items built by or for a vehicle manufacturer like Harley-Davidson must meet rigid quality and safety standards. This is not to suggest that other manufacturers do not make good products. There are aftermarket designers and fabricators who offer exceptionally high quality components. But for the new rider or those who do not know their way around the motorcycle aftermarket, I would recommend factory authorized accessories.

Larger dealerships carry every kind of practical accessory you might need or want. Take the time to browse dealership settings, not just your local store but also those dealers in other parts of the country. Often, your local dealer will stock only accessories that suit the region. A Florida or Southern California store would be unlikely to consider riders who brace for blizzards in Boston or Grand Rapids. When summer travel takes you all over North America, glean ideas from dealerships and motorcycle shops outside your climate zone.

FIG. 11-3. On tour, you can find dealerships like Harley-Davidson of Reno (shown) that carry different types of accessories and riding apparel.

0021251'

FIG. 11-4. For street riding around the neighborhood, a clean custom look makes it! Accessories can add a functional passenger seat, a sissy bar, pillion pad, a luggage rack and even a windshield—in minutes. Goal here is quick dress-down for an evening run up the main drag of Mayberry. When dawn comes, your cycle is quickly readied for comfort on the open highway.

0021175

FIG. 11-5. Sometimes a windshield offers a better view in the rain. If you and your passenger would rather view scenery than fight whiplash every time a gust of side wind hits your helmets, consider a windshield of quality Lexan plastic. FAR: Rear passenger comfort is as important as the operator's. Certain models look "cool" in stripped down form, but rear passengers need sturdy pegs to place their feet out of harm's way, and a secure backrest to keep from sailing off the back of the cycle under hard acceleration.

0021535/0021127

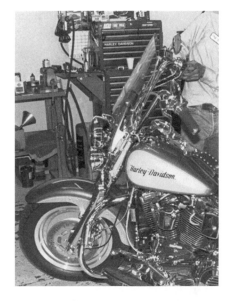

FIG. 11-6. Lower profile seats, custom buddy seats, easier riding seats and better padded seats are just some of the options. Typically, owners pick a pattern theme and motif that suits their style.

0021174

FIG. 11-7. Engine dress-up items, like chrome covers and rocker boxes, add distinctive appearance and embellish already pleasing lines and shapes of the engine.

0021159

FIG. 11-8. Some items look great while adding utility. These chrome "reduced-reach" hand control levers offer best of both worlds. Custom pegs, durable black cushion grips and an appropriate handlebar can serve as attractive and functional items, too.

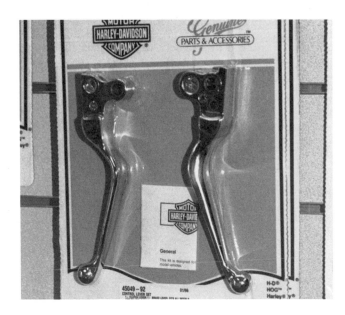

FIG. 11-9. Beginning with 1996 model Sportsters, 3.3 gallon fuel tank offers greater fuel capacity. Using correct installation kit, you can retrofit this more functional tank back to 1986 Evolution XL models. Always be certain your accessories come with proper mounting hardware to serve your cycle. Note captured essence of classic "peanut" style tank.

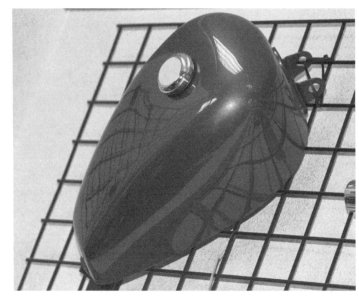

Form Over Function

Special trim items and custom accessories have enticed Harley-Davidson owners for all of this company's history. Who's to say that a versatile cycle cannot look better? Considering the quality of Harley-Davidson chrome trim items, it's no wonder that buyers continue to dress up their machines.

Purely Functional Accessories

Operating a motorcycle demands every bit of your attention. Your riding posture, the chassis height and a passenger's comfort and safety each contribute to the quality of your riding experience.

Rather than condemn a motorcycle for its vibration level, discomfort, poor ride quality or handling, consider available options. Harley-Davidson knows that riders have special needs and desires. Here, accessories come into play.

FIG. 11-10. Chrome switch housings and master cylinder covers can turn a smart looking cycle into a dazzling art-form.

0021041

FIG. 11-11. Evolution motorcycles come with a variety of factory trim and finish. Often, your cycle is great in every respect, but you might prefer a chrome piece or fender like one of the other models offers. Harley-Davidson recognizes this need, and retrofit kits for these parts allow their use on other cycles. Interchangeability proves useful here.

0021280

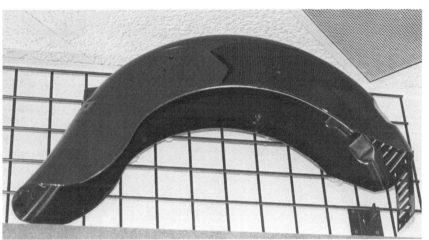

FIG. 11-12. Belt secondary drives have proven themselves. Using the correct kit for your model, chain drive Evolution cycles can be retrofitted with belt drive systems. Although somewhat costly, these kits reduce maintenance, noise and normal vibration inherent in roller chains. Form and function go together here.

0021098

Safety First

A common pitfall in accessorizing any type of motor vehicle is the risk of compromising its safety engineering. Again, this is why Harley-Davidson factory accessories make sense. Used on the right application and properly installed, these components can safely meet your needs.

Show bikes can project any kind of image. If you ride a cycle on the highway, however, always consider your cycle's safety and function. Likely, far more Harley-Davidsons than necessary have wrecked because of unsafe modifications. When in doubt, use only factory recommended accessories, intended for installation on your cycle.

WARNING —
Changing or adding footpegs and floorboards can alter your leg location and riding posture. Make certain that you can easily reach the ground with your feet to maintain balance at a stop. Harley-Davidson's accessory catalog keynotes which models can be fitted with these products.

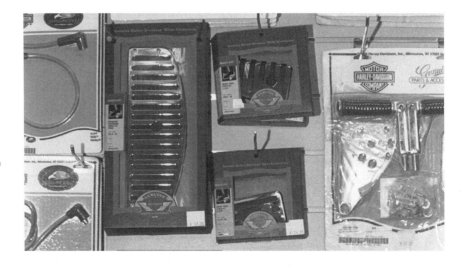

Fig. 11-13. For those who like floorboards, Harley-Davidson offers retrofit kits for Evolution motorcycles. Use caution when selecting running boards and footpegs. Your foot and leg location proves crucial to balance and safety.

0021851

Fig. 11-14. Place riding safety and posture above all other considerations. You may look cool with a set of footpegs mounted high on front frame down tubes, but this approach could prove deadly in a situation where you need to balance or stop quickly. Avoid hasty innovation.

0021852

FIG. 11-15. You could easily compromise your safety and that of a passenger by improperly installing accessories. Add-ons, like these saddlebags and lighting, require electrical wiring and other tasks. When wiring, care must be taken to preserve integrity of lighting system and factory wiring harnesses. (See later section in this chapter.)

0021448

INSTRUMENTS FOR ENGINE SURVIVAL

Just as proper mirrors provide a sense for road and traffic conditions, monitoring equipment can enhance your understanding of the engine's operating condition. Of all the accessories made, gauges that provide better engine monitoring serve a vital role.

FIG. 11-16. This oil pressure gauge kit, complete with installation instructions, fits '82 and later Shovelhead and Evolution 1340cc engines. Do not hesitate to invest in such an accessory. Learn your engine's normal operating parameters, and watch for tell-tale signs of trouble.

0021120

FIG. 11-17. Simple method of monitoring oil temperature is with oil dipstick temp gauge. Operating much like a meat thermometer, this gauge can keep your valuable engine from overcooking. Find a safe way to check this gauge regularly when operating your cycle in various climates. Know when oil is cold, normal and too hot. Adjust your riding accordingly.

0021854

FIG. 11-18. This liquid-filled oil pressure gauge kit helps monitor oil pressure of 1340cc engine. Some of us prefer precise readings of oil pressure. Like other Harley-Davidson accessories, kit includes all pieces to complete installation plus a full set of instructions.

0021855

FIG. 11-19. Oil cooler kits have created plenty of controversy. As oil flow is critical to engine survival, there is only one line of oil coolers that I would recommend: Genuine Harley-Davidson Motoring Accessories. Deluxe combination oil cooler/thermostat, shown here, will provide both oil cooling and a means for allowing engine to warm normally and quickly. Always opt for a thermostat on an oil cooler system.

0021856

FIG. 11-20. If your speedometer is hard to read, an aftermarket instrument may work better. Several classic faces are available for all year models. Select one you would like to read regularly. This could help maintain your good driving record.

0021857

FIG. 11-21. A quality ta-
chometer is far more than a
fancy and distinctive gauge.
By monitoring your engine's
rpm, you can improve fuel
economy, reduce powertrain
stress and choose precise
points to make gear changes.
This is a powerful on-board
tool for preserving your valuable investment.

0021213

FIG. 11-22. Voltmeter moni-
tors condition of charge system and battery. Practical
retrofit kits fit Evolution motorcycles. Gauge can mount
near handlebar, on fairing or
at any other easy to view location.

0021858

FIG. 11-23. Although a tool,
not an instrument, 1-Amp
Battery Charger Kit or Battery Tender allows a slight
trickle charge of your delicate
battery. This device would
make starting far easier in
cold fall and winter weather.
Consider using these kinds of
chargers for overnight parking on trips when you must
leave your cycle un-garaged.
Battery Tender serves long-
term storage of your motorcycle.

0021859

A BRIGHTER ROAD AHEAD

Some of the more functional Harley-Davidson upgrades and accessories involve lighting. Legal light requirements have changed considerably over the years, and lights are better today than ever. Harley-Davidson helps make earlier models safer by offering kits to upgrade lighting.

FIG. 11-24. Some lights are simply attractive. Added to a classy cycle, they can also increase brightness and night visibility. Add-on running lamps and turn signal lamps enhance other motorists' view of your motorcycle.

0021265

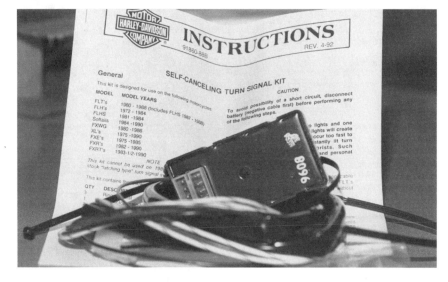

FIG. 11-25. 'Self-Cancelling Turn Signal Kit,' another Harley-Davidson accessory, is available as a retrofit. Depending upon which 1990 or earlier Evolution model you have, this device will either monitor time-and-distance or time-only, then cancel turn signal appropriately. Device also serves as a four-way flasher. Kit is available through your dealer under part #91860-88B and fits specific models.

0021860

READY FOR ROADSIDE SERVICE

Nobody wants a flat tire, and some think carrying a tire repair kit will ward off such a fate. Superstition is a leap for me, but carrying tire repair tools does make sense. Along with a quality tire pressure gauge, and even a set of tire levers for on-the-road tire changes, the following items are of great value for roadside repairs.

FIG. 11-26. Harley-Davidson offers a practical and useful Deluxe Tire Repair Kit. Kit contains necessary hard and soft tools to service a flat tire in an emergency situation. "Enginair" pump is handy for filling tire with air. Kit is compact, and you can replenish supplies. (See Chapter 8 for details on tire service.)

0021861

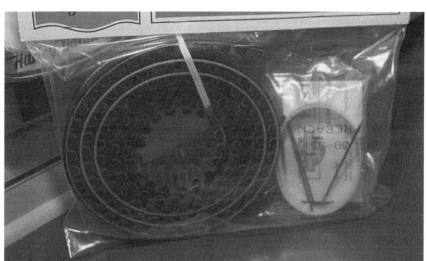

FIG. 11-27. Most Evolution cycles use belt secondary drive systems. For road emergencies, a belt repair kit can make the difference. Select a kit specifically for your cycle, and carry it with your saddlebag tools. If you ever need this kit, you'll be glad it's along.

0021866

FIG. 11-28. Chain breaker is a must tool for some chain repairs. If you or your group need to perform an emergency roller chain repair, this tool is vital. Carry extra master links and chain repair links, too.

00218865

FIG. 11-29. Although a tune-up tool for regular timing checks, this timing hole plug can prove valuable if you find yourself doing ignition repairs on the road. Part #96291-96 is for 1340cc engines, #96290-96 works for XL engines, and #96295-65TA (not shown) fits all engines.

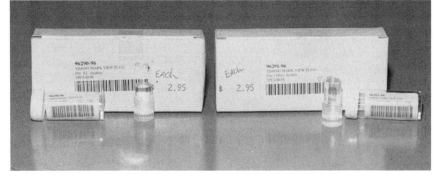

0021864

SECURITY ADD-ONS

Your Evolution motorcycle is popular, sometimes with the wrong people. At times this popularity leads to theft of small parts and even whole motorcycles. There are various security measures that can deter impromptu and even well planned crimes of this sort.

FIG. 11-30. Padlocks are a first line deterrent to theft. Bar & Shield locks, Kryptonite Fork Locks, Diskus Padlocks and Super Tough Cable Lock #8600 each offer protection for your motorcycle. This official Harley-Davidson Universal Mount Helmet Lock (right), part #45732-86, can secure your helmet. Consider such an investment as cheap insurance.

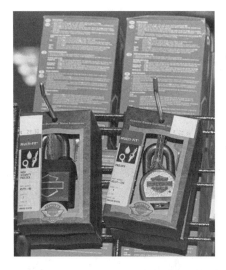

0021867/0021868

FIG. 11-31. Voltage drop and motion detector alarm systems make sense. Outside your motel window, it would certainly get attention if an alarm went off due to someone trying to move your cycle. On rare occasions, these kinds of alarms can "false" and wake up a motel full of folks for no real reason. When working properly, however, this is excellent protection against theft in this kind of setting.

0021309

INSTALLATION TIPS

Installing accessories can provide either hours of pleasure or a weekend full of frustration—followed by a trip to the dealership's service department. Fortunately, Harley-Davidson Motoring Accessories each come with full instructions and installation details. This can tip the scale in favor of easier electrical hookups and a safer retrofit job.

Experience accounts for some general details that apply to any accessory installation. I will share some of these points and trust that you will find them helpful. The goal is to preserve your cycle's finish, trim, electrical system integrity and reliability. Follow these details and those outlined in your accessory's installation instructions.

FIG. 11-32. Your fuel tank, fairing and other parts have expensive, high quality paint jobs. Many trim items involve removing existing trim and installing replacement pieces. To protect finish from damage and accidental dents or scratches by your tools, you can create cardboard or foamboard guards to protect these pieces. Hold guards in place with masking tape while you replace parts.

0021164

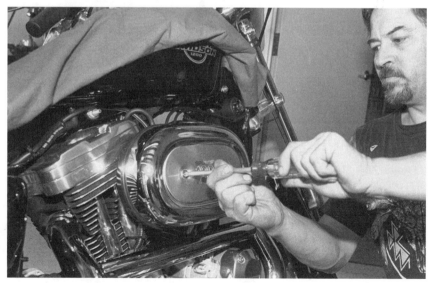

FIG. 11-33. Use of correct, high quality tools is a must. You can cause damage to yourself and your valuable Evolution motorcycle by using either the wrong tools or worn tools. When removing fasteners with Allen, Phillips, Torx or clutch-head screws, make certain that your tool tips are of correct size and in top condition. This will assure a snug fit and less likelihood of slipping out or twisting material from a fastener's head.

0021513

FIG. 11-34. In cases where fasteners are too tight for hand loosening, an impact driver will often reduce risk of damage to fastener. These drivers were originally introduced for work on motorcycles. I have used this particular tool for over twenty years. It has prevented damage to many screws and allowed re-use of hardware that would otherwise be ruined during disassembly. Air tools can sometimes do well here, *but be cautious*. An out of control air operated device can cause a lot of damage.

FIG. 11-35. When installing larger items like new custom wheels, tires and fork components, become familiar with installation instructions. Also read your factory service manual section describing this kind of service work. Make certain that any change you make is an enhancement to your machine and not a potential risk of injury.

FIG. 11-36. Use a torque wrench to secure parts. When in doubt about how tight, check your factory service manual for recommended settings. Torque wrenches come in all sizes, including this handy inch-pound type. Use these precision tools to assure proper tightening without over-torquing. You can prevent grief by using the right tools.

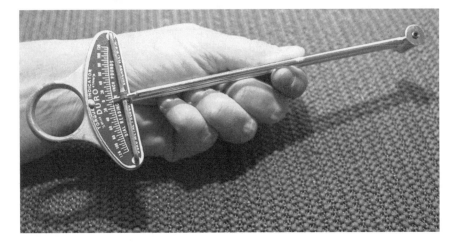

FIG. 11-37. When installing accessories, you need to tap into correct circuits and use fused wiring that will handle amperage. Whenever in doubt, read instructions and review wiring diagram in your factory service manual. Consult your dealership service department, if necessary, to assure that you have tapped into the right circuit.

0021374

FIG. 11-38. Wiring connections and splices are critical. There is more likelihood that your cycle will experience a problem here than at any other location in the electrical system. Although piggy-back and crimp type splices are an industry standard, I still rely upon silver solder, heat shrink insulation/tubing and careful taping of wires.

0021873

FIG. 11-39. Route wires using extreme caution. Make certain that no wire route passes over a sharp edge. Allow for vibration and violent shaking, common perils for motorcycle electrical wiring. Mimic factory wiring, and if practical, route your new wires through small plastic sleeve tubing. This makes for a nice appearance and prevents risk of chafing and nicks. Tape ends of sleeve to keep out moisture and debris.

0021874

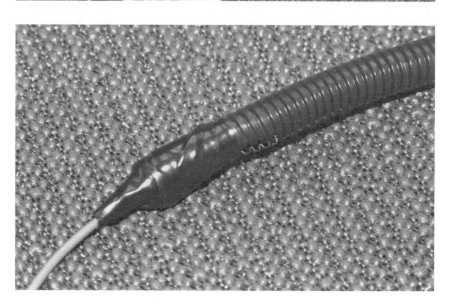

FIG. 11-40. Amperage demands determine wire gauge. Longer runs of wire demand heavier gauge (smaller number numerically). Follow instructions for the accessory, and do not overload wire or circuits. Route in shortest and safest practical manner to reduce resistance and loads on your cycle's electrical system.

0021875

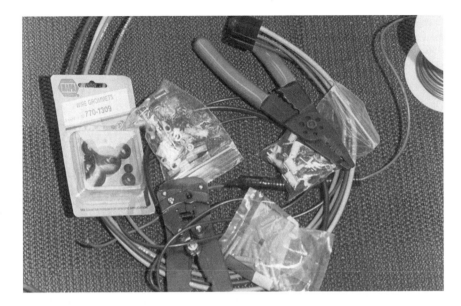

FIG. 11-41. Battery upgrades include both a Heavy-Duty High-Cranking Premium Battery and an Improved Low-Maintenance Battery. These batteries are available for all Evolution motorcycles. They complement high output alternators on cycles with added electrical accessories.

0021876

If you plan to add many electrical accessory devices, consider installing a high output alternator and heavy duty battery. Harley-Davidson offers a Super High-Output 38-Amp Charging System Kit that provides 50% more charging amperage at an idle than a stock alternator, and 30% more output at highway speeds. Pre-'89 1340cc models can benefit from a less expensive 32-amp alternator upgrade that claims a 50% gain in output.

NOTE —
For more details on electrical system work and troubleshooting, see earlier chapter covering electrical details. You will find techniques for identifying live circuits, ways to determine amperage flow and details on other electrical concerns.

EVOLUTION CYCLE AS ART OBJECT

For many owners, personalizing their motorcycle takes on an even more delicate note. Striving to enhance the already superior paint, chrome and powdercoat finish of these cycles, there is an entire industry built around custom paint and engraving work.

At Harley-Davidson Owners Group (HOG) Rallies and gatherings of motorcyclists at Daytona Speed Week, Sturgis and all places in between, you will find artists who specialize in Harley-Davidsons. If motorcycling has become an intimate part of your life and life-style, you might consider paying this kind of compliment to your machine.

FIG. 11-42. Pinstriping has been an artform as far back as the carriage trade. No custom motorcycle is without the brushwork of such an artist. Specialists can create original artwork that will make a distinctive and personal statement on your motorcycle.

0021060

FIG. 11-43. Windshield engraving is another area where art takes over. Beautiful and distinctive patterns can make your statement across mirrors, windshields and fairings. This artist sets up her booth at rallies. She can do your cycle while you wait or leave you free to enjoy other sights at the show.

0021189

Bar & Shield Dress Code

The most distinctive pattern in Harley-Davidson riders' wardrobes is the two-color scheme of black and orange. Next to colors, the most popularly recognized phenomena is the use of leather—wherever possible!

FIG. 11-44. Leather riding apparel dates to Harley-Davidson's early history. Leather will outlast most other materials and provides good protection from "gravel rash" in the event of an accident. Pick a helmet with top Snell and D.O.T. rankings.

0021877

FIG. 11-45. Never wear sandals or open shoes while riding. Sensible and handsome boots can provide both protection from gravel rash and ankle support in the event of a mishap. Nobody plans to have an accident, but if you ever need protection, this is your best insurance.

0021879

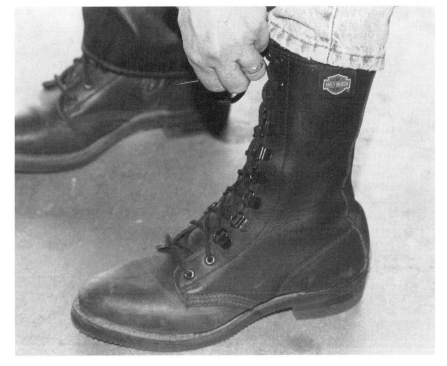

FIG. 11-46. Gloves can keep your hands warm and fingers functioning when temperatures drop. Remember, chill factors at highway speeds can turn a cool fall day into a numbing ride. Leather riding apparel and gloves will easily block wind and reduce chill factor. Dress according to climate, and don't start a ride by getting a tank top sunburn, only to find your teeth chattering when the sun drops. Temperatures vary rapidly on a cycle at speed, so dress appropriately and stay safely covered.

00212880

FIG. 11-47. To enjoy your ride and thereafter, stay well hydrated and protected from extreme heat and a scorching sun. Find a practical way to carry plenty of fresh drinking water on long distance runs. For bright sunny days and trips alongside snow fields, wear a UV-blocking faceshield or sunglasses, and use plenty of sun screen!

00218233

12

DETAILING AND STORING YOUR HARLEY-DAVIDSON

Precise parts fitup and a superior finish set your Evolution motorcycle apart from all others. Harley-Davidson's patented paint processes, tasteful trim and artful striping have garnered the attention of high ticket automobile manufacturers. Your cycle's valuable finish and trim are worth preserving. With proper care, your motorcycle can have a showroom fresh look for years.

DETAILING AND PROTECTING COSMETICS

Detailing your motorcycle begins with a thorough wash. Many owners ride in hot climates, dust, scorching sun and abrasive wind. Unlike a desert camel, however, there's no protective hair or hide to seal the elements from your Harley-Davidson's paint finish.

Magnetic abrasives cling tenaciously to paint pores, while scorching sun and road salts oxidize trim and rubber. A cleaner must be gentle enough to leave healthy paint intact, yet still cut and flush the grit from paint.

There are many commercial car wash solutions on the market. The objective with any good car soap is to dissolve road oils and gently flush dirt away.

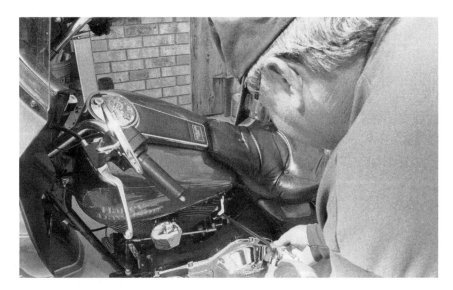

FIG. 12-1. Local car wash or a home pressure washer will remove major debris after a hard day of riding. However, be cautious about forcing water into carburetor, ignition and electrical areas. Pressure washing reduces risk of rubbing abrasive material into expensive urethane finish or scratching chrome by hand washing method.

FIG. 12-2. A rubber nosed spray nozzle, car wash solution, horse hair brush and a genuine English chamois are tools for a safe wash job. (See appendix for suppliers.)

FIG. 12-3. Washing technique is important. For a safe wash job around grit and abrasives, avoid scratching your cycle's finish. *A sponge or wash cloth is hazardous.* Special car wash mitts work much better, but hand pressure can still cause grit to press into paint or drag across the surface. I use a horse hair brush, applied gently.

(Although dishwashing liquids can work well, they are often too harsh.) Commercial products can include a complete cleaning system, chemically engineered to work with specific waxes or polishes.

Eastwood Company, a mail order supplier at Malvern, Pennsylvania, offers specialty detail supplies for auto and truck restorers and show cars. Eastwood's tools and products can protect your Harley-Davidson's special finish and extend its good looks for years. Your dealer also offers products formulated to work with the patented Evolution Era paint processes.

My approach begins with a pressure washer that attaches to a compressed air source and garden hose. This siphon washer can easily clean surface dirt away, and you can adjust pressure and volume for more control than a commercial car wash.

After spraying harmful debris away, you can hand wash the bike with a gentle horse hair brush. This reduces risk of scratches yet still massages foaming soap into microscopic pores of finish. Your motorcycle's surfaces will clean up easily, followed by a gentle rinse of clear water.

Quick Work of Waxing Chores

Most Harley-Davidson owners can find better things to do with their weekends than wash and polish a vehicle. The majority would agree that riding adventurous roads is what cycling is all about—surely more fun than performing a wax job! In recent years, however, equipment has drastically sped up detailing work. Shifting away from disc-sander type buffers, the orbital polishers now appear everywhere—and for good reason.

FIG. 12-4. Either hand waxing or use of a random orbital waxer/polisher is your best bet. Quality units are available from retail suppliers. Use very gentle pressure and take your time.

FIG. 12-5. This buffer bonnet's grey debris followed a thorough wash. An orbital buffer, used with a wide range of detailing chemicals, can gently strip/clean, apply wax or polish and buff the finish to a high luster. Uniform buffing action, as opposed to sluggish, ineffective hand waxing, will encourage use of an orbital buffer on accessible surfaces.

While a disc buffer can leave paint or clearcoat full of swirls, gentle orbital buffing offers first-time detailers a chance to do a professional polishing job without ruining an expensive paint finish.

Carnauba based semi-paste wax, mixed with a liquid polish, works best with the orbital buffer. Although the buffer easily works with other chemical products, the combination polish and wax allows a faster, more thorough job. Carnauba based waxes provide better paint breathing and protection from at-

FIG. 12-6. Finishes raked with disc buffer swirls respond impressively to orbital buffing with quality "Swirl Remover" (available from Eastwood Company and auto paint supplies). Applied directly to buffer pad, this non-scratching substance is more like a polish than a rubbing compound. I've played with ultra-fine sanding scratches left by 1200 grit wet-sanding paper and found that an orbital buffer can remove all traces in minutes—without cutting deeply into finish.

FIG. 12-7. Buffer will lay down a uniform blend of carnauba wax, providing a protective layer. Surface oxidized material transfers to buffing pads. You can easily hand wax hard to reach areas with the remaining wax/polish on the polishing bonnet. Install a clean bonnet and begin orbital buffing. In minutes, surface will glisten from every angle! Hand buffing with a terrycloth towel brings high lustre to hard to reach areas.

mospheric hazards. Apply wax and polish solution simultaneously to terry cloth buffing bonnet. Movement of orbital buffer is easy to master, much like operating a floor polisher. Application of wax/polish to painted and accessible surfaces will take about fifteen to twenty minutes.

As for risk of removing paint from orbital buffing, I once interviewed Loren E. Doppelt, Senior Product Manager for Waxmaster/Chamberlain. Loren noted, "I've buffed and polished a sample hood at car shows. The hood receives 1,000 buffings before we routinely re-paint it...Frankly, even then, there's no evidence that the paint is damaged."

Conventional hand waxing, a tedious, unfulfilling task, is now passe. An orbital buffer produces professional results the first time out. For a sharp appearance, treat your motorcycle to polishing jobs with a smaller random orbital buffer and quality carnauba wax/polish.

Quick Tips To A Better Detail Job

1) Wash your cycle thoroughly. Use bug and tar remover and other specially formulated chemicals to treat problem areas.

2) When using a buffer, make sure polish and waxes are compatible. Chemical bases differ, and some chemicals react adversely when mixed.

3) Use several terrycloth towels when hand waxing. Don't apply towels used for buffing the sides and lower areas of your cycle to upper or fuel tank surfaces. This will avoid introducing harmful road oxidants, oil film and corrosives to upper areas of your motorcycle.

4) Always wax your cycle in the shade. Many polishes and waxes have chemistry that will evaporate rapidly in direct sunlight. A hot paint surface is also more vulnerable to scratching and damage.

5) Apply polish directly to the cloth or bonnet. Pouring it onto the painted surface may cause uneven chemical action, including stains.

6) Avoid use of any product that seals paint permanently. Such materials may prevent normal expansion and contraction of paint and seldom offer protection against UV radiation. Auto painters lament the fish-eye effect that results when re-painting finishes that were treated with permanent sealers.

7) Invest in the miracles of modern science. Special detailing chemicals not only leave more time for riding your motorcycle, but they often provide superior results.

8) Allow vinyl surfaces to breathe. Most vinyl has a chemically engineered "topcoat" that needs protection. Choose your vinyl treatment carefully.

9) Use a small detail brush to reach difficult areas. A freshly polished finish draws attention to those small crevices and crannies that you miss. A few extra minutes make the difference between a show-stopper and a shoddy job.

10) Pay attention to quality. There's a reason for higher priced products, and all waxes are not the same. The longest lasting stuff may not serve your paint finish best. Look for breathable Carnauba and antioxidants. They can extend the life of your motorcycle's finish.

The Rest of the Details

When your cycle's paint finish comes back to life, a sparkling surface with deeply colored lustre, there's an incentive to complete the detailing chores. Here, too, I recommend fast, high quality chemical products for highlighting the trim.

Flat stainless steel and chrome moldings respond readily to the gentle buffing action of the orbital machine, and the balance of this hardware will polish easily by hand. Rubber and vinyl, the two most vulnerable materials after paint, require a hand-applied combination cleaner/protectant product that will counter oxidation.

The principal cause of oxidation on your cycle's painted surfaces and rubber is sunlight. Use of a protective UV-blocker agent on vinyl, leather and plastic trim extends the life of these materials. I heartily recommend 303 Protectant for this job.

A gentle cleaner, 303 claims to provide a protective barrier against oxidation without damaging vinyl's topcoat chemistry. Sensitive vinyl surfaces must flex and breathe. Any coating that either draws away the special surface chemistry or seals the topcoat from breathing will eventually cause embrittlement. Avoid silicone oils and other chemistry that leave a "wet" look on vinyl. In my experience, 303 Protectant delivers the best protection.

FIG. 12-8. The boating and outdoor equipment industries highly recommend 303 Protectant for canvas, vinyl and fiberglass. 303 can protect tires, dash pads, rubber seals and rubber cushions. Orvis says that this product can also extend your flyfishing casts—a claim worth testing!

FIG. 12-9. Permatex's Indian Head Rubber Lubricant has a long history. Claims have it harmless to vinyl, rubber and canvas, with many uses around your cycle. This substance also works as a tire mounting lubricant. Used regularly on shock bushings and other chassis/frame rubber, this lubricant can enhance service life.

FIG. 12-10. Alloy and spoke rims respond to a thorough cleaning and light coat of carnauba wax. When chrome spoke wheels become dull, hand rubbing with a metal polish such as Simichrome does the trick. If wheel surface has oxidized, polishing with a die-grinder driven light buffer pad will restore its surface.

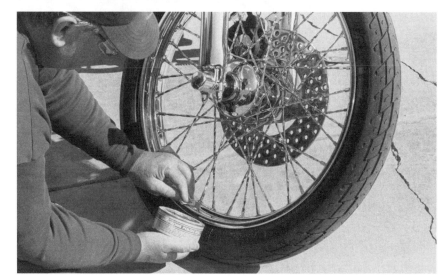

Stripping Film and Wax Buildup

Improperly applied waxes and polishes, particularly those which seal the paint surface, will permit oxidation and yellowing. The worst example is the desert or beach community cycle with a dulled color base coat and a yellowed "clearcoat" finish.

Some aftermarket paint sealant/protectant products also pose a threat to paint. Claiming long term paint protection and ease of maintenance, many of these products actually smother the original paint. Sealed and unable to breathe, the treated paint or urethane clear coat surface succumbs to cracking, weather checking and other damage caused by ultraviolet sunlight.

The most common cause of wax buildup is poor application technique. Such a paint finish likely had untreated surface oxidation, and uneven hand rubbing has built up successive layers of wax. Although most one-step waxes and polishes employ a cleaner to cut through and loosen old layered wax, this chemistry often fails to do a thorough job.

After using a random orbital buffer and professional chemical products, it's obvious why hand polishing leads to wax buildup. A motorcycle waxed regularly by hand will turn a terrycloth buffer bonnet blacker than the tires! Successive layers of wax simply seal off the paint. Paint cracking or severe fade then develops. A proper wax job should lightly coat the surface and allow paint to breathe.

"Chemistry 101" For Detailers

Effective detailing is knowing which chemicals to use on a given surface. For washing your cycle, look for solutions that prevent streaking. Professional car soaps remove very little wax and allow several cleanings between re-wax jobs. Tar and spot removers are actually high-grade cleaning solvents designed for safe work around painted finishes and upholstery.

Caution: Although tar and spot remover safely removes grease, gum, most stains, adhesives and undercoating, it may affect the topcoat of some vinyl and plastic items. Read labels carefully. These chemicals are also useful for removing wax and silicone before painting stripes or applying touchup.

Rubber dressing and protectants generally have a polymer or silicone base. Renewing tires, pedal and running board pads, and vinyl materials is as easy as applying the right chemistry to the surface. Some materials require slight hand buffing.

Rubbing and finishing compounds have several uses. Cleaning or cutting into the painted surface, these materials remove dull paint, "orange peel" and water spots. These products can be abrasive, so use extreme care. Often, a fresh repaint or even new clear coatings require color sanding, which leaves a mildly scratched, dull surface. Power (orbital) buffing with non-abrasive chemical compounds can make the finish smooth and shiny.

Products like Carecraft's Swirl Remover fit a special niche. Carecraft calls its product a buffing cleaner capable of removing fine scratches and oxidation. Swirl Remover contains no wax or silicone, yet it lubricates the buffer pad. As a follow-up to rubbing compound or a poor detail job, Swirl Remover has no harsh abrasives and can be a mild, effective alternative for restoring a slightly oxidized finish.

Additionally, there are treatments and cleaners for chrome, stainless steel and every other material found on a motorcycle. The concern here is chemical compatibility. With questionable materials, always test chemicals first. Discoloration and damage can result from improper use or poor mixing of chemicals.

Let modern tools and chemistry do the work. Save your time and energy for friends and fun rides!

Use a chemical finishing compound and an orbital buffer to reverse potential damage from wax buildup. (Avoid the use of rubbing compounds. They are abrasive and remove clearcoat or paint.) The goal is to eliminate old wax and gently lift oxidized, dead paint from below the wax. A yellowed finish simply means that oxidation has occurred. This damage is often reversible with the use of an orbital buffer and a chemical swirl remover.

Once the finishing or cleaning compound has removed wax and oxidized paint, the surface will regain its luster. The fresh finish can receive a coat of quality polish or wax.

LONG-TERM STORAGE OF YOUR CYCLE

Many motorcycles stay parked for long periods of time. Some cycles are strictly for warm weather, summer riding. Your cycle might undergo long periods of storage, and this can require special care.

When storing your Harley-Davidson for long periods, consider the temperature, air quality and humidity. Major areas of concern are the engine, transmission and electrical system, the frame, chrome and painted trim, the fuel system, tires and braking system.

Preserving your cycle's painted surfaces and upholstery involves many products used for detailing work. For painted surfaces, a hefty coat of wax, lightly orbital buffed for even distribution, will help protect the finish. For long storage, apply two coats of a carnauba-base wax, buffing lightly. (A coat of cosmoline has been the long-term storage approach for severe climate or extreme salt air environment.)

Vinyl upholstery, tire sidewalls and any other plastic or rubber areas require a liberal coating of an antioxidant protectant like 303.

Wax all chrome with a quality product. (Clean first with Simichrome if necessary.) Apply a liberal coating everywhere, even on spokes and nipples. Especially in salt-air regions, take every precaution to eliminate oxidation.

Once the trim, frame/chassis, wheels and tires have been thoroughly protected, you should blanket the cycle with a *breathable* and fitted cover. An enclosed garage, barn or storage shed will further protect your bike from elemental damage. Prevent exposure to bird droppings, tree sap and other corrosive hazards that might impair wax protection and destroy valuable paint.

Engine and Chassis Protection

Most Harley-Davidson dealerships can prep a cycle for "winter storage." You may prefer to sublet winter prep work to your dealer. I will share some procedures that are important, and you can decide whether this is within the scope of your ability.

If the engine will set for a very long period, or if high humidity and varied temperatures are a factor, protect the engine's cylinder walls, valve guides, valve seats, valves and piston rings. Remove spark plugs and squirt approximately two tablespoons of Harley-Davidson motor oil, Marvel Mystery Oil or a similar fine lubricant into each cylinder.

Reinstall spark plugs, and with spark leads disconnected, crank the engine just a few revolutions. This will coat cylinder walls and other bare metal in the upper cylinders with a film of protective oil. Leave spark wires disconnected as a safety measure during storage.

After the storage period, before attempting a start up, crank the engine over with the spark wires removed. This will pump excess oil from the cylinders. Remove and clean the spark plugs in solvent or install a fresh set of spark plugs before attempting to start the engine.

Reinstall spark wires. Start the engine, maintaining the lowest practical rpm during start-up and initial warm-up. Oil pressure should register immediately upon start-up, quickly cancelling the oil pressure light.

FIG. 12-11. Before storing your cycle, change the engine oil and install a new oil filter. Run engine through warm up and assure clean oil flow throughout the system. Clean and oil (if required) the air filter element. Make sure that it fits securely. Apply 303 Protectant to secondary drive belt.

FIG. 12-12. Harley-Davidson procedure for protecting fuel tank from rust and corrosion during storage is to drain tank completely and coat inside with a spray rust preventative. This requires mild flushing of the tank (using gasoline) before re-starting engine. (Dispose of gasoline safely, in an environmentally friendly manner.) Modern aftermarket tank cleaning and coating treatments (shown) can simplify tank protection.

FIG. 12-13. If you decide to leave your fuel tank full during storage, fuel stagnation and carburetor/injector gumming is a major concern. Harley-Davidson suggests use of a gasoline stabilizer, added to a full tank of fuel. Turn off fuel petcock, drain carburetor by loosening fuel bowl drain screw slightly, and tighten drain screw when all fuel has drained from carburetor bowl.

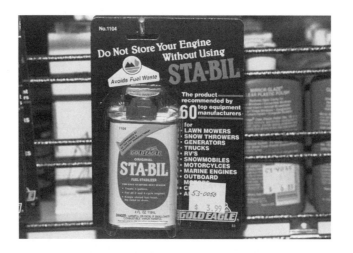

FIG. 12-14. Harley-Davidson also recommends adjusting primary chain before storage. (See earlier service chapter in this book.) Unless you have recently changed gear and primary oils, do so. Likewise, it would be wise to repack wheel bearings and install new axle/wheel bearing seals.

FIG. 12-15. Raise frame to support your cycle securely off ground. (Be absolutely certain that bike is stable and will not fall over or get knocked down during storage period!) This will protect tires from belt damage. Inflate tires to normal pressures. I wipe a coating of 303 Protectant on sidewalls and tread surfaces to help prevent oxidation.

FIG. 12-16. For long storage, Harley-Davidson recommends filling oil tank and either pinching off or removing and plugging line from oil tank bottom to oil pump fill fitting. This will prevent oil from seeping past check ball and into crankcase. If you disconnect line (which I would do to prevent hose damage), make a suitable plug for end of open hose. Carefully cap off inlet at oil pump feed line to prevent contamination.

Use of Proper Brake Fluid and Storage

Conventional (non-silicone) hydraulic brake fluid is hygroscopic and readily bonds with water. When a hydraulic cylinder vents to atmosphere, the brake system is especially vulnerable to moisture contamination. Eventually, especially if you store such a vehicle for long periods, moisture can seep into the system, lower the boiling point of the brake fluid, cause oxidation damage and pit or corrode the hydraulic brake cylinders.

For this reason, Harley-Davidson recommends D.O.T. 5 level brake fluid only. This is non-hygroscopic silicone based fluid, which resists heat and boil-out to a much higher degree and will not draw moisture. When adding brake fluid to your Evolution cycle, *always use D.O.T. 5 fluid*, available from your Harley-Davidson dealership.

Never mix D.O.T. 5 brake fluid with any non-silicone based conventional brake fluid. These substances are totally incompatible, and damage to your braking system could result. Your brakes could fail completely, and an accident could occur. Always use clean D.O.T. 5 brake fluid during routine service.

If someone introduces conventional D.O.T. 3 or other non-silicone brake fluid into your Harley-Davidson's system, you must flush the system with denatured alcohol or a specially formulated hydraulic brake system flushing compound, then disassemble each caliper and the master cylinders. Air dry the lines and cylinders. Coat cylinder bores with D.O.T. 5 brake fluid, then install new rubber seals. Fill/bleed the system with clean D.O.T. 5 grade brake fluid. (See earlier chapter for details on brake work.)

APPENDIX 1: SOURCES

MANUALS AND OTHER BOOKS

Your best source of information for the repair and maintenance of an Evolution era Harley-Davidson motorcycle is the *Genuine Service Manual* and the *Owner's Handbook* for your specific model. The only limitations are your knowledge and training in motorcycle repair, proper tools, work space and parts availability.

All Evolution era manuals are currently available through your local dealership. Each of these OEM level guides refers to a specific model range. Unlike many OEM automotive service manuals, the Harley-Davidson manuals cover every area of the motorcycle. One book for your cycle will suffice.

Parts catalogs from reputable aftermarket suppliers of performance chassis and engine components can also serve as reference guides for fitup and interchangeability of various pieces. From catalogs, you can also learn what areas of the cycle require special attention and possible modifications.

For those seeking a deeper historical overview of Harley-Davidson as a company and world renowned manufacturer, I heartily recommend a copy of David K. Wright's notable book, *The Harley-Davidson Motor Company: An Official Ninety-Year History*. This illustrated narrative, with a foreword by Willie G. Davidson, offers an intimate account of the facts, circumstances and personalities that led the Harley-Davidson Motor Company from a fledgling operation in 1903 to the most visible and marketable motorcycle mark in history. Although there are many books written to the subject of Harley-Davidson and its fabulous motorcycles, in my view, David K. Wright has done more research than any other historian.

Riders interested in learning more about the techniques and mindset of successful motorcycle road racers will find Keith Code's books of great interest. Keith Code's Superbike School and exposure to professional road racing served as the foundation for two classic books: *A Twist of the Wrist* and *The Soft Science of Road Racing Motorcycles*.

Racing a motorcycle is not for the faint of heart, yet Keith Code has taught many thousands of everyday road riders to recognize the handling techniques that can drastically improve a rider's skill and, consequently, safety....Great reading and valuable insight.

PARTS

Your Evolution motorcycle is popular, and parts availability seldom presents a problem. The local Harley-Davidson dealership can provide pieces for every Evolution cycle built, including Genuine Harley-Davidson and Screamin' Eagle performance components. In addition, you will find a variety of aftermarket parts sources throughout the United States, Canada and other countries.

For quality filters and oil products, I rely on Harley-Davidson for "Genuine" replacement service parts and lubricants. I do, however, use K&N replacement air and oil filters whenever practical. For milder street-use, powertrain or chassis build-ups, I begin with Genuine Harley-Davidson parts.

Fuel System, Induction and Air Filtration

K&N Engineering
P.O. Box 1329
Riverside, CA 92502
714-684-9762
Filtration products

Mikuni American Corporation
Carburetor Division
8910 Mikuni Ave.
Northridge, CA 91324-3496
HSR42, HSR45 and other performance carburetors

Paxton Superchargers
1260 Calle Suarte
Camarillo, CA 93012
310-450-4800
Supercharger specialists

Pingel
2076 C 11th Avenue
Adams, WI 53910
1-608-339-7999
Valves for fuel tanks that offer high volume flow

Rivera Engineering
12532 Lambert Road
Whittier, CA 90606
310-907-2600
SU carburetor kits and much more

S&S/Super E Carburetor
(See your S&S dealer or contact
S&S Cycle Co.
Rt. 2, Co. G Box 215
Viola, Wisconsin 54664
608-627-1497.)
High performance products

Electrical & Electronic Ignition Enhancements

Accel Ignition (See your Accel dealer)
Mega-Fire adjustable spark curve ignition

Compu-Fire/Engine Electronics
909-598-5485
Elite 1 Ignition Modules and other electronic ignition enhancements

CRANE/HI-4 Ignition
See your Crane dealer for ignition enhancements

J&S Engineering (Electronics)
Box 2199
Garden Grove, CA 92642-2199
714-534-6975
Advanced electronic ignition and performance spark retard system

Jacobs Electronics
500 N. Baird St.
Midland, TX 79701
1-800-626-8800
Ignition specialty items and enhancements

MSD/Autotronic Controls Corp.
1490 Henry Brennan Drive
El Paso, TX 79936
915-857-5200
Quality ignition enhancements

SGS Enterprises/Magnum Security System
1560-1 Newbury Road, Suite 233
Newbury Park, CA 91320
1-800-480-0677
Magnum Passive Motorcycle Security System

Aftermarket High Performance & Racing

Andrews Products, Inc.
5212 Shapland Ave.
Rosemont, IL 60018
312-992-4014
Camshafts, gearcases, close-ratio gearboxes, belt drives, and more

Balance Masters/Suntech Innovations
1-800-786-8324
"Active Engine Balancing" products

Barnett Tool & Engineering
P.O. Box 2826
Santa Fe Springs, CA 90670
310-941-1284
Clutch assemblies for heavy duty use

Bartels Performance Products
3237 Carter Avenue
Marina Del Rey, CA 90292
310-578-9888
Head work, intake manifolds, tuned exhausts and full line of racing and street performance pieces; highly recognized among performance buffs

Competition Cams/CompCams
3406 Democrat Road
Memphis, TN 38118
1-800-967-1066
Camshafts for any level; V-Thunder line of lifters, cast iron lifter blocks, high performance pushrods

Crane Cams/Fireball Cams
530 Fentress Blvd.
Daytona Beach, FL 32114
904-258-6174
Camshafts and performance valvetrain components

Doug Fisher International
10640 S. Garfield Ave.
South Gate, CA 90280
310-861-6882
D.F.I. Vibration Damper, complete engine balancing facilities

Edelbrock
(See your local Edelbrock dealer or call 1-310-782-2900)
Performance cylinder heads, intake manifolds, Edelbrock/JE Pistons and QuikSilver carburetors

Hemi Design Performance Products
708-652-5450
Segmented racing and street hemi-heads with matching pistons

Lockhart Oil Coolers
151 Calle Iglesia
San Clemente, CA 92673
714-498-9090
Thermostatically controlled engine oil cooler kits

M-6 Chain Tensioner
8439 White Oak, Ste. 109
Rancho Cucamonga, CA 91730
1-800-M6-IN-USA
Retrofit automatic primary chain tensioner assemblies

Merch Performance, Inc.
RR2 Red Deer
Alberta, CANADA T4N-5E2
403-346-1221
Big-bore kits, stroker kits, custom machining, stud kits and cylinder heads

Mid-U.S.A. Motorcycle Parts
4937 Fyler Ave.
St. Louis, MO 63139
1-800-632-0024
"Fast Time" adjustable pushrods by V-Thunder

Nempco/The Biker's Choice
P.O. Box 311
Guilderland Center, NY 12085
Outlet for TVA5 torsional vibration absorber and a full line of aftermarket products

RB Racing
1625 W. 134th Street
Gardena, CA 90249
310-515-5720/FAX: 310-515-5782
Tuned exhaust systems for use with or without oxy-sensors; retrofit programmable electronic fuel injection; exhaust turbocharging for street, pro-street and pro-gas competition

Rivera Engineering
12532 Lambert Road
Whittier, CA 90606
310-907-2600

Aftermarket engineering and manufacturing firm noted for geartrain, clutch, chassis and engine developments

Ross Forged Pistons
12901 Yukon
Hawthorne, CA 90250
1-310-644-9779
Stock and custom forged pistons

S&S Cycle Co.
Rt. 2, Co. G Box 215
Viola, Wisconsin 54664
608-627-1497
Complete and race-ready high performance engine assemblies, custom cylinders, heads, camshafts, gearcase assemblies and aftermarket high performance components

S.T.D. Development Company
P.O. Box 3583
Chatsworth, CA 91313
818-998-8226
Transmission cases, engine cases, cylinder heads and upgrade castings for racing and high performance

SuperTrapp Exhaust
(See your dealer or call 1-216-265-8400.)
Stainless steel 2-into-1 exhaust headers

United Engine and Machine Co.
4909 Goni Road
Carson City, NV 89706
702-884-1299
Hypereutectic T6 Alloy KB Performance Pistons and kits

Wiseco Pistons
7201 Industrial Park Blvd.
Mentor, OH 44060-5396
1-800-321-1364
Manufacturer of high performance pistons

Suspension/Chassis

Arlen Ness
16520 East 14th Street
San Leandro, CA 94578
510-276-3395
Performance frame kits and custom billet wheels

Forking by Frank
945 Pitner
Evanston, IL 60202
708-869-6792
Custom fork assemblies

KT Components/Sofspension
(See your KT Components dealer)
Sofspension torsion bar system for Softail models

Paughco, Inc.
P.O. Box 3390

Carson City, NV 89702
702-246-5738
Full line of frame, restoration and custom accessory parts

Storz Performance, Inc./Ceriani Forks
239 S. Olive Street
Ventura, CA 93001
805-641-9540
Ceriani forks

White Brothers
24845 Corbit Place
Yorba Linda, CA 92687
714-692-3404
Inverted forks, lowering kits, exhaust systems, shocks
and chassis upgrades

Brakes, Wheels and Tires

Avon Tires, Ltd.
P.O. Box 336
Edmonds, WA 98020
1-800-624-7470

Dunlop Tire
(See your Harley-Davidson dealer or Dunlop dealer.)

Goodyear Tire & Rubber Company
(See your local dealer)

Performance Machine, Inc.
P.O. Box 1739
Paramount, CA 90723
310-634-6532
Four-piston disc brake calipers, upgrades and wheels

RC Components
140 Hunters Court
Bowling Green, KY 42103
502-842-6000
Aluminum 4-piston chrome or polished brake calipers

Rev-Tech Custom Chrome
16100 Jacqueline Ct.
Morgan Hill, CA 95037
1-800-729-3332
Custom brake systems and a full line of aftermarket
products

Steel Eagle Products
6051 N. 56th Ave.
Glendale, AZ 85301
602-435-2926
Custom wheels in chrome and alloy

Wildwood Chrome Calipers
(See your Wildwood dealer)
Chrome single and dual calipers

Specialty Tools

*Many Harley-Davidson repair and overhaul procedures
involve the use of specialty tools available only through
your local dealership. You may find some of these tools
through the suppliers below, as Harley-Davidson recommends Snap-On tools for many of the repairs.*

Easco/K.D. Tools
Niche specialty tools for awkward jobs
See your local tool supplier

Snap-On Tools
Contact your local Snap-On dealer

Riding and Technical Schools

AMI, Inc.
3042 W. International Speedway Blvd.
Daytona Beach, FL 32124
1-800-874-0645
Harley-Davidson mechanic's school for 1936 to Evo era
cycles

I.C.S./School of Motorcycle Repair
925 Oak Street
Scranton, PA 18515
1-800-595-5505, Ext. 9786
At home correspondence course in motorcycle mechanics

Motorcycle Mechanics Institute
2844 W. Deer Valley Road
Phoenix, AZ 85027
602-869-9644
Harley-Davidson Training Center for motorcycle technicians

Motorcycle Safety Foundation Rider Education Courses
1-800-447-4700 for the nearest course

Penguin Racing School
P.O. Box 852
Searsport, ME 04974
207-548-2100
"Nation's oldest motorcycle road-racing school..."

State Administered Rider-Education Programs
(44 states currently offer administered rider training
programs. Check with your local D.M.V. office for details.)

Evolution Era Artwork

Eric Herrmann Studios
3945 E. Waltann Lane
Phoenix, AZ 85032
602-482-1421 (Fax: 602-867-8841)
Fine art paintings, prints of originals and etched glass art
sculptures of Harley-Davidson motorcycles

APPENDIX 2: SPARE PARTS
FOR THE OPEN ROAD

Your properly maintained Harley-Davidson motorcycle may never break down on the road. Yet for long trips, bringing along a sensible set of tools and spare parts can safeguard your adventure and provide a greater degree of self-reliance.

Store your tools and spare parts securely. Try to balance your tools and luggage to assure that the cycle will handle safely. Tools and spare parts can be heavy, so mount them low in your cycle's chassis (bottom of the saddlebags) to maintain a safe center-of-gravity.

NOTE —
Always carry a quality first aid kit. Stow a ground cloth for making repairs and to serve as an emergency shelter from the weather.

Tools for Roadside Fixes

1. A set of combination open/box end wrenches and a set of pliers

2. A compact volt-ohmmeter

3. An induction ammeter and starter current meter

4. Flare nut wrench set or plumber's small chain wrench

5. Wire repair/connector kit and crimping pliers

6. Tools to break down and repair a tubeless or tube type motorcycle tire

7. CO_2 tire inflation kit, tire patches and tire removal tools

Spare Parts for the Long Ride

1. Fuses and/or relays and tail/stop light bulbs

2. Some 12-, 14-, and 16-gauge automotive wire

3. Two rolls of electrical tape

4. Solderless crimp connectors and terminals

5. Small roll of duct tape

6. Spare fuel hose and quality hose clamps

7. Small tube of silicone gasket sealant

8. Small tube of metal mender (Permatex's LocWeld or equivalent)

9. Tube of liquid thread locker

10. Teflon tape

11. Clean and sealed silicone D.O.T. 5 brake fluid

12. A tire valve stem (tubeless) and valve cores

13. H-D's kit for repairing both tube and tubeless tires

14. An oil filter and at least a quart of oil

15. Clean shop rags or towels

16. Air cleaner element (or use a K&N washable filter)

17. If practical, mount a C.B. radio on your cycle or carry a cellular telephone

APPENDIX 3: NEW OR REBUILT ENGINE BREAK-IN

There is little information available on the proper break-in of a new or freshly rebuilt engine. Your motorcycle engine's performance and longevity depend upon correct break-in methods. The following procedures parallel those recommended by Sealed Power Corporation, a major supplier of hard parts to the engine remanufacturing industry. I have relied upon these findings for many years.

> **CAUTION —**
> *These run-in schedules are good basic procedures to follow for engine break-in. They are recommended as a practical guide for engine rebuilders who are not advised of specific factory run-in schedules. If available, follow Harley-Davidson's guidelines for engine break-in.*

Engine Run-in Procedure (engine in frame/chassis)

Before starting the engine, make preliminary adjustments to the carburetor. If applicable, adjust tappets (aftermarket adjustable performance types), and set or verify ignition timing. Always install a new oil and air filter. Prime the engine lubrication system before attempting to start the engine. Clean crankcase ventilation components and the breather system. Carefully check crankcase and gearbox oil levels.

When an engine is started for the first time, the most common cause of bearing scuff and seizure is a dry start. This can happen in the short length of time before the oil, under pressure, is delivered to bearings and other vital parts. Pre-priming the oil system can be accomplished with a pressure tank or pre-lubricator attached to the system or by mechanically driving or priming the oil pump to supply the necessary oil throughout all oil passages.

Initial Starting Steps (before run-in schedule)

1) Start engine and establish throttle setting at a fast idle (1000 to 1500 RPM), and watch oil pressure gauge. If oil pressure is not observed immediately, shut engine down and check back on assembly of oil pump and lubricating system. When engine running is resumed, continue at the fast idle until the engine reaches normal operating temperature.

2) Stop engine and recheck oil levels.

3) Make necessary adjustments to carburet or, ignition timing, tappets (only if you have installed adjustable pushrods, and if they are readily accessible).

4) Re-torque cylinder heads following Harley-Davidson's recommendations. (Use aftermarket manufacturer's guidelines for Edelbrock, S & S Cycle and other aftermarket heads.)

5) Check for oil leaks, making corrections where necessary.

Engine Run-in Schedule

Set freshly rebuilt engine for a brisk idle. Put the motorcycle under a moderate load and accelerate to 50 miles per hour with alternate deceleration. Continue this intermittent cycling under this load for at least 50 miles. Additional time is desirable. *Keep the cycle moving, and never let the engine overheat during this procedure.*

Harmful Practices

1) *Avoid lugging under any load condition.* Lugging takes place when the motorcycle does not readily respond as the hand grip throttle rotates. Engine speed is too low, and the engine cannot develop sufficient horsepower to pull the load. (Downshift and keep rpm up.)

2) *Avoid long periods of idling.* Excessive idling will increase engine temperature and can result in incomplete burning of fuel. Unburned fuel washes lubricating oil off cylinder walls and results in diluted crankcase oil and restricted (poor) lubrication to all moving parts. The relatively dry cylinder walls depend upon oil throw-off to lubricate them; a speed above a slow idle is necessary for this. Long idling periods produce glazing of cylinder walls, which is detrimental to ring seating.

3) *Avoid stopping your engine too quickly.* When an engine has completed the test run-in schedule, or at any time the engine is heavily worked, it is a good policy to disengage the load from the engine and decelerate gradually. Allow the engine to idle for a brief period before turning the ignition to the off position.

A moment of smooth idling will allow the engine to stabilize and begin to cool gradually. This promotes a desirable dissipation of heat from any localized area of concentrated temperature. In extremely cold weather, such good practice avoids the rapid cooling that can cause valve and seat warpage, cylinder barrel distortion, and such.

APPENDIX 4: HARDWARE GRADING

Using safe, correct hardware is a vital part of any repair. New fastener upgrades and liquid thread locker can affect torque settings. When you follow torque guidelines, clean all hardware thoroughly and note whether the tightening torque is for dry or lubricated threads.

CAUTION —
Lubricating the threads will alter torque settings. Liquid thread locker creates slight drag. You must increase torque settings, using the manufacturer's recommendation, to overcome this drag.

In your factory service manual, torque charts and references appear throughout each repair and service section. Below are typical torque specifications and a bolt identification chart that provide *maximum torque settings* for bolts not listed in your manual's repair sections. (This may prove useful for mounting accessories and aftermarket components.)

In the charts below, you will find domestic bolt sizes and grades, as these have been the traditional Harley-Davidson hardware types. Metric specifications will serve those components and accessories that have moved to the metric standard, primarily off-shore built accessories.

Unless otherwise noted in your official Harley-Davidson service manual, maximum torque specifications reflect the use of clean and dry threads. Reduce torque by Harley-Davidson's recommended percentages when threads are lubricated with engine oil.

CAUTION —
Some assemblies call for high grade steel hardware screwed into softer alloy threads. In such instances, tightening hardware to the maximum torque allowance may exceed the strength of the casting's alloy threads. This could result in stripped casting threads. Always adhere to Harley-Davidson's recommended torque settings for such an assembly.

Metric Thread and Grade Identification

Metric and SAE thread notations differ. Common metric fastener strength property classes are 8.8, 9.8, 10.8 and 12.9, with the class identification embossed on the head of each bolt. Some metric nuts will be marked with single digit strength identification numbers on the nut face.

CAUTION —
SAE strength classes range from grade 2 to 8 with line or dot identifications embossed on each bolt or nut head. Markings correspond to two lines less than the actual grade. (Example: A Grade 8 bolt will have 6 embossed lines on the bolt head; a Grade 5 bolt will have 3 embossed lines on the bolt head, etc.)

Inch (5/16–18)		Metric (M8–1.25)	
Thread major diameter In inches	5/16	Thread major diameter in millimeters	M8
Number of threads per inch	18	Distance between threads in millimeters	1.25

Contrast between U.S. (inch) and Metric hardware Grading.

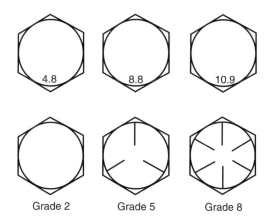

Grade 2   Grade 5   Grade 8

On metric bolts (top), the identification/class numbers correspond to bolt strength. Higher numbers represent an increase in strength. For SAE classified bolts (bottom), markings on top of bolt or nut head indicate grade. More marks or dots represent an increase in tensile strength. The number of marks is always 2 less than the actual grade classification.

Bolt Torque

Bolt size	Grade 5		Grade 8	
	Nm	ft-lb (in-lb)	Nm	ft-lb (in-lb
1/4-20	11	(95)	14	(125)
1/4-28	11	(95)	17	(150)
5/16-18	23	(200)	31	(270)
5/16-24	27	20	34	25
3/8-16	41	30	54	40
3/8-24	48	35	61	45
7/16-14	68	50	88	65
7/16-20	75	55	95	70
1/2-13	102	75	136	100
1/2-20	115	85	149	110
9/16-12	142	105	183	135
9/16-18	156	115	203	150
5/8-11	203	150	264	195
5/8-18	217	160	285	210
3/4-16	237	175	305	225

Harley-Davidson continues the use of U.S. grade bolts and nuts. Above is one hardware manufacturer's maximum recommended torque for U.S. bolts. See the Harley-Davidson shop manual for torque settings at each hardware/fastener on your motorcycle.

Metric Hex Head Cap Screws

Suggested Assembly Torques in Foot-Pounds (Inch-Pounds)								
	Property Class 8.8		Property Class 9.8		Property Class 10.9		Property Class 12.9	
DIA	Dry threads	Lubricated threads	Dry threads	Lubricated threads	Dry threads	Lubricated threads	Dry threads	Lubricated threads
M4	(27.5)	(17)	(30)	(18)	(38.5)	(24)	(53)	(32.5)
M5	(56.5)	(33.5)	(61)	(37)	(78)	(47)	(107)	(65)
M6	(95)	(57.5)	(103)	(61)	(132)	(79)	(180)	(109)
M8	19	12	21	13	27	16	37	22
M10	39	23	42	25	53	32	73	44
M12	67	40	73	44	92	55	127	76
M14	107	64	116	69	148	89	203	122
M16	167	100	181	108	230	138	316	190
M20	325	195	352	211	449	269	617	370
M24	562	337	609	366	775	465	1066	640
M30	1117	670	1210	726	1540	924	2188	1271

Metric hardware has found its way into some Harley-Davidson accessories. Above is one hardware manufacturer's maximum recommended torque settings for metric cap screws. By comparing torque limits and load capacities with U.S. graded bolts, you can determine the approximate strength of metric hardware.

Automotive Books From Robert Bentley

ENTHUSIAST BOOKS

The Racing Driver *Denis Jenkinson*
ISBN 0-8376-0201-7

Maximum Boost: Designing, Testing, and Installing Turbocharger Systems *Corky Bell*
ISBN 0-8376-0160-6

Volkswagen Inspection/Maintenance (I/M) Emission Test Handbook: 1980-1997
Volkswagen of America ISBN 0-8376-0394.3

Volkswagen Sport Tuning for Street and Competition
Per Schroeder ISBN 0-8376-0146-0

Jeep Owner's Bible™ *Moses Ludel*
ISBN 0-8376-0154-1

Ford F-Series Pickup Owner's Bible™
Moses Ludel ISBN 0-8376-0152-5

Chevrolet & GMC Light Truck Owner's Bible™ *Moses Ludel*
ISBN 0-8376-0157-6

Toyota Truck & Land Cruiser Owner's Bible™ *Moses Ludel*
ISBN 0-8376-0159-2

Chevrolet by the Numbers™**: 1955-1959**
Alan Colvin ISBN 0-8376-0875-9

Chevrolet by the Numbers™**: 1960-1964**
Alan Colvin ISBN 0-8376-0936-4

Chevrolet by the Numbers™**: 1965-1969**
Alan Colvin ISBN 0-8376-0956-9

Chevrolet by the Numbers™**: 1970-1975**
Alan Colvin ISBN 0-8376-0927-5

Alfa Romeo Owner's Bible™ *Pat Braden with foreword by Don Black*
ISBN 0-8376-0707-9

The BMW Enthusiast's Companion *BMW Car Club of America*
ISBN 0-8376-0321-8

Sports Car and Competition Driving *Paul Frère with foreword by Phil Hill*
ISBN 0-8376-0202-5

The Technique of Motor Racing *Piero Taruffi with foreword by Juan Manuel Fangio*
ISBN 0-8376-0228-9

Race Car Aerodynamics *Joseph Katz*
ISBN 0-8376-0142-8

Think To Win *Don Alexander with foreword by Mark Martin*
ISBN 0-8376-0070-7

The Design and Tuning of Competition Engines *Philip H. Smith, 6th edition revised by David N. Wenner* ISBN 0-8376-0140-1

Vintage Racing British Sports Cars *Terry Jackson with foreword by Stirling Moss*
ISBN 0-8376-0153-3

New Directions in Suspension Design: Making the Fast Car Faster *Colin Campbell*
ISBN 0-8376-0150-9

The Scientific Design of Exhaust and Intake Systems *Philip H. Smith and John C. Morrison* ISBN 0-8376-0309-9

FUEL INJECTION

Ford Fuel Injection and Electronic Engine Control: 1988-1993 *Charles O. Probst, SAE*
ISBN 0-8376-0301-3

Ford Fuel Injection and Electronic Engine Control: 1980-1987 *Charles O. Probst, SAE*
ISBN 0-8376-0302-1

Bosch Fuel Injection and Engine Management *Charles O. Probst, SAE*
ISBN 0-8376-0300-5

VOLKSWAGEN OFFICIAL SERVICE MANUALS

Eurovan Official Factory Repair Manual: 1992-1999 *Volkswagen of America*
ISBN 0-8376-0335-8

Passat Official Factory Repair Manual: 1995-1997 *Volkswagen of America*
ISBN 0-8376-0380-3

Jetta, Golf, GTI, Cabrio Service Manual: 1993-1997, including Jetta_///_ **and Golf**_///_
Robert Bentley ISBN 0-8376-0365-X

GTI, Golf, and Jetta Service Manual: 1985-1992 Gasoline, Diesel, and Turbo Diesel, including 16V *Robert Bentley* ISBN 0-8376-0342-0

Corrado Official Factory Repair Manual: 1990-1994 *Volkswagen United States*
ISBN 0-8376-0387-0

Passat Official Factory Repair Manual: 1990-1993, including Wagon *Volkswagen United States* ISBN 0-8376-0378-1

Cabriolet and Scirocco Service Manual: 1985-1993, including 16V *Robert Bentley*
ISBN 0-8376-0362-5

Volkswagen Fox Service Manual: 1987-1993, including GL, GL Sport and Wagon *Robert Bentley* ISBN 0-8376-0340-4

Vanagon Official Factory Repair Manual: 1980-1991 including Diesel Engine, Syncro, and Camper *Volkswagen United States* ISBN 0-8376-0336-6

Rabbit, Scirocco, Jetta Service Manual: 1980-1984 Gasoline Models, including Pickup Truck, Convertible, and GTI *Robert Bentley* ISBN 0-8376-0183-5

Rabbit, Jetta Service Manual: 1977-1984 Diesel Models, including Pickup Truck and Turbo Diesel *Robert Bentley*
ISBN 0-8376-0184-3

Rabbit, Scirocco Service Manual: 1975-1979 Gasoline Models *Robert Bentley* ISBN 0-8376-0107-X

Dasher Service Manual: 1974-1981 including Diesel *Robert Bentley*
ISBN 0-8376-0083-9

Super Beetle, Beetle and Karmann Ghia Official Service Manual Type 1: 1970-1979
Volkswagen United States
ISBN 0-8376-0096-0

Beetle and Karmann Ghia Official Service Manual Type 1: 1966-1969 *Volkswagen United States* ISBN 0-8376-0416-8

Station Wagon/Bus Official Service Manual Type 2: 1968-1979 *Volkswagen United States* ISBN 0-8376-0094-4

Fastback and Squareback Official Service Manual Type 3: 1968-1973 *Volkswagen United States*
ISBN 0-8376-0057-X

AUDI OFFICIAL SERVICE MANUALS

Audi 100, A6 Official Factory Repair Manual: 1992-1997, including S4, S6, quattro and Wagon models.
Audi of America. ISBN 0-8376-0374-9

Audi 80, 90, Coupe Quattro Official Factory Repair Manual: 1988-1992 including 80 Quattro, 90 Quattro and 20-valve models *Audi of America*
ISBN 0-8376-0367-6

Audi 100, 200 Official Factory Repair Manual: 1988-1991 *Audi of America*
ISBN 0-8376-0372-2

Audi 5000S, 5000CS Official Factory Repair Manual: 1984-1988 Gasoline, Turbo, and Turbo Diesel, including Wagon and Quattro *Audi of America*
ISBN 0-8376-0370-6

Audi 5000, 5000S Official Factory Repair Manual: 1977-1983 Gasoline and Turbo Gasoline, Diesel and Turbo Diesel
Audi of America ISBN 0-8376-0352-8

Audi 4000S, 4000CS, and Coupe GT Official Factory Repair Manual: 1984-1987 including Quattro and Quattro Turbo *Audi of America* ISBN 0-8376-0373-0

BMW SERVICE MANUALS

BMW 5-Series Service Manual: 1982-1988 528e, 533i, 535i, 535is *Robert Bentley*
ISBN 0-8376-0318-8

BMW 3-Series Service Manual: 1984-1990 318i, 325, 325e(es), 325i(is), and 325i Convertible *Robert Bentley*
ISBN 0-8376-0325-0

SAAB OFFICIAL SERVICE MANUALS

Saab 900 16 Valve Official Service Manual: 1985-1993 *Robert Bentley* ISBN 0-8376-0312-9

Saab 900 8 Valve Official Service Manual: 1981-1988 *Robert Bentley* ISBN 0-8376-0310-2

Robert Bentley has published service manuals and automobile books since 1950. Please write Robert Bentley, Inc., Publishers, at 1734 Massachusetts Avenue, Cambridge, MA 02138, visit our web site at http://www.rb.com, or call 1-800-423-4595 for a free copy of our complete catalog, including titles and service manuals for **Jaguar**, **Triumph**, **Austin-Healey**, **MG**, **Volvo**, and other cars.

Brake master cylinders, 172; bleeding, 179–81; fluids, 84, 173, 178, 180–81; leaks, 179; piston position, 174; repairs, 70

Brake pads: inspection, 45, 84; replacement, 172, 173, 175–79

Brake rotors, 177, 206–7; inspection, 45; repairs, 69, 70

Brakes, 10, 13, 34, 157, 172; bleeding, 178, 179–81; dual disc brakes, conversion to, 206–7; grease, 177, 179; improvements, 9; inspection, 45; parts, sources for, 260; repair tools, 70, 158; service, 172–81; upgrades, 205–7. See also *Front brake*; *Rear brake*

Braking: counter-steer swerve and, 62; skills, 55–57

Breaker bar, 71

British motorcycles, 13, 14, 16

Brushes, worn, 131

Buell cafe racer, 13, 15, 16, 24, 32, 34–36, 199; suspension, adjusting, 203; tires, 209; torque, 220. See also *Unit construction engine/transmission*

Bump start, 52

Bushings, 139; connecting rod, 133, 134, 140; inspection, 141; rear swing arm, 192, 197, 198; replacing, 140; wear, 131, 134, 137, 196

Butterfly valves, 52, 103

Buying a motorcycle, 25–46; choice of model, 30–32, 183, 201–2; identification of models, 25–29; new motorcycle, 46; pre-owned cycle, 36–46

C

C. B. radio, 261

Cables: inspection, 50; lubrication, 83

Calipers, brake. See *Brake calipers*

Camshaft lobe(s), 22; flat, 124; measuring, 139; wear, 70, 128, 138

Camshaft(s): bearings, failure of, 125; ignition and, 214–15; repairs, 70; timing gears, 75, 141; upgrades, 215–17, 220; wear, 123, 127–28, 137

Carburetor, 22, 30, 122; adjustments, 104–6, 263; constant velocity (C. V.), 52, 103–5, 199; plugged passages, 128; rebuilding, 128–29; tuning of, 72, 102–6, 128–29; upgrades, 210–14

Carburetor needle, sticking of, 124, 125, 128

Carnauba wax, 247–48, 250, 252

Casting cracks, 123, 125

Catalytic converter, 129, 220

Chain. See *Primary chain drive and chaincase*; *Secondary chain*

Chain breaker, 235

Chaincase, primary. See *Primary chain drive and chaincase*

Charging. See *Battery charging*

Chassis: choice of, 183, 201–2; development of, 5–9; identification codes, 28; parts, sources for, 259–60; storage of, 252–55; tuning, 184–98, 201–5

Chisels, 70

Choke, 48, 52, 53, 105

Choppers, 9, 11–12, 184

Chrome, protection of, 252

Chrome accessories/trim, 227–29

Circuits. See *Wiring*

Classic model motorcycle, 17, 18

Cleaning, 142; battery, 74, 94, 129–30; carburetor, 128; drain plug, 86, 88; fork tube caps, 195; motorcycle finish, 245–52; primary chaincase, 86, 151; prior to oil change, 80–81; secondary chain, 90; secondary drive belt, 91; spark plug threads, 98; throttle, 83; wheel bearings, 163–64

Clinometer, 171–72

Clothing, 60, 65, 68, 225, 241–43

Cluster riding, 61

Clutch: adjustment, 131, 145–48, 152; disengaging, 146, 152; drag, 146; dry type, 145, 223; failed, 131; high apply pressure, 223; inspection, 42–43; overhaul tips, 149–52; proper functioning, 143; quick access, 34; racing, 223; slipping, 146; troubleshooting, 145–46, 152; upgrades, 222–24; wear, 149

Clutch cable: adjustment, 145; damaged, 131; free-play, 146–47, 149; replacement, 145, 148–49

Clutch cover, 86–87

Clutch lever, 13; adjustment, 145; free-play, 146–47, 149; movement of, 51; orientation to, 48, 49

Clutch plates: binding, 131; repair, 150–51; worn, 145

Code, Keith, 54, 257

Color-coding of parts, 128, 141

Compensating sprocket, 151

Compression: checking with remote starter switch, 73; low, 123–24; normal, 127

Compression braking, 55–56

Compression gauge, 75, 123

Compression test, 41, 75, 123–24

Connecting rod bearings, wear of, 137

Connecting rod bushings: abnormal noises, 133; replacing, 140; wear, 134

Connecting rods, 22; abnormal noises, 133; damage, 125

Constant velocity (C. V.) carburetor, 52, 103–5, 199

Continuity/ohm test, 115–16

Continuity tester, 73

Cornering. See *Turning the motorcycle*

Counter-steering, 58, 59, 62

Cover, motorcycle, 252

Crankcase: emission system, 199; location of, 22–23; pressure, 135; storage protection, 255

Crankcase breathing system, 22, 128, 135, 211, 219, 263

Crankpin, 22, 221

Crankshaft, 132, 143, 221; inspection, 141; measuring, 139; sprocket nut, 151; sublet of assembly work, 71; wear, 134

Crankshaft bearings, 124, 221; abnormal noises, 133; failure of, 125; wear, 137

Curve: riding through, 61; stopping on, 61, 62

Customized motorcycles, 33; factory, 9, 11–12, 18, 44; paint work, 241; value of, 46

C.V. carburetor. See *Constant velocity (C. V.) carburetor*

Cylinder barrel, 124, 139, 140

Cylinder base gaskets, 142

D

E

WARNING —

- *Motorcycle service, repair, and modification is serious business. You must be alert, use common sense, and exercise good judgement to prevent personal injury.*

- *Before using this book or beginning any work on your vehicle, thoroughly read the Warning on the copyright page, and any Warnings and Cautions listed on page 277.*

- *Always read a complete procedure before you begin the work. Pay special attention to any Warnings and Cautions, or any other information, that accompanies that procedure.*

WARNING —
• *Motorcycle service, repair, and modification is serious business. You must be alert, use common sense, and exercise good judgement to prevent personal injury.*

• *Before using this book or beginning any work on your vehicle, thoroughly read the Warning on the copyright page, and any Warnings and Cautions listed on page 277.*

• *Always read a complete procedure before you begin the work. Pay special attention to any Warnings and Cautions, or any other information, that accompanies that procedure.*

Valves, 128, 216, 219; grinding, 71, 137, 138; longterm storage protection, 252; replacement, 138; wear, 134, 137, 138
Valve seats, 219; cutting, 138; longterm storage protection, 252; wear, 138
Valve springs, 138, 216
Valve stems: cutting, 139; inspection, 138; measuring, 139; seized, 125; tires, 158, 169
Valve timing, 127–28
Valvetrain, 122, 124; abnormal noises, 133, 134; damage, 125; Evolution engine, 21; wear, 138
Vibration dampers, 223–24
Viewing plug, timing, plastic, 100
Visual emissions inspections, 211
V.O.E.S. See *Vacuum Operated Electric Switch (V.O.E.S.)*
Voltage, 109; drop alarm, 236; drop test, 116–18; tests, 71, 113–18
Voltage regulator, 109, 119
Voltmeter, 74, 112, 114–15, 233; short circuit test, 115–16; starter test, 120
Volt-ohmmeter, 73, 76, 111, 112, 119, 261; alternator tests, 130; analog, 112, 113; battery testing, 118; digital, 71, 72, 76, 112, 115; safe use of, 118; short circuit test, 116. See also *Ohmmeter; Voltmeter*
VR1000 motorcycle, 13, 15, 17, 34, 199
V-twin engine, 2. See also *OHV V-twin engine*

W

Warm-up, engine, 52–53, 152, 153, 253
Waxing, 247–49, 251–52
Weight, shifting of, 58
Wet-plate clutch, 143, 145, 222–23. See also *Clutch*
Wet storage battery, 107. See also *Battery*
Wheel bearings: cleaning, 163–64; end-play, 164–65; inspection, 45; repacking, 159, 162, 164, 254; selective fit spacers, 165; service, 162–66
Wheel spoke nipples, 161, 162
Wheel rims: cleaning/polishing, 250; factory rim offset, 161; inspection, 50; rim protectors, 168; runout, 159, 160; service, 158–62; trueness, 159, 160, 161; tubeless tire, 158

Wheels, 157; alignment, 158, 170–72; balancing, 159; cast, 9, 10, 26, 28, 158–59, 206, 208; hubs, 162–66; inspection for damage, 44; installation, 238; laced spoked, 9, 158–62, 206–7; parts, sources for, 260; power transmitted to rear, 143; service, 158–66; types, 158; wobble, 64. See also *Tires*
Wheel truing stand, 159
Windshield: aftermarket accessory, 227; engraving, 241
Wire gauge, 98
Wire harness, 116
Wiring, 111; of accessories, 231, 239–40; charge circuit, 119; continuity test, 115; ignition, 126; inspection, 46; repair, 261; short circuit test, 115–16; spark plug, 215
Wrenches, 69, 70, 71, 72, 261. See also *Torque wrenches*
Wrist pins, 140; fitting, 71; loose, sound of, 133; replacing, 140
WR motorcycle, 16

X

XLA Sportster motorcycle, 14
XLCH Sportster motorcycle, 14
XLCR Sportster motorcycle, 16
XL Evolution engine, 21, 26, 27; induction system, 22; inspection plate, 143; primary chain/transmission lubricant, 87–88; transmission, 144
XLH Sportster motorcycle, 14, 20, 27–28; 883 Deluxe model, 35, 36; 883 Hugger model, 26, 205
XL Sportster motorcycle, 14, 17, 18, 24; brake upgrades, 206; engine, 4; fuel tanks, 228; shifter parts, location of, 154; shifter pawl adjustment, 153; transmission repair, 154
X-model motorcycle, 27
XR750 motorcycle, 13, 15, 16–17, 34, 199
XR1000 Sportster motorcycle, 16, 34

Please read these Warnings and Cautions before proceeding with maintenance and repair work.

WARNING—

• Do not reuse self-locking nuts or any other fasteners that are fatigued or deformed in normal use. They are designed to be used only once, and become unreliable and may fail when used a second time. This includes, but is not limited to, bolts, washers, self-locking nuts, circlips and cotter pins that secure the subframe, control arms, stabilizer bar, ball joints and other suspension, steering and brake components. Always replace these fasteners with new parts.

• Never work under a lifted vehicle unless it is solidly supported on stands designed for the purpose. Do not support a vehicle on cinder blocks, hollow tiles, or other props that may crumble under continuous load. Do not work under a vehicle that is supported solely by a jack.

• When working on your vehicle make sure that the ground is level. Disconnect the battery ground strap to prevent others from starting the vehicle while you are working on it.

• Never run the engine unless the work area is well ventilated. Carbon monoxide kills.

• Friction materials such as brake or clutch discs may contain asbestos fibers. Do not create dust by grinding, sanding, or by cleaning with compressed air. Avoid breathing asbestos fibers and asbestos dust. Breathing asbestos can cause serious diseases such as asbestosis or cancer, and may result in death.

• Tie long hair behind your head. Do not wear a necktie, a scarf, loose clothing, or a necklace when you work near machine tools or running engines. If your hair, clothing, or jewelry were to get caught in the machinery, severe injury could result.

• Disconnect the battery ground strap whenever you work on the fuel system or the electrical system. When you work around fuel, do not smoke or work near heaters or other fire hazards. Keep an approved fire extinguisher handy.

• Finger rings should be removed so that they cannot cause electrical shorts, get caught in running machinery, or be crushed by heavy parts.

• Catch draining fuel, oil, or brake fluid in suitable containers. Do not use food or beverage containers that might mislead someone into drinking from them. Store flammable fluids away from fire hazards. Wipe up spills at once, but do not store the oily rags, which can ignite and burn spontaneously.

• Always observe good workshop practices. Wear approved eye protection when you operate machine tools, work with battery acid, hydraulic presses, gear pullers, spring compressors, or use tools that require impact, such as hammers, drifts and punches. Gloves or other protective clothing should be worn whenever the job requires it.

• Some aerosol tire inflators are highly flammable. Use extreme care when repairing a tire that may have been inflated using an aerosol tire inflator. Keep sparks, open flame or other sources of ignition away from the tire repair area. Inflate and deflate the tire at least four times before breaking the bead from the rim. Completely remove the tire from the rim before attempting any repair.

• Keep sparks, lighted matches, and open flames away from the top of the battery. If hydrogen gas escaping from the cap vents is ignited, it will ignite gas trapped in the cells and cause the battery to explode.

• Do not attempt to work on your vehicle if you do not feel well. You can increase the danger of injury to yourself and others if you are tired, upset or have taken medicine or any other substance that may impair you from being fully alert.

• Illuminate your work area adequately but safely. A fluorescent worklight is preferable to an incandescent worklight. Use a portable safety light for working inside or under the vehicle. Make sure the bulb is enclosed by a wire cage. The hot filament of an accidentally broken bulb can ignite spilled fuel or oil.

CAUTION—

• If you lack the skills, tools and equipment, or a suitable workshop for any procedure described in this book, we suggest you leave such repairs to an authorized Harley-Davidson dealer or other qualified shop. We especially urge you to consult an authorized Harley-Davidson dealer before beginning repairs on any vehicle that may still be covered wholly or in part by any of the extensive warranties issued by Harley-Davidson.

• Harley-Davidson is constantly improving its vehicles and sometimes these changes, both in parts and specifications, are made applicable to earlier models.   Always check with your authorized Harley-Davidson dealer for the latest parts and service information, including Service Bulletins.

• Before starting a job, make certain that you have all the necessary tools and parts on hand. Read all the instructions thoroughly; do not attempt shortcuts. Use tools appropriate to the work, and use only use only genuine Harley-Davidson parts or parts with equivalent characteristics, including but not limited to, type, strength, and material meeting Harley-Davidson specifications. Makeshift tools, parts, and procedures will not make good repairs, and may result in vehicle malfunction of possible personal injury.

• Use pneumatic and electric tools only to loosen threaded parts and fasteners. Never use these tools to tighten fasteners, especially on light alloy parts.

• Be mindful of the environment and ecology. Before you drain the crankcase, find out the proper way to dispose of the oil. Do not pour oil onto the ground, down a drain, or into a stream, pond, or lake. Consult local ordinances that govern the handling and disposal of chemicals and wastes.

• Do not quick-charge the battery (for boost starting) for longer than one minute, and do not exceed 15.0 volts at the battery with the boosting cables attached. Wait at least one minute before boosting the battery a second time.

• Harley-Davidson offers extensive warranties. Therefore, before deciding to repair or modify a Harley-Davidson that may still be covered wholly or in part by any warranties issued by Harley-Davidson, consult your authorized Harley-Davidson dealer.

Please read the Safety Notice and disclaimer on the Copyright page.

ACKNOWLEDGMENTS

Assembling detailed facts and photos for this book required the cooperation of many individuals and companies. Their time, patience, and enthusiasm for Harley-Davidson motorcycles helped enhance the substance and graphic impact of this work.

I owe special thanks to Bud and Patty Evans, owners of Harley-Davidson of Reno, who graciously placed their service, parts and sales operations at my disposal. This gratitude extends to managers Kent Stephens and Niall Weatherspoon, plus Tim Conway, Phil Pasqual, Phil Amman, Will Roemer, Dirk Nanney, Tom Evans, Chuck Moffit, Lewis Olvera, Rick Adair and the rest of the dealership's staff.

Harley-Davidson's Reno HOG Rally provided photo access to cut-away powertrain displays plus the wisdom of Service Operations Trainer Robert Follett. Through such events, Harley-Davidson demonstrates its commitment to owners.

In addition to the large number of photos shot within the service department at Harley-Davidson of Reno, I photographed several service-related tasks at Carson Custom Cycles (Carson City, Nevada). Ron McBroom, Rick Shaward and shop owner Larry Perkins generously provided this backdrop.

Notably, my appreciation reaches to the exceptional cooperation provided by individual Harley-Davidson owners, in particular Duane and Toni Heiny, and Steve and Peggy Shaw. Their meticulously maintained Evolution cycles, particularly Toni's stunning Heritage Softail Classic and Steve's nimble Buell, appear throughout the book.

Big Mike Darrah, Carson City's acclaimed motorcycle safety instructor, also offered his time, a full-dresser and top riding talent before my camera. Cycles made available by Dennis Taylor, Danny Lyons, Robert Patrucco and Richard Reese, plus the participants at the 1995 Bridgeport, California Harley-Davidson gathering and that summer's HOG Rally at Reno, Nevada, further round out the graphics.

Brent Howerton, life friend and living witness to our high school days of motorcycling antics, remains a continuing source of levity and support for my projects. He can readily account for each of them.

As no book project fails to drag our most intimate ties into the fray, I must once more commend my wife Donna and son Jacob for their patience and acceptance around this demanding project.

ABOUT THE AUTHOR

Moses Ludel's first two-wheeled American iron was a 1955 Allstate-Cushman bought for eight dollars, the day's wages at a summer gas station job. After graduating to motorcycles, including a variety of British bikes and America's Harley-Davidson V-twins, the author eventually became the operator of an independent motorcycle repair shop where he painstakingly serviced and rebuilt these machines.

A degree from the University of Oregon led to automotive photo-journalism. Moses's technical stories and columns, now totaling over 1800 works, have appeared in *Popular Hot Rodding*, *Guide to Muscle Cars*, *Super Street Truck*, *Corvette Fever*, *Truckin'*, *Fabulous Mustangs*, *Super Ford*, *Four Wheeler*, *Off-Road*, *Sport Truck*, *Trailer Life*, *Motorhome*, *4x4 Magazine Japan*, *4WD SUV*, *Chevy Truck*, *Jp Magazine*, Microsoft's *MSN-Motorsite* on the internet, and the Portland *Oregonian* newspaper.

In 1992, Robert Bentley Publishers released Moses' first book, the widely acclaimed *Jeep Owner's Bible*. The author's subsequent book releases were the *Ford F-Series Pickup Owner's Bible*, the *Chevrolet & GMC Light Truck Owner's Bible* and his most recent work, the *Toyota Truck & Land Cruiser Owner's Bible*.

The *Harley-Davidson Evolution V-Twin Owner's Bible* provides the kind of photography and attention to detail that have drawn enthusiasts to each of Moses Ludel's previous books. In the author's words, this in-depth volume is a "tribute, illustrated celebration and guidebook for the thorough enjoyment and proper care of America's premier motorcycles, the Harley-Davidson Evolution Era V-twins!"

Note: Unless otherwise indicated, all photographs in this book are by the author.